DICTATORS
AND
DISCIPLES

From Caesar to Stalin

A Psychoanalytic Interpretation of History

by
Gustav Bychowski, M. D.

Preface by Carl Binger, M. D.

INTERNATIONAL UNIVERSITIES PRESS
New York   New York

To the ever mourned memory of my only son Jan Ryszard, Navigator in the R.A.F. Polish Squadron, killed in action on May 22, 1944, who gave his young life fighting for a better world.

FOREWORD

Julius Caesar, Oliver Cromwell, Robespierre, Hitler, Stalin! A rogue's gallery or a galaxy of supermen and demigods? All but the one who is still among the living met with a violent death. Cromwell cheated the hangman by dying of tertian ague but his body was disinterred and hung on the gallows. "Sic semper tyrannis!"

In a cool and lucid and eloquent book, Dr. Bychowski tells the story of the rise and fall of these dictators, what forces flung them into the zenith of history, determined their orbits, attracted other bodies to them and finally hurtled them like spent meteorites into the crater of their devastation.

Here is an epic theme for a scholar, challenged to study "man's inhumanity to man". It is no gossipy chronicle, but a serious and well-documented attempt to find an underlying principle.

Since the author is distinguished as a psychiatrist and psychoanalyst it is to be expected that his interpretation of history will be a psychological one without, however, any underestimation of the strength of social and economic forces. He does not foist his interpretations on his reader. He is far too skilled a clinician to do so. Instead he allows history to tell its story, only interposing his own constructions when the facts have all but convinced us.

The appearance of this book is well timed, when the pattern of the recent past has become a little clearer and the shadow of coming events is not yet inexorably cast. Nor is it quixotic to hope that by insight and understanding the gloom of this shadow might still be lifted.

These preparatory remarks will, I hope, serve as champagne to a ship at the launching. Whatever waves of opinion Dr. Bychowski's book encounters, the reader may be confident that the man on the bridge has charted his course with a discerning and experienced eye and a steady purpose.

CARL BINGER

CONTENTS

PREFACE

When, in 1935, I paid my last visit to Sigmund Freud, I asked him what contribution he thought psychoanalysis might eventually make to the solution of the appalling crisis with which our civilization was threatened. "How can we," I said, "devote our time and energy to curing a few individuals at a time like this when our entire civilization, our very existence, is imperiled?" Freud replied that in his opinion we could not hope to save mankind, but could best help by advancing and popularizing our psychoanalytic knowledge, so that eventually it would become public property, a part of universal thought, so to speak. Then, in the distant future, the day might come when these horrifying reactions of the collective psyche would no longer be possible.

The years went by and my clinical and psychoanalytic work prevented me from devoting myself to other problems. Then came the war and the invasion of my country—Poland. I was driven from my home, and my normal activity, like everyone else's, was forcibly interrupted. At this moment of personal distress my mind became focused on man's history which I tried to interpret with the help of psychoanalytic concepts.

The present work deals with a problem that is perhaps the center of today's social and political life. Dictatorship has brought in its wake consequences so portentous that both psychologists and sociologists are compelled to give grave thought to all its aspects. And anyone who loves liberty is bound to ponder deeply over the origin and causes of this evil and the possibilities of preventing and curing it.

Just as prophylaxis is the ideal goal of medicine, so prevention should be our goal in dealing with diseases of society. But effective prevention of disease presupposes its accurate diagnosis. The analyses of some past and present dictatorships that are presented in this book are intended to help us discover the general principles that could govern the origin, course and final elimination of dictatorship.

These principles, arising out of the complexity of all social phenomena, relate to the social, economic, and psychologic fields. The last named interests me most especially, therefore I have deliberately placed the other aspects of the question in the background although I fully grant their importance to a real understanding of dictatorship.

This study of the personal psychology of dictators and of the collective psychology which constitutes the foundations of dictatorship is primarily based on the great discoveries of psychoanalysis to which Freud devoted two monumental works: *Totem and Taboo,* and *Group Psychology and the Analysis of the Ego.* The former presents a cluster of brilliant hypotheses about the origin of religion and morals in human society. The latter is a masterful analysis of the principles governing collective psychology and of the evolution of the ego. In addition to Freud's writings I have also based this study on the classical works of Le Bon. It was he who, before the emergence of psychoanalysis, applied the principles of social psychology to studies of the French Revolution and socialism. My own studies led me to deal with particular problems of collective and historical psychology. And here in this work it is my hope to make contributions to a new science, the psychoanalytic interpretation of history.

WHAT IS DICTATORSHIP?

I do not propose to dwell too long on the definition of dictatorship, for surely there can be no semantic quarrel over the word. So perhaps the simplest method of approach is along the line of etymology. Accordingly, we arrive at the parent word, "to dictate" from which "dictatorship" is derived. In this derivation is implicit at the same time the manner in which one individual imposes his will on his society. Two additional features are required to make this definition complete. The first concerns the character of the dictation, namely, its inflexibility, and the second concerns the origin of dictatorship. Its basis is not derived from the devolution of power or of prerogatives, but on power and prerogatives arbitrarily assumed by the person of the dictator.

Thus dictatorship differs from monarchic power even of the most despotic brand. In a monarchy, the accession to power presents no problem; it is regulated by custom. Therefore, the only question that arises is why his subjects tolerate the rule of a despotic monarch. Where a dictator is concerned, we must first pose the question, "How does he acquire power?" before considering the problem of how he holds on to it. We are not interested in the technique of the coup d'état which leads to dictatorship. What concerns us is rather the situation which makes a coup d'état possible, to wit, the historical, sociological, and psychological aspects of a given situation.

JULIUS CAESAR AND THE DEATH
OF THE REPUBLIC *

The course of Roman history ** can serve as a perfect illustration of Freud's theory expounded in *Totem and Taboo,* according to which the earliest form of society was marked by a struggle between the primal father of the horde and his sons who banded together in order to overthrow him and divide the females among themselves. Thus, about nineteen hundred years before Freud pointed out this pattern, the Roman king was killed, the Republic was established and its path of development was apparently bound for democracy. However, the collective mind still cherished deep longing for the guiding and ruling parent. In a period of misery and social upheaval, the vortex produced Caesar, one of the "sons" who gave promise of being a substitute for the great and good father. Although he was an aristocrat, he was able to persuade the populace that his heart beat for them and he won their love by assuming the role of the savior of freedom and liberator from oppression. But physical circumstances, which found their counterpart in Caesar's own unconscious mind, compelled him to act as a tyrant. His rule sounded the death knell of the Roman republic; instead of creating freedom, he demolished it. But in thus defeating his own alleged purpose, he defeated himself, and perished at the hands of his former friends.

Caesar's death, however, failed to save the Republic. The

* Reprinted from the *Journal of Clinical Psychopathology,* vol. 7, no. 4, April, 1946.

** For a brief chronology to all chapters, see pp. 253 ff.

image of the heroic father-leader had been planted so deeply in the minds of the people that it could not be eradicated by an act of individual annihilation. The memory of the beloved Caesar merged with the old parental image and underwent a process of idealization and deification. Incorporated in the collective ego-ideal, it then helped foster the growth of the institution of Imperators.

Caesar's rise had been prepared by the tyranny of Sulla. Just prior to Sulla, the power of the aristocracy had been declining rapidly, the plebeians had been seething with revolt while the power of Rome had been threatened by Mithridates, King of Pontus. The rebellious plebeians had neither sufficient strength nor adequate leaders to win a decisive victory. Their revolts, of which the one headed by Marius was the most serious, contributed only to a general weakening of the whole structure, and at the same time increased the feeling of universal uncertainty and paved the way for reaction.

Sulla's dictatorship was, as Ferrero said in *The Greatness and Decline of Rome,* (1) * ". . . an initial and sanguinary triumph of an oligarchy of murderers, slaves, indigent nobles, unscrupulous adventurers, rapacious usurers and mercenaries over an immense state of oppressed millions who, in a paroxysm of fury, made a vain attempt at revolt."

In brief, the social situation at that time was characterized by extremely high tension in the class struggle, by despair on the part of some, and fear and a sense of impending danger on the part of others.

This was the moment when Sulla entered the political arena. Because he felt insecure as a representative of the ruling and threatened oligarchy, he proceeded with utter ruthlessness to safeguard his own security. His actions betrayed no doubts or vacillations, for his mind was set on destroying all the rebellious forces, on seizing absolute and

* For all references, see pp. 258 ff.

unopposed power, on ruling by force, on holding in his own hands all the means of exercising force and on gaining control over the whole people whom he proposed to turn into a supine mob.

He shrank from nothing to achieve his objective. His absolute and ruthless selfishness, both personal and class-selfishness, was not based on any pretense of ideology. Not for one moment did he hesitate to make peace at considerable sacrifices with Rome's worst enemy, Mithridates. Nor did he feel bound by any considerations for tradition. To secure lumber for war machines, he cut down the groves of the Lyceum and the century old plane trees of the Academy, in the shade of which Plato had once taught. This was one of the earliest symbols of the attitude of dictators toward the giants of thought. Sulla in his greed, however, desired to affix to his absolute power the sanction of the people's approval. So great was the general weakness in this state of profound confusion, and so terrible was his cruelty, that he easily succeeded in his purpose and raised his power to a level of absolutism such as had never been seen before, a power which, contrary to all tradition, was not limited in duration or by delegation of any of its authority. "The terrible massacre in the Circus gave even the dullest Roman to understand that in the matter of tyranny, there had been an exchange, but not a deliverance." (2)

But was it all really so new and unexpected, was there no precedent for it in the previous course of Roman history? Not, of course, during the time of the republican regime; but if we go further back, we can easily perceive that the dictatorship was but a regression to the old regime of kings. This historical regression was characterized by Mommsen as follows: "The new office was none other than the old kinghood, which after all also consisted in a voluntary obligation on the part of the citizenry to render obedience to one from their midst as to their absolute lord." And in a melancholy vein Mommsen concludes: "There had been a little too much defeat in the oligarchy's last victory." (3)

Sulla wiped out all the rights of the citizenry and turned them into a terrorized and cowardly mob. "In his palatial abode he received with indifference the homage of Rome's most distinguished personages, who with hatred in their hearts came humbly to render obeisance to the master of life and death." (1)

While they feared and hated him, he had nothing for them but contempt, such as a strong and ruthless egoist with his jungle logic feels for weaklings whom he has succeeded in cowing and in making utterly subservient to himself.

Sulla handled his own personal interests as well as those of his friends as if they were matters of state. As his ambitions did not reach beyond salvaging his own prerogatives, he quickly relinquished power the moment he could do so without danger to himself and his friends. After he had stepped down, it turned out that the latest "monarch" had, been, according to his own lights at least, an upright republican. Once out of office he retired completely to private life, a life of epicurean pleasure and idleness.

"His conduct," says the wise Plutarch, "fixed a stigma upon offices of great power which were thought to work a change in men's previous characters, and render them capricious, vain, and cruel. However, whether this is a change and reversal of nature, brought about by fortune or rather a revelation, when a man is an authority, of underlying baseness, were matters for determination in some other treatise." (2)

Nevertheless, psychologically, Sulla's dictatorship and restoration prepared the Roman people for the advent of a new ruler. Independent political thought had deteriorated to such an extent, the need for leaning on a strong leader was so acute, that the desire for turning the helm of government over to one man utterly undermined the foundations on which the commonwealth could have been built anew. "Sulla decimated the knights, muzzled the tribunate and curbed the consuls. But even Sulla could not abolish his own example and preclude a successor to his domination." (4)

Accordingly, when the new man came along who not only craved power, but also possessed all the necessary qualifications for a real ruler, his ambitions coincided with the covert desires of a large part of the public. "Romans gave way before the good fortune of the man and accepted the bit, and regarding the monarchy as a respite from the evil of the civil wars, they appointed him dictator for life." (5)

Caesar's plans and ambitions were settled even before he entered public life. His desire to be a master had been aroused in his youth. Suetonius reports his reaction when contemplating the portrait of Alexander the Great in the temple of Hercules at Gades. "He heaved a sigh, and as if out of patience with his own incapacity in having as yet done nothing noteworthy at a time of life when Alexander had already brought the world to his feet, he straightway asked for his discharge, to grasp the first opportunity for greater enterprises at Rome."

Immediately after this report, Suetonius, with deep perception, points to deeper and older motives of this desire for ruling the earth. "Furthermore, when he was dismayed by a dream the following night, (for he thought that he had offered violence to his mother), the soothsayers inspired him with high hopes by their interpretation which was: that he was destined to rule the world, since the mother whom he had seen in his power was none other than the earth, which is regarded as the common parent of all mankind." (6)

This lust for power found a justification in the family tradition of the proud patrician. Was he not an heir of kings and even of Gods? "In the eulogy of his aunt, he spoke in the following terms of her paternal and maternal ancestry and that of his own father . . . 'our stock, therefore, has at once the sanctity of Kings, whose power is supreme among mortal men and the claim to reverence which attaches to the Gods, who hold sway over Kings themselves'."

It must have been a particularly humiliating experience for such a man to have to hide from Sulla, the Dictator, like the commonest of criminals. Through his wife, who was a sister of Marius, Caesar was linked by marriage with the Marian Revolution. Therefore, Sulla, bent on consolidating his power, asked him to divorce her. Caesar, sensing the imminent danger, fled to Rome where, suffering from a severe attack of quartan ague, he had to change his hiding place almost every night. Finally, he was obliged to beg mercy from the Dictator, through the good offices of friends in positions of influence.

Such an experience, in a period of general strife, and disintegrating social forms and ideals, may have caused a deep resentment in him and deepened his resolve to reach a position where never again would he be preyed upon. Why should not he, who was a descendent of Kings and Gods, and felt in himself the fiber of a ruler be on top in this strife, why should not he be the one to be feared and obeyed?

In another characteristic accident, while on a mission in the provinces, Caesar was captured by pirates. He behaved quietly while waiting for the ransom money to arrive, but he told his captors that some day he would crucify them all. Once freed, he promptly fulfilled his promise. At first, he asked the Governor to punish them but when this official replied that he would consider the matter at his leisure, Caesar took revenge into his own hands and crucified the malefactors. The good Suetonius cites as an instance of Caesar's clemency the fact that before the pirates were crucified he had their throats cut.

Here again we have an example of Caesar's reaction to the feelings of being overpowered and humiliated. These

attitudes, full of resentment and threatened pride, prevailed
till his later years and occasionally were manifested even in
the period of his established power. Caesar did not rise when
the Senate came to greet him; yet he was furious when at
their next meeting one member of the College did not rise
at his entrance. He mocked him bitterly: "Come then,
Aquile, take back the republic from me, you mighty tribune." And then for some time when publicly announcing
his decisions he would add in a biting tone: "That is, if
Aquile allows it."

Caesar's erotic interests and activities were intense and of
an obviously bisexual character. His homosexuality was a
notorious cause of scandal and subjected Caesar to shafts of
banter throughout his life, and this at a time when standards
of sexual morality were much more tolerant than ours. His
relation with Nicomedes, King of Bithynia, has come down
as infamy. During one of his triumphs he was greeted as a
queen, and in his Gallic triumphs soldiers shouted: "All the
Gauls did Caesar vanquish, but Nicomedes vanquished him.
Lo! Now Caesar rides in triumph, victor over all the Gauls;
Nicomedes does not triumph, he who subdued the conqueror."

Caesar was not too much disturbed by this reputation.
It was as if he made it a point of honor to show that even
such a "queen" could be a real king. The following episode
is very characteristic of his defiant attitude. Caesar received
the command of Gaul only after having overcome the opposition of his enemies. Transported with joy at this success,
he could not keep from boasting a few days later before a
crowded house that having gained his heart's desire to the
grief and lamentation of his opponents, he would from that
time on ride on heads. When someone remarked that that
would not be an easy matter for any woman, he replied,
"that Semiramis, too, had been a queen in Syria". He also
mentioned the Amazons.

We can also understand the report that he was fastidious about his person and that he delighted in elaborate clothes, pearls and gems, by taking into account the strain of homosexuality and narcissism in his personality.

Caesar also had many love affairs with queens. In one of his speeches, the elder Curio calls him "omnium mulierum virum et omnium virorum mulierem". Apparently his desires were boundless because he is said to have ordered a bill drawn making it lawful for Caesar to marry whatever wives he wished and as many as he wished. This was another manifestation of the rebellious son trying to return to the privileged position of the powerful father of the primitive tribe, the ruler of all the females. Even his beloved Servilia prostituted her own daughter, Tertia, to Caesar.

Caesar's overweening desire to show off and impress people may have been a compensation for his passive homosexuality and a manifestation of his tremendous exhibitionism. The circuses he offered to the Romans were so lavish that a bill was passed limiting the number of gladiators. He even used the death of his daughter as an opportunity to give an extraordinary feast in her memory, a thing quite without precedent in the annals of Rome. He was always trying to impress foreign princes and the people of remote provinces. "All were thunder-struck by his actions and wondered what their purpose could be."

The purpose, however, soon became clear and obvious. Cicero says that Caesar ever had upon his lips these lines of Euripides: "If wrong may ever be right, for a throne's sake were wrong most right; be God in all else feared." (4)

However, his ambition reached further than merely safeguarding his own interests. It encompassed the destinies of the entire nation, of the country at large. Not only did his own ego-ideal compare and identify itself with ideals of the country's expansion and power, but Rome's people themselves, or at least substantial numbers of them, saw in Caesar the incarnation of their own profound desires and ideals. He was worshipped as a general, as a symbol of Rome's might; he was obeyed not only out of fear, but out of deep-seated love and faith. His rule seemed sufficiently justified and substantiated, and the obedience and deference to Caesar which dwelled in the hearts of his subjects gradually became integral components of the collective ego-ideal.

"Caesar's monarchy was not an oriental despotism by the grace of God, but a monarchy such as was founded by Pericles and later by Cromwell, to wit, a representation of the nation by an individual of the highest type and a man in whom unlimited confidence reposed." Nevertheless, the regression to monarchy was complete; "there was not one feature in Caesar's state that could not have been found in the old kingdom." (3)

Surveying the road over which Caesar traveled to power, we may perceive certain definitive factors. Despite all the internal weaknesses of the commonwealth, the republican traditions were still too deeply imbedded in the minds of the citizenry to permit an autocratic regime being introduced without the use of force. Accordingly, when Pompey, having won his victories in the East, decided, after protracted hesitations, to return to Italy (62 B. C.), and instead of declaring himself the ruler, dismissed his troops and proceeded to Rome accompanied by only a small retinue, he was doomed to failure. Loath to apply force, he imagined that all would yield to his will without pressure and that, by keeping within the bounds of the law, he might be able to hold the position of the foremost citizen and depositary of the people's will, as well as the Senate's trust and, if necessary, might act as the commonwealth's commander-in-chief. In the meantime, however, the mood of the Romans had changed rapidly, due to rumors about the dismissal of his troops; the submissiveness with which his return had been expected in Rome was replaced by a general opposition. He did not offer the display of strength necessary to impress the mind of the masses.

"He had evidently formed the plan of making himself master without employing arms; he reckoned upon destroying the republic by a slow and internal revolution and by preserving as much as possible, in so illegal an attempt, the outward form of legality." (7)

Caesar's basic principle of action was first and foremost to solicit the support of the people. It should be remembered that at the outset of his career he had been the leader of the democratic party. Another factor to be kept in mind is that he started his consulship by enforcing the agrarian laws, which amounted to practically an agrarian reform on a vast scale. The enforcement of these laws required the application of force and the ruthless crushing of the opposition of the aristocracy. In this way, the future imperator posed as a champion of the people, who could not help seeing in him a protector and a friend, in other words, a kind-hearted parent.

The sharp word of Sallust applies excellently to his method of political activity: "Bonum publicum simulantes pro sua quisque potestate certabant." (While pretending common good, they strove merely for their own power.) (8) As a matter of fact this was quite a common procedure at that time: "Nobody ever sought power for himself and the enslavement of others without invoking libertas and such fair names . . . and centuries later when the phrase Vindex Libertatis appears on the coinage, it indicates armed usurpation attempted or successful, the removal of either a pretender or a tyrant." (4)

After resigning his consulship, Caesar lingered with the troops, whom he was supposed to lead to the provinces, in the vicinity of Rome, so as to be able to bring pressure to bear on the course of events in the capital. Tribune Clodius, whom Caesar installed in office, proposed four laws, three of which were intended to gain the favor of the masses and to curtail the power of the Senate.

The campaign in Gaul gave Caesar both fame and power. To influence public opinion in his favor, he published his memoirs on the Gallic war and at the same time intensified the process of corrupting the people, which he had been carrying on for several years past with the immense funds he had amassed in Gaul as part of the spoils of war.

Caesar practiced corruption on an enormous scale. Almost every year, during the winter, he returned from Cisalpine Gaul with the treasures of the Gauls. In one day, at Lucca, two hundred Senators could be counted in his apartment and one hundred and twenty lictors at the door, all soliciting favors of varying sorts. His party consisted to a great extent of rascals. Cicero was very much afraid of them when Caesar arrived with his band to visit him at Formiae. "There is not a rascal in all Italy," said he, "who is not with him." Atticus called his retinue an infernal troop.

The troops were utterly loyal and deeply devoted to Caesar, for they saw in him not only a great general, but a generous benefactor as well, who held in his hand their future fortunes and the promise of security for their old age, a matter of no mean import to the veterans. He had a deep understanding of their psychology and knew how to handle them as is illustrated in the famous mutiny scene described in *De Bello Gallico*.

In the course of the civil war, Caesar succeeded in overpowering the old republican and aristocratic Rome, a goal that he had pursued from the beginning of his political career. Even before that time he had tried to undermine the prestige of the aristocracy, for its members had prevented him from getting the Egyptian Command. He restored the trophies commemorating the victories of Marius, which Sulla had long since demolished; on the other hand, he tried to gain the sympathy of dissatisfied and frustrated groups and individuals. "He was the sole and ever-ready help of all who were in legal difficulties or in debt, and of young spendthrifts, excepting only those whose burden of guilt or of poverty was so heavy or who were so given to riotous living, that even he could not save them; 'what they needed,' he told them, 'was a civil war'." (6)

The chain of victories with which Caesar overthrew the old republican liberties started with the battle at Pharsalia and ended with Scipio's defeat at Tapsos; the deeply symbolic suicide of Marius Pontius Cato, commander of the Utica garrison, added another sinister detail to the unfolding drama. The Senate, overawed and subservient to the conqueror, proffered to Caesar its support, dictatorship for a period of ten years, supervision over public morality (praefectus morum), the power to appoint public officials, the privilege of the floor in the Senate ahead of all others, and other prerogatives.

"The Republic," Caesar was wont to say, "is a name without a body or shape and Sulla who relinquished dictatorship was a dunce." In keeping with these cynical strictures, all of Caesar's actions aimed exclusively at consolidating and strengthening his absolute power. In this endeavor, he could never be satisfied since as Plutarch explains, he was driven by an "emulation of himself" (an excellent way of describing his insatiable ego-ideal). By identifying his own career with the fate of the country, he safeguarded the integrity and the indivisibility of the realm and at the same time secured his own position.

The uprising in Spain was the last attempt at survival of the foundering commonwealth; its fate, however, had been sealed by the Battle at Munda. "But destiny, it would seem," says Plutarch, "is not so much unexpected, as it is unavoidable." Caesar returned to Rome and contrary to tradition, which frowned on celebrating victories won in civil wars, he made a solemn entry into the capital. On this

triumphant entrance, homage and honors were showered
on him in profusion and while he was being extolled to the
skies, there set in at the same time a wave of vilification
of all the existing government authorities, particularly the
Senate, which was the object of Caesar's special aversion.
The crowning point of the encomiums heaped upon the
dictator was the idolatry, which among other things made
of him the creator of true liberty. Among the monuments
erected on Capitol Hill to the Roman kings, the statue
of Caesar the Liberator was set next to the memorial in
honor of the legendary Brutus and in close proximity to the
temple of the Goddess of Liberty. Soon in the temples
throughout the Roman realm, statues of Caesar began to
be erected, sacrificial offerings were made before them and
a special chapter of priests was erected to worship him as a
God.

Caesar proceeded to reduce beyond all measure the prestige of the Senate and the consulship, institutions that had
at all times been universally respected. He made a large
number of his soldiers, many of them ruffians and aliens,
senators and he mocked the consulship when, upon the
death of Consul Fabius on December 31, in the year 45
B.C., he ordered one Caninius Rabilus elected consul for
the few remaining hours of that day.

He was indeed a true dictator. Gradually, all the institutions around which the life of the state and the body
politic revolved, were destroyed and degraded, while all
power and authority became centered in his person, which
he had surrounded with an aura of omnipotence. These
two processes were complementary to each other. Once
all the formerly revered institutions were shattered, it was
easier for power and authority to become attached to the
one person who had brought this about; and the higher
the position of such a personage in the social hierarchy, the
easier it was for him to crush the remnants of old traditions

and customs. There is no doubt that the cult of Caesar became deeply rooted in the people's psyche and this worship the dictator sought continually to augment by all possible means. Unquestionably Caesar's real and intrinsic greatness was of material assistance in this process. Consequently, the old ideals were slowly replaced in the collective mind by the ideal of an imperator, on whom rested the greatness of the nation and the state. Thus it became gradually easier to show him submission and obedience. In fact, it became a matter of course, and the "father of the country" was turned into an adored father of the nation.

The attempt on Caesar's life might seem to contradict this interpretation. On the contrary, we believe that the tragedy enacted on the fateful Ides of March and the consequences of that tragedy substantiate our conclusions.

In the opinion of the people the commonwealth was dying. Small wonder that in some of the more conscious Romans this fact evoked despair, which was but a natural reaction resulting from the shattering of old ties and ideals. It was then only natural that some of the prominent Republicans either really believed or tried to make themselves believe that Caesar would restore the old Republican freedom. In this respect, changes in the attitude of Cicero are very characteristic and reflect these deep vacillations of the Roman mind. In his *Pro Marcello,* Cicero exulted in the growth of Caesar's power and counselled him about the expectations of the Romans. "For your glory," wrote Cicero, "I take it, consists in the tidings spread through the world of great services done to friends or to your country or to mankind. You have yet to reconstruct the Republic."

It was not a matter of accident that the assassins belonged to the circle closest to Caesar, Brutus himself playing the part of Caesar's son, as it were. Some of the men who slew the dictator had worshipped him just like all the rest of the people and firmly believed that he would restore the oldtime liberty. Consequently, the firmer their belief and their affection had been, the greater became their disillusionment. Those who expected a rebirth of liberty from the benign father's sense of justice and from his power, understood too late that they had been serving a tyrant who, under the pretext of safeguarding liberty, had concentrated complete power into his own hands. "Most open and deadly hatred was produced by Caesar's passion for royal power." (5) All at once the benign father became an evil and ruthless parent, a despotic ruler of the old tribe, who engendered in his sons both hatred and rebellion. Thus in slaying the false liberator, they themselves became "liberators" to posterity.

Certainly they believed not only in the old Republic but in the privileges of their own class which seemed deeply threatened or even abolished by the Dictator. A summary analysis of Brutus and of his associates will be illuminating on this point. The relationship between Caesar and Brutus is so well known that we will recall only a few points here.

When Brutus was accused of opposing him, Caesar said: "What? Think ye not that Brutus can wait for this poor flesh?" It was then a fact that Caesar not only spared him the punishment meted out to others of his party, but admitted him to his closest intimacy. "Brutus had as large a share in Caesar's power as he wished." After Pharsalus, Brutus gave up a lost cause, received pardon from Caesar, high favors, a provincial command and finally the praetorship. Caesar spared Brutus and apparently loved him—out of regard for Servilia. As a young man, he had been intimate with Servilia, Brutus' mother, who was madly in love with him. Brutus was born when this passion was in full blaze and Caesar had some grounds for believing that Brutus was his own son. Caesar cherished him and could not look upon him as a prospective rival, but rather as a devoted friend and successor. Brutus, however, had indicated clearly by his actions and writings what was his attitude toward the mighty parent.

Before taking up arms against Caesar he had already, at least once, turned symbolically against his father. He sided with Pompey at whose instigation his legal father had been put to death. Brutus wrote: "Our ancestors thought that we ought not to endure a tyrant even if he were our own father . . . to have more authority than the laws and the senate is a right that I should not grant to my father himself."

The posthumous influence of Cato, that paragon of republican virtue, asserted itself in Brutus who was his beloved nephew. Brutus composed a pamphlet in honor of the Republican who took his life, true to his principles. "There were deeper causes still in Brutus' resolve to slay the tyrant—envy of Caesar and the memory of Caesar's amours with Servilia, public and notorious. Above all, to Brutus and to Cato, who stood by the ancient ideals, it seemed that Caesar, avid for splendor, glory and power, ready to use his birth and station to subvert his own class, was an ominous type, the monarchic aristocrat, recalling the Kings of Rome and fatal to any Republic." (4)

Nevertheless, in Brutus' attitude toward Caesar, there was so much attachment that his whole position was somewhat Hamletic and he had to be induced by long pressure to take part in the conspiracy.

Among the remaining liberators there were Caesar's closest friends and his best generals. "The new party of the Liberators was not homogeneous in origin or in motive. The resentment of the pardoned Pompeians, frustrated ambitions, personal feuds and personal interests masked by the profession of high principle, family tradition and the primacy of civic virtue over private virtue, all these were in the game. Yet in the forefront of this varied company stood trusted officers of the Dictator, the generals of the Gallic and Civil Wars, rewarded already for service or designated for high office." (4)

We can presume that they took part in the conspiracy not only to save freedom but also out of envy of the limit-less glory and supremacy of one who was supposed to be only "primus inter pares". The sons objected to one of them assuming the power of the hated parent.

Nor does the behavior of the eight hundred senators who saw Caesar killed without uttering a word of protest necessarily testify to their passionate desire for freedom. "They owed to him the honor of sitting in the curia. They begged for his protection and lived on his favors . . . all the time this horrible struggle lasted, while like a beast attacked by the hunters, he strove among the swords drawn against him, they remained motionless on their seats, and all their courage consisted in fleeing when Brutus beside the bleeding corpse assayed to speak." (5)

From this dramatic picture, the conclusion can only be that their need of and love for him remained only to the degree he maintained his strength, and could be looked upon as a means for support. They were ready to give him up as soon as a seemingly stronger force emerged, a force that dared to oppose the Divine Parent himself. It is in reference to that event that Cicero, while discussing friend-ship wrote these memorable words: "It is on the day when the oppressors of their country fall that we see clearly that they have no friends . . . a tyrant cannot have friends." (7)

Thus we see how the road led from the old democracy, through the aristocratic and oligarchic regime to a con-centration of absolute power in one individual. The re-gression to the old monarchy seemed complete. On Caesar's statue somebody wrote: "First of all was Brutus consul, since he drove the Kings from Rome; since this man drove out the consuls, he at last is made our King."

However, the subsequent results of Caesar's assassination in March of the year 44 B.C. are particularly instructive. The conspirators had been of the opinion that with the slaying of Caesar the most difficult part of their task had been accomplished and that once the tyrant was dead, the road to the reconstruction of liberty was open. It turned out, however, that it was easier to remove the man than his deeds, above all the changes, which had been partly wrought and partly completed by him in the collective psyche of the Romans. "Caesar was no longer, but the conspirators after having killed the man and accomplished what they thought to be the most difficult part of their undertaking, suddenly perceived his deeds rise before them and block their way." (1)

The objective hopelessness of the conspirators was reflected in their psychology. They became stricken with fears and feelings of guilt, which paralyzed their future actions. Directly after the assassination, they behaved like Hamlets. They were unable to act even when their course of action appeared with clarity in their mind. Both Caesar's assassins and Hamlet struggled with the image of the father toward whom their feelings were deeply ambivalent.

And what were the reactions of the people to Caesar's death? Did they breathe a sigh of relief on being liberated from oppression and did they eagerly grasp their long-lost liberty?

On the contrary, the people felt helpless and forlorn. "Now that their great protector was gone, the masses felt left to shift for themselves, bereft of leadership, without any support other than the impotent remnants of Clodius' associates." (1) The Senate dispersed in panic. The conspirators proceeded to the Forum, there to announce to the people the glad tidings, but they found no response from the multitude.

The feeling of an irreparable loss and of helplessness increased considerably after Caesar's last will and testament had become known. Once more the magnanimous picture of the benign and almighty father stood revealed before the eyes of the stricken mourners. "When it was found that the will of Caesar gave to every single Roman seventy-five drachmas and left to the people his gardens beyond the Tiber . . . an astonishing kindliness and yearning for Caesar seized the citizens." (9)

The excitement of the masses reached its height during Caesar's solemn funeral. Spontaneously, a huge pyre was erected, on which the mortal remains of the leader were consigned to the flames, while the mob with flaming torches tried to set fire to the abodes of the conspirators. Thus, symbolically, they expressed both their love for the dead leader and their hatred of his enemies. Out of the glowing fire of these inner metamorphoses came into being a supreme idealization of Caesar, who now definitely and irrevocably took his place among the gods.

Accordingly, the struggle waged by the triumvirate against Caesar's assassins acquired a religious sanction. Thus on the triumvirate devolved a particle, so to speak, of Caesar's power, who in that way posthumously, as it were, continued to function as a dictator. Each of the future triumvirs endeavored to be the living exponent of that dictatorship and all three together managed to wipe out what was left of the old commonwealth. Octavian marched on Rome, forcing the senate to confer the consulship upon him. This accomplished, he for all time to come deprived that most venerable of the commonwealth's institutions of any and all significance. The battle at Philippi spelled the final defeat of the republican party and with it the cause of the commonwealth became definitely lost. No effort, however heroic, was able to save what to all intents and purposes had been moribund in the collective psyche for many years past.

The universal disorganization which set in after Caesar's death was perfectly consonant with the gradual decay of the old bases of public life. The terrorism and the proscriptions liberally applied by the triumvirs aimed at nipping in the bud all attempts at opposition and kept the Romans in a state of subservience while the struggle with the Republican faction was going on. The edict of the triumvirate outlawed 700 senators and 2,000 nobles; throughout the length and breadth of the realm there spread a veritable orgy of persecutions, murders and unbridled passions. All the foundations of ethics and an orderly community life crumbled.

This is the picture Ferrero offers of moral disintegration in post-Caesarean Rome. "There were wives who succeeded in having entered on the fatal lists husbands whom they detested or who, while making their husbands believe that they were attempting to save them, turned them over to the hangmen. There even had been sons who betrayed the hiding places of their fathers." (1)

The general break-up also eventually engulfed both armies, which after the battle at Philippi held in their hands the decision on Rome's fate and over which the commanders lost all control and authority.

"Liberty was dead, the armies proceeded to accept as their commanders the triumvirs, who due thereto seemed to all and sundry to be holding power for all time to come."

All of these happenings, all of this dramatic struggle between the principles of democracy and despotism ended as if the end had been predestined. All fluctuations and struggles notwithstanding, the old principle of monocracy prevailed in the end.

"The battle at Philippi," Ferrero says, "only confirmed what had already been decided at Pharsalus." (1)

What is our interpretation of the final stages of this struggle?

The dictator became the personification of an ideal, the incarnation of the ego-ideal and at the same time of the powerful guardian parent. Surrounded with the halo of almighty power, he tapped the sources hidden in the collective mind, the very sources from which religious sentiment flows. Accordingly, the image of Caesar became the material out of which a deity was evolved. "Caesar was numbered among the Gods, not only by a formal decree, but also in the conviction of the vulgar."

With the entire affection concentrated on the dictator's image alone, all other authoritative factors paled into insignificance, relinquishing to the dictator's image the last remnants of their own emotional value. Thus in the collective mind, the dictator became more and more the only personification of power, just as in public life he had been the only factor of government, while fear, obedience, affection and adoration were in turn the four pivotal elements of the people's attitude toward him. Each of these emotional ties is distinctly exclusive and tends to concentrate around one person only, thus strikingly accentuating its origin from the primeval relationship between parent and son. Such a tie has traces of a dictatorial character in its very origin, as it admits of no distribution and eliminates all rivals.

As the broad masses of the people lost faith in their own strength and in their own democratic institutions, their need for leaning on a strong father increased. The mind of the masses executed an ever-increasing regression to childhood, with all of the latter's feeling of dependence, helplessness and weakness, resulting in worship of personages who may give help, support and, above all, strength. The weaker the ego, the stronger the anxiety and the need for support.

Such regression perforce brings in its wake another specific type of regression, which under certain conditions may be observed in the collective psyche. Both thought and emotion descend from the high level of abstraction to concrete, that is, more primitive attitudes. Instead of the ideal of the republic, there comes to the fore, just as in the days of old, the patriarch, the monarch, the general, the imperator, in one word, the father with all his good and evil attributes.

The death of this new father-substitute merits specific attention. Again there occurred a mighty upheaval in the mind of the masses, which had begun to be stabilized. The despair caused by the loss of the beloved parent could not help producing a feeling of weakness and defenselessness. The melancholy mood, which the collective mind is unable to endure for a protracted period of time, became liquidated in two ways. Once by the flames, which as we saw, symbolized on the one hand the affection for the departed and on the other hand the craving for the destruction of his murderers who were considered as felons and vile rivals. Hence, the possibility of a revolutionary and even anarchistic flare-up. Secondly by the extraordinary idealization of the dead Caesar, which manifested itself in the erection of a mausoleum dedicated not only to the memory of his person, but also to his position in the world of reality. Thus the process of his deification, which had begun while he was alive, was completed.

One need not despair for a man who had been elevated to the heights of divinity.

From this deep source originated the growing absolutism of the Roman monarchy. All imperators were objects of divine worship, their glory and majesty were a natural expression of their position in the collective mind, in which their images became integrated into the ego-ideal, thus joining up with the most ancient images of the divine father.

Let us add a few more words about the funeral pyre which was supposed to exalt the great deceased and annihilate his assassins. From studies of pyromania, we know that setting fire has a definite symbolic and economic meaning. It serves to express both essential drives postulated by psychoanalytic theory. Arson is a discharge of both the erotic and the destructive libido; it is a symbol of both love and hate. (10) Jaspers has described servant-girls from the country who, longing for their native home and detesting the home of their employer, destroyed the latter by flames. (11) In one of my own cases, frustrated love found its outlet in a fire which symbolically destroyed surrounding reality.

We may assume that the funeral pyre after Caesar's death expressed not only the ardent love which burned in the souls of the people, but also their whole repressed aggressiveness toward the beloved yet austere father. After such a discharge, the process of idealization and deification could develop without any obstacles. It was symbolic that in later years Horace in his Odes could omit all mention of Caesar, the Dictator. "Only the Julium Sidus is there—the soul of Caesar, purged of all earthly stain, transmuted into a comet and lending celestial auspices to the ascension of Caesar's heir." (4) It was largely from this idealization that Augustus derived his strength and splendor.

OLIVER CROMWELL
AND
THE PURITAN REVOLUTION *

The record of the Cromwell dictatorship is very instructive, for it reveals certain basic laws of the individual and the collective psyche.

Modern research has shown us the silhouette of a great revolutionist, dictator and statesman and has given us an opportunity of studying him from more angles than Carlyle's hero worship permitted. The monographic studies by Firth, Morley, Gardiner, Buchan, Hayward, Stirling Taylor, the analysis by Kittel, the essay by Onken as well as Carlyle's older work have served as my source material in this essay. (1)—(9)

A moderately well-to-do member of the landed gentry, Cromwell was brought up in a Puritan environment. We know virtually nothing about his relationship with his father, always a significant factor in the formation of personality. We do know, on the other hand, that his relationship to his mother was exceedingly close, that the future Lord Protector relied greatly on her opinion and authority and that even in the midst of pressing state tasks, he never retired without first paying her a visit. The strict educator of his early school years was the Puritan Dr. Thomas Beard, who instilled into the regicide-to-be the principles of Puritan fanaticism, a belief in the constant intervention of Providence in human affairs, and a conviction that the Pope and Antichrist were the same. The role played by this

* Reprinted from *The Journal of Clinical Psychopathology*, vol. 7, no. 2, October, 1945.

teacher in shaping Cromwell's ideals was so great that when the latter had already become a member of Parliament, he dedicated to his former pedagogue one of his early brief, violent and unfinished speeches.

Calvinism, as a point of departure for Puritanism, was the fundamental medium through which Cromwell regarded the world and its affairs. This tendency, deeply rooted in early youth, became increasingly evident as Cromwell matured politically and participated more in public affairs.

We need not go into detail here about the contents of the Calvinistic doctrine. We should like to emphasize, however, the inexorable severity of its teachings on predestination and eternal perdition on the one hand and the omnipotent grace of salvation on the other. The uncompromising austerity of the superego imposed a continuous and unusually vigilant repression, while the repressed impulses reappeared under the guise of an ever menacing Satan. Hence, the seventeenth century saw a million witches burned at the stake—of whom not a few met their death in England and even in Cromwell's native locality.

Cromwell's Bible was not the Bible of contemporary man. It had not passed through the filter of critical exegesis. It was to him what it still is today to the absolutely orthodox Jew, namely, the Book of books, the sole revealed word of God, in which every phrase, every text is equally binding and holy. The God to whom Cromwell turned directly, throughout his entire life, on every question and in every crisis, was the real Lord of Hosts of the Old Testament, whose direct intervention in all human affairs could not possibly be doubted.

As far as other elements in Cromwell's mental development are concerned, mention must be made of the old family antagonisms with respect to the monarchy: The protoplast of the family, Thomas Cromwell, Earl of Essex, Minister of Henry VIII, was executed because of his excessive

zeal in support of the Reformation and his part in the
King's marriage to the soon hated Anne of Cleves. Some
scholars surmise that the future regicide may have met
his future victim, later the King of England, on his family
estate in his youth.

The meagre facts in our possession regarding the early
years of Cromwell indicate the presence of markedly neurotic traits, or more precisely, phobias and death fears
resulting from a religious feeling of guilt and sinfulness.
He would not infrequently rouse the local doctor at night
in the belief that he was dying. Later, in the first period of
his sojourn in London, he likewise consulted a physician,
who in his notes characterized him as "valde melancholi-
cus".

In subsequent years Cromwell often returned to his old,
allegedly great sins. He writes as follows to his cousin:
"You know what my manner of life hath been. Oh, I lived
and loved darkness, and hated the life, I was the chief of
sinners. This is true, I hated godliness, yet God had mercy
on me." Of course, one should not deduce from these
ex post facto reflections of a neurotic that the conduct of
the youthful Cromwell was indeed deserving of condemnation. We know full well how deceptive such a neurotic
perspective can be. There is only a bare possibility that the
outbursts of a childish or boyish temperament, whether of
an aggressive or an aggressive-erotic character, merited such
a severe appraisal from the neurotic superego.

Then there was the mysterious moment of religious con-
version which restored to Cromwell a seeming calm, al-
leviated his fears and awakened within him the hope or
perhaps even the certainty of salvation. But in the course of
time this calm was broken by periods of gloomy despair.
One of Cromwell's friends describes his state of mind and
the spiritual crisis he underwent at that time as follows:
"This great man is risen from a very low and afflicted con-

dition, one that hath suffered very great troubles of soul, lying a long time under more terrors and temptations, and at the same time in a very low condition for outward things. In this school of afflictions he was kept till he had learned the lesson of the cross, till his will was broken into submission to the will of God." Religion, one of the students contends, was implanted in his soul by means of the hammer and fire and did not illuminate his understanding with a gentle light.

Henceforth Cromwell's activity was increasingly steeped in a religious atmosphere, as if he wished to prove himself worthy by his deeds, as if he were anxious to provide God with proof of his gratitude for the mercy shown him. It appears natural that his attempts also tended to protect others from transgression, to offer redemption from old and future sins and above all to stifle the ever present, though repressed, feeling of guilt.

His growing self-confidence, together with an ardent sense and need of justice, gained for Cromwell a leading position among his neighbors and finally a seat in Parliament. Several minor matters in which he became interested in the province bear witness to his fervent sympathy for the wronged and to his fanatical passion for justice. Nonetheless, even in these early activities, the uncontrolled violence of his temperament was fully in evidence, resulting in sharp censure being heaped upon him.

In Parliament he was gradually drawn into the whirlpool of the House's fight with the King, in which religious considerations came to the fore. The conflict with Archbishop Laud assumed in his eyes the proportions of a war against the diabolic intrigues of papism, while the King's attempted coups against independence and the guaranteed rights of Parliament appeared to him directed not only against the rights of the citizens but also against the sole certain and unmistakable means of saving the human soul.

In this way, the political fight became closely identified with the religious struggle, acquiring holy sanction and consuming intensity.

During these battles Cromwell had ample opportunity to study the methods of violence which doubtless found a true echo in his turbulent soul. Force was the prerogative of the King, but Parliament also permitted itself forcibly to detain the speaker, who, intimidated by the King, was eager to close the debate and leave the chamber. We shall see later that the influence of these examples was twofold. In the first place, they aroused a natural desire to react, secondly, they served as an example which the mentality of Cromwell accepted easily—just as if the attacked unconsciously identified himself with the aggressors. It appears probable that this capacity to react violently on the one hand and to step into the antagonist's shoes on the other are among those factors which predestine an individual to become the representative of a fighting, oppositional group. Needless to say, they by no means necessarily imply that he has all the other qualifications for a leader.

To gain a better appreciation of the antagonism between the King and Parliament at that time, one must understand the experiences of the collective psyche against the framework of which this battle was being waged. The coalescence between the House and the monarch was very close and strong. There has come down to us an authentic report by Thomas Alaured, M.P., which tells us that during the scenes which accompanied the fight for the petition of rights, the members of the House wept when the moment to oppose the King arrived. In opposing him they felt as if they were cutting into their own flesh. Their superego was closely tied up with the tradition of royalty and only their strong sense of the wrongs they had suffered at the monarch's hands and of his illegal acts was able to break these ties and array Parliament against him.

Accordingly, the violence of the members' passions increased proportionately to their steadily mounting grievances and the gradual straining of their ties of loyalty. The course of future events showed, that these ties—strained though they became to some extent—were never completely broken.

In any event, these reflections make it easier to understand why Cromwell, with all the violence of his temperament, and his absolute belief in the righteousness of the cause he championed, displayed a certain amount of vacillation in his subsequent relations with the King and even attempted to save him. The ambivalence which he showed in this and many other matters was therefore not an exclusively individual characteristic.

It is a matter of common knowledge that Cromwell defended the King before the council of war and declared, after the King had escaped, that "it is some time wiser to allow the murderer to escape". When, in the course of deliberations on the King's fate, Goffe, who represented the army, declared having had a revelation to the effect that the army was committing a sin by entering into negotiations with the enemies of God, in other words with Charles Stuart, Cromwell replied that he did not believe in individual revelations and that the King's fate did not appear to him at all as having been "prejudicated". It was obvious that, all his revolutionary activity notwithstanding, the desire to preserve the monarchy in any form whatsoever, as a foundation stone of the social order, constituted one of the basic motives that guided his actions for a considerable period of time. Eminently characteristic in this connection is the following statement he made: "Therefore I shall move what we shall centre upon. If it have but the face of authority, if it be but a hare swimming over the Thames, I will take hold of it rather than let it go."

When the fugitive King sent one of his trusted retainers

to Cromwell with a message, he received the answer that the regicide-to-be was ready to do everything for him with the exception of sacrificing his own self. The sincerity of his reply is remarkable and at the same time it bears witness to the strength of the ties of loyalty which were not to be rent asunder for some time to come.

Cromwell's negotiations with the royalists were so protracted that they aroused serious suspicions within the army.

It was only the course of events, the ever-recurring treachery of the King on the one hand and his own glorious victories on the other, which helped Cromwell to shake off the old bonds, to lay aside his doubts and strike the decisive blows. The victories he won constituted in his eyes proof positive of the righteousness of God's cause and made of the conqueror the leader and savior of an embattled people.

In spite of all internal restraints and obvious manifestations of ambivalence, the struggle against the King, conducted toward the end with utter ruthlessness, was brought eventually to a tragic climax. Cromwell, who, as history records, quickly distinguished himself on the battlefield, was also the moving spirit, in fact the very soul, of the regicidal drama.

From the moment he took up the fight, he was absolutely certain that the cause for which he fought was just. In his successes on the battlefield he saw the visible sign of divine grace which could manifest itself only in a cause as just as the suppression of a tyrant, the restoration of freedom and of respect for the law. "Good laws, nay, the best laws, were no advantages when will was set above law."

The very beginning of the struggle in Parliament disclosed the basic characteristics of Cromwell's nature, violent, absolutist in thought, guided by powerful emotions and secure in the feeling that he was unconditionally right. In this connection a rather characteristic illustration is furnished by Cromwell's struggle against the bishops in which he took—very early in the contest—a most radical and un-compromising stand. He was one of the so-called "root and branch men", a group which aimed at extirpating the insti-tution of bishops at its very roots. In Cromwell's mind this question became the test of the purity of his own infallible faith, the crux of his innermost religious beliefs. It was also associated with the treacherous and despotic per-sonality of the King. Thus, the struggle assumed the dynamic impetus and the coloring of religious absolutism.

In battle he was not only a great commander, but a leader as well, inspired by a sense of a mission to be fulfilled, a representative on earth of the Lord of Hosts. He went into the fray chanting psalms and endeavored to imbue his troops with the same spirit, training them to iron discipline and austere piety. Thus the revolutionary general became something of a biblical prophet-commander in whom each new victory strengthened his conviction of the grandeur and justice of his mission.

There is no need to point out in this connection to what extent the King's resistance and above all his incorrigible treachery intensified the unyielding determination of the victorious general and fanatical leader.

But when in the last act of the tragedy Charles found himself in his foe's power, doubts began to assail not only the captive's immediate jailors, but the soul of the general himself. Nevertheless, the tragic solution of the quarrel was bound to come and come soon.

The King's doom was demanded by the army whose feats, just like his own, Cromwell viewed as a direct act of Provi-dence. The successive stages of war which led him—until then an unknown and modest member of the landed gentry —from victory to victory, gave him food for meditation on the ways in which Providence was accomplishing its holy and just objectives. Since, however, he was at the same time achieving his own purpose—both conscious and unconscious

—the two categories of objectives merged more and more strongly with each other, until at last the dividing line between his own desires and the dispositions of Providence became completely blotted out thus throwing wide open the approach to the most glorious rationalization of his own desires and impulses.

When therefore the Lord's Anointed found himself in the custody of Cromwell's soldiery and within reach of the latter's chastising arm, the desire to destroy his captive was perforce bound to supercede any and all reservations. Nobert Hammon, his cousin and friend, who was entrusted with guarding the King turned to Cromwell voicing his doubts, awed by the horror of the situation and the possibilities which it implied. Above all he was terrified by the burden of his own responsibility. To allay his doubts Cromwell replied: "I am such a one as thou didst formerly know, having a body of sin and death, but I thank God, through Jesus Christ our Lord there is condemnation through much infirmity, and I wait for the redemption. If thou wilt seek to know the mind of God in all that chain of Providence whereby God brought thee thither, and that Person to thee, now before and since, God ordered him, and affairs concerning him; and then tell me, whether there be not some glorious and high meaning in all this above what thou hast yet attained . . ." A compromise with the King would have been an act of base hypocrisy. Was it not obvious that the glorious divine revelations were not aiming at such an objective? By the same token, the determination of the army which refused to permit a compromise was an act of Providence.

It seems that the sense of divine sanction in relation to a deed as atrocious as the killing of the monarch afforded Cromwell a feeling of peculiar, painful satisfaction. In connection with the appointment by the House of Commons of a board, which was to try the case against the King, Cromwell is reported to have said: "If any man had deliberately designed such a thing he would be the greatest traitor in the world, but the Providence of God had cast it upon them."

Cromwell followed all the stages of the King's case with passionate interest, for this matter was of the most material importance and eminently personal interest to him. The following incident will serve as an illustration. The board entrusted with conducting the King's trial held a session on the morning of the day of the trial, so as to find the proper legal formula under which to try him. In the course of the debate, the news arrived that the King was being brought in, that he was ascending the stairs leading up from the river. "At which Cromwell ran to the window, looking on the King as he came up the garden; he turned as white as the wall . . . then turning to the board said thus: 'My masters, he is come; he is come and now we are doing that great work that the whole nation will be full of. Therefore I desire you let us resolve here what answer we shall give the King when he comes before us, for the first question he will ask us will be by what authority and commission we do try him'."

While the trial was running its course, Cromwell's inflexible will time and again overcame the hesitancy of the judges as well as all protests and opposition from outside sources. He had resolved that the King must perish and once he resolved anything he was inflexible.

Cromwell's mental condition all during this tragic achievement of his was quite peculiar. Witnesses relate that his behavior was marked by considerable exaltation and anxiety. He is reported to have coerced one of the judges into signing the verdict and to have broken out into loud laughter while doing it, while he smeared up another judge's face with ink.

But even after the King had been executed Cromwell did

not experience a complete measure of appeasement. "He was in a strange, unbalanced mood, half of exaltation and half of melancholy." To a psychoanalyst these two antithetic definitions have an explicit meaning of their own. And then under cover of night the regicide came to the coffin in which reposed the remains of the Stuart King, pried open the lid with his sword and gazing for a long time into the dead man's face, whispered over and over again: "Cruel necessity."

From this we are bound to infer that the King's execution, though it satisfied Cromwell's deepest personal desires, failed to give him peace of mind. Most likely there remained within him a sense of guilt, perhaps even something akin to an unconscious grief. The struggle, however, was not yet over and ever new tasks, such as the war with Scotland and the expeditions to Ireland claimed Cromwell's attention. The attitude of the army which carried its general to the top, surrounded him with affection and implicit trust and saw in him the guarantee of its own liberty as well as of its rights and prerogatives, heightened the commander's self-satisfaction and concurred with his own desires. The collective sanction he thus received coincided with his own innermost religious sanction which more and more assumed the character of a conviction of his own mission. Thus there was gradually consummated the process of the systematic rationalization of his own desires which, because they were elevated to the idealistic level of a holy mission, assumed the character of absolute infallibility. In this way developed Cromwell's very personal and unfailing *historiosophy* which was borne out by all of his successes of which he had such a generous measure and the very nature of which is best expressed by a passage from a letter to Richard Meyer, the father of his daughter-in-law. "Truly our work is neither from our own brains nor from our courage and strength, but we follow the Lord who goeth before, and gather what he scattered that so all may appear to be from him." Here also belongs the indignation with which he explained to the Scottish clergy that the battle of Dunbar, that miraculous revelation, that mighty and strange appearance of God, was not a commonplace occurrence. In the same manner he later on cautioned the Irish that should they offer resistance they would have to expect what divine Providence might inflict upon them, "in that which is falsely called the Chance of War".

Let us at this juncture turn our attention away from the focal personality of Cromwell to examine the psyche of the English people. The struggle against the King was being waged by a portion of the landed gentry and of the well-to-do middle-class. In the eyes of the people at large and of an overwhelming majority of the aristocracy, the King never ceased for a moment to be the Anointed of the Lord and the very thought of opposing him was bound to arouse horror, since it aimed at the most essential foundations of the superego. The army, at first only a tool in the hands of Parliament, very soon made itself independent and formed its own objectives and ideals. The negative side of these objectives and ideals was the struggle against the "tyrant", whereas their positive side was the securing of power and privileges. Once it became apparent that even a King could be done away with without the world crumbling as the result, there was no cause to relinquish power and turn it back to its original holder, the Parliament, weakened as it already had been by the first great "purge" executed by Colonel Pride. Let us take note, in this connection, of the highly important fact that the purge in question had as its objective the removal from the House of Commons of all those members who might have opposed the execution of the King. Thus it was possible to have a unanimous but subservient Parliament, a body which having once abdicated its own ego ideal, was bound to become a feeble and impotent tool in the hands of the new rulers.

The social background of the revolution began to take shape very soon. Under the guise of militant and victorious puritanism the bourgeoisie began to take power, thus giving rise, for the first time in English history, to a party of middle-class democracy. Nor were more radical elements, including communistic "Levellers", lacking. Their political aspirations were—quite in keeping with the spirit of the period—steeped in mysticism. Before their eyes hovered as the ultimate ideal and objective of the struggle, a sublimated vision of the community life of the early Christians. Opinions, quite unusual for that period, were voiced, that private property in general and the ownership of land in particular were the work of Satan. The personnel of Cromwell's own army, even in the highest grades, included individuals who came from the very lowest strata of society. Colonel Pride, who executed the famous purge of Parliament was a driver by profession, Cornet Joyce who captured the King and delivered him into the army's hands was a tailor, Colonel Gordon was a lackey, and so forth. The Puritans of whom the "Long Parliament" was mostly composed, were recruited chiefly from the bourgeoisie. During the civil war, the southern and eastern portions of England, which were by far the wealthiest and the most industrialized, sided with Parliament. In these sections a nobility of the new type, contaminated by tendencies pervading the bourgeoisie, then in the process of formation, was in the ascendency. On the King's side stood the northwestern counties, which were economically backward and still preserved a substantial measure of the feudal economic system. The King's partisans, the so-called "Cavaliers", were the direct successors of the old-time feudal nobles. (10)

When the King was escorted from the court along the

street, the soldiers shouted loudly "execution, execution". The windows, however, and the store fronts were full of people many of whom wept or prayed aloud for the King. Popular sentiment was on the side of the King who by his actions at the time of the execution and his last words addressed to the people strengthened the emotional ties linking him to the great family of the English people.

When the executioner, wearing a mask, showed to the people the head of the Stuart King, a groan broke forth from the assembled multitude (as related by an eye-witness), "such a groan, as I never heard before and desire I may never hear again".

Next ensued a scene, strange and ghastly in its stark horror. Men and women paying money for being allowed to approach the corpse, dipped their kerchiefs in the still fresh blood, and tore out the King's long hair, which they preserved as a relic. This scene evokes memories of a totemistic feast in the dim past. Children bereaved by the loss of an adored father want to gain possession of at least some part of his remains to preserve in that way something of his mysterious force. This incident symbolically depicts the relationship between the King and the people. The nation did not become reconciled to the loss of its King by violence. The elements of kingship which dwelled within the dead monarch remained alive in the mind of his subjects. The near future was to bear witness to that.

For the moment a chill of horror shook the country. A halo of martyrdom and glory descended upon the murdered monarch. The people were quick to think that Charles had been the best of rulers and a most innocent martyr. In vain did old Milton complain that the people "with a besotted and degenerate baseness of spirit, except some few who yet retain in them the old English fortitude and love of freedom, are ready to fall down flat and give adoration to the image and memory of this man, who hath offered at more cunning fetches to undermine our liberties and put tyranny into an art, than any British King before him."

The course of events and Cromwell's subsequent actions made him master of the entire United Kingdom. The real and final silhouette of the dictator became visible against a background of battles and political manoeuvres.

As a warrior Cromwell was not only a general and a strategist; battles were his joy, the slaying of his foes his delight. "The repeated evidence of Oliver Cromwell's joy at the slaying of his enemies is a continual fact which cannot be neglected as a very substantial part of his character." (7) In a letter to Walton, written after a battle, he described to him the death of the latter's son on the field of glory in these words: "As he lay dying, young Walton said one thing lay upon his spirit. I asked him what it was. He told me it was that God had not suffered him to be more the executioner of His enemies."

Combat gave him happiness since it afforded him the opportunity to practice and to gratify his innate sadism and violence in a manner which not only did not run counter to the exigencies of his superego, but on the contrary, was supposed to have been ordained by the latter. In another letter to the same Walton, Cromwell assures him that, "we study the glory of God, the honour and liberty of Parliament, for which we unanimously fight without sitting our own interest".

Cromwell's violent nature manifested itself with increasing clarity in his first moves in Parliament. It was obvious that he brooked no opposition and when meeting it he not only wanted to convince, but also to smash his opponent. This was still more the case when an opponent seemed to attack his sacred religious tenets, of which the justness even in the smallest details was in his eyes a dogma not permitting of the slightest doubt. When riots broke out in Ireland, Cromwell, then an ordinary member of Parliament, contributed his entire annual income to defray the costs of the expedition against the execrated Papists. Neither then nor at any later time did he bother to penetrate more deeply into the causes underlying the quarrel with Ireland. Blinded by hatred, he was unable to perceive the shadow of England's guilt, but saw in the Irish riots a manifestation of Papism's rebellious spirit and a splendid opportunity for a ruthless crusade.

During the expedition to Ireland Cromwell seems to have given completely free rein to his nature. His cruelty knew no bounds, at his behest the population of entire cities was put to the sword, and generations of mothers were later to frighten their children by the very sound of his name. And all this in the name of the holy tenets of the Puritan faith, all to the greater glory of the Almighty Lord of Hosts. "In Drogheda," his biographer says of Cromwell, "the puritan agent of God behaved as a homicidal lunatic."

Each step in the war in Ireland was in Cromwell's opinion ordained by God. After the exceptionally sanguinary capture of Drogheda he stated with obvious contentment when reporting the events of the assault and of the destruction of the enemy army and population: "The officers and soldiers of this garrison were the flower of all their army." The ultimate cause, however, of that blood bath was God: "I am persuaded that this is a righteous judgment of God upon these barbarous wretches who have imbrued their hands in so much innocent blood."

When analyzing Cromwell's actions during the campaign in Ireland in the light of his own utterances and letters, we perceive an inflexibility and vindictiveness which are not at all mitigated by flashes of forbearance and even pity which occur from time to time. Cromwell attempted to spare the town of Wexford by giving it a chance to surrender. The general, however, did not succeed in checking his soldiery which perpetrated an appalling carnage in that hapless town

as well as in so many others. But he did not regret what
happened. After all, he had done everything in his power
and was now quite contented that Providence had ruled
otherwise. The slaughter which had been such a perfect
success no longer burdened anyone's conscience: "And indeed it had not without cause been deeply set upon our
hearts, that we intending better to this place than so great
a ruin, hoping the town might be of more use to you and
your army, yet God would not have it so, but, by an unexpected Providence, in this righteous justice, brought a just
judgment upon them, causing them to become a prey to the
soldiers, who in their piracies had made preys of so many
families and made with their bloods to answer the cruelties
which they had exercised upon the lives of diverse poor
Protestants."

To Cromwell each battle became a veritable judgment of
God. The following passage admirably portrays his mood—
he was then but a rising general—at the outset of a battle:
"I can say this of Naseby, that when I saw the enemy draw
up and march in gallant order toward us, and we a company
of poor ignorant men, to seek how to order all the horses—
I could not, riding alone about my business but smile to
God in praise in assurance of victory, because God would
by things that are not bring to naught things that are." A
few days after the victory at Preston, he wrote as follows
to the governor of Scotland: "The witness that God hath
borne against your army doth at once manifest, if you deny
me in this we must make a second appeal to God, a second
appeal to the Ordeal of Battle." That, however, was but an
isolated incident in the general scheme of things. What an
average man called events, were to a Christian "dispensations, manifestations, providences, appearances of God".
There was no such thing as fate or chance, each battle was
an appeal to God.

To Cromwell each victory seemed a proof of divine grace

and he deemed himself, as Carlyle said, "a minister of divine justice, an executor of God's verdicts on God's enemies". Disobedience to God was disobedience to Cromwell and vice versa. His own principles and commands emanated directly from God, he thought, and therefore had to be carried out with utter ruthlessness. Even when he attempted to show some degree of kindness and forbearance towards the vanquished he made it contingent upon implicit compliance with every one of his commands. Otherwise, woe to them for offending the holy cause of God and Cromwell.

The sense of justice, at all times very strong in Cromwell, was gradually and very noticeably assuming the character of a vindictive and ruthless fanaticism. Defeats suffered by his enemies were always in his eyes a well-deserved punishment, his own victories an infallible sign of God's justice. He himself was becoming a representative of a super-justice, an instrument of God, the chosen man who had a great mission to perform.

The violence and ruthlessness he displayed on the field of battle were but one manifestation of his general tendencies which now came to the surface more and more strongly. The primitive phobias of his early youth became transformed into an everlasting unsatiated religious fanaticism, as if his consciousness of sin and guilt was seeking assuagement in applying the inflexible principles of an austere and aggressive superego. That controlling force, never ceasing in its demands, increased not only its aggressiveness and ruthlessness, but also extended the purview of its influence and domination. The austere morality of the "parliament of saints", convened and directed by the dictator, penetrated, as we know, into all the phases of community, family and personal life, subjecting everything to strict control and censorship. The country was slowly transformed into a school, into a large correctional institution managed by neurotic, sadistically aggressive schoolmasters. If we stop to

consider the trend in the method of government followed
by a man who, even at the time of his struggle for power,
displayed tendencies indicating a magnanimous tolerance,
we perceive in its full magnitude the problem: how does
the dictator's soul become callous, how do elements of
aggressiveness and ruthlessness gain ascendency over Eros.
What did after all prevent England's ruler from carrying
out a program which Barebone developed in such inspiring
words in a speech before Parliament: "We should be pitiful
. . . and tender towards all thought of different judgments,
love all, tender all, cherish and countenance all, in all things
that are good . . ."

These words reflect strong tendencies towards sympathy
and tolerance which Cromwell vainly endeavored to put into
practical operation. In a speech before the "Short Parliament" he advocated tolerance and love towards all "sheep
and lambkin" even the "poorest and most erring". To the
envoy of Louis XIV who interceded with him on behalf
of the Catholics he promised—and with obvious sincerity—
a far-reaching tolerance and referred to how many of them
he had already saved from the fire, "the furious fire of
persecution which tyrannized their conscience, and arbitrarily confiscated their substances". He showed himself
equally favorably disposed towards the plan of granting full
rights to the Jews and in the face of obstacles raised by the
clergy, pledged to them his grace and protection, without,
however, being able to grant them full equality of rights.
Finally to the Quakers, who under the Commonwealth and
in the beginning of the Protectorship were persecuted and
imprisoned, he showed considerable mildness and understanding. During a personal interview between the Lord
Protector and the leader of the Quakers, the famous preacher
Fox, the two religious antagonists established a contact,
which in the end brought about a radical change of policy
with regard to the Quakers. In a circular notice to all jus-

tices of the peace, Cromwell declared that, far though it was from his mind to approve of the erroneous practices and tenets of the Quakers still, since these practices and tenets originated from the spirit of error rather than from malicious opposition to authority, they should be pitied and treated as people afflicted with visions, freed from prisons and handled in the future with kindness rather than with severity.

If these noble intentions on Cromwell's part could not always materialize, if stark reality so often and so glaringly gave them the lie, the fault lies not exclusively and possibly not even primarily with the dictator's contrary, unconscious tendencies, but with the manner of thinking and the ruthlessness of his satellites, the entire ruling clique which surrounded him. His principles, his superego, lived projected as a variety of reflections in the minds of that clique, regardless whether it consisted of fanatical clergymen or of "saints from the Short Parliament", or of the Council of Thirteen or finally of his comrades-in-arms. In all of them, the principles constituting Cromwell's superego (or rather its upper conscious strata) found not only a multiple, but also a coarsened, more rigid, and even distorted reflection. This phenomenon can be explained on the one hand by the general rules governing the collective psyche, which level down more subtle individual mentalities, and on the other hand by the contrast between a personality of genius and average minds, which gladly content themselves with ready-made formulas and systems.

Accordingly, even if Cromwell had really wanted to proceed along the lines of his better tendencies, he was prevented from doing so by the demon of his unconscious mind as well as by the demon of the collectivity. Thus it would not be entirely fair to hold Cromwell alone responsible for all the absurdities and exaggerations of the Puritan regime, for all that prying, hypocritical, bigoted, and moralizing despotism.

Cromwell rode into the lists for the purpose of freeing the country from the despotism of the Stuarts and the bishops. To replace the monarchy, a republic, the Commonwealth, was established and Cromwell became its first servant, its first protector. Was he not "a poor worm and a weak servant of God" as he wrote of himself in a letter to his son at the outset of the Scottish war? "You see how I am employed, I need pity. Great place and business in the world is not worth the looking after . . . I have not sought these things; truly I have been called unto them by the Lord, and therefore am not without some assurance that he will enable His poor worn and weak servant to do His will."

At another time he strikes so fervid a tone of modesty as to savor of self-mortification and this at a moment when after his glorious victory at Naseby he had every reason to be justly proud. He wrote to the House of Commons: "It may be thought that some praises are due to those gallant men of whose valour so much mention is made; their humble suit to you and all that have an interest in this blessing is that, in the remembrance of God's praises, they may be forgotten. It is their joy that they are instruments of God's glory and their country's good. It is their honour that God vouchsafes to sense them . . ."

Foregoing all recognition of his own merits, humbling himself completely before God's will, the valiant knight discovers in himself tones of kindness and tolerance. Further on in the above missive he takes exception to any limitation of the freedom of conscience. The struggle was being waged for the sake of the victory of the divine cause and of virtue; accordingly all of God's children should be protected and surrounded with care.

But this tone was so foreign to the mentality of the High

Assembly that when publishing both of Cromwell's above missives it omitted from each of them the pertinent passages. Which shows, as Gardiner says, that the very idea of tolerance, in whatever shape, was at that time accessible only to a small select group.

Cromwell at times contrived to see some particular sublimity in renouncing power and even in completely effacing his own person. Exalted to the highest pitch he referred in an almost ecstatic speech before the "Parliament of Saints" to the examples set by Moses and Paul "who could wish themselves blotted out of God's book for the sake of the whole people".

And here again we see the other side of the medal. The ruthless dictator who had so quickly assumed an enormous power in the country, seemed to regret his prominent position, to humble himself, to hesitate before making weighty decisions, to display even something akin to weakness. Moreover, he rejected the royal crown offered to him although he most obviously aspired to it. It is plain that he did not feel sufficiently strong to overcome restraints in his innermost being and the opposition of a portion of the army. These hesitations and the sense of weakness—deeply hidden, to be sure, but manifesting themselves from time to time— as well as the fear of a final supreme preferment, supplement the picture of the leader, who after exterminating the lawful ruler, by quick stages became himself a dictator.

An analysis of his relationship to Parliament seems most essential for a proper understanding of Cromwell as a ruler as well as for the understanding of the very nature of the mental processes taking place within him.

A republic, as Buchan aptly remarked, cannot be established by simply decapitating the monarchy. The mental make-up of the various social groups was just as far removed from the Commonwealth as was the psyche of Cromwell himself. His attitude with regard to the democratic principle of majority rule, without which a republic is well-nigh unthinkable, is best reflected in a conversation with E. Calamy (which, incidentally, occurred in the later years of the Protectorship). The latter informed him that out of every ten people in England nine were against him, to which Cromwell replied: "But what if I disarmed those nine and put a sword into the hands of each tenth person?"

At first it might have seemed that Cromwell, since he was Parliament's champion and protector would collaborate with it, the more so, as it was to Parliament that he in fact owed his power. However, the situation very soon became completely reversed. In a considerable measure, Parliament's own weakness and clumsiness, its unproductivity, though it was covered up by much talk and excessive solicitude for its own rights and prerogatives, contributed to this turn of events. A body of such a type, lacking support among the broad masses of the people and opposed by a determined and strong-willed army, had no chance of survival.

This phase of events, however, is of less interest to us. We mention it merely to round out the picture and to avoid the appearance of one-sidedness. By the same token, we must not overlook Cromwell's patience and forbearance in the initial stages, his protracted and persevering negotiations with Parliament until at last, driven to the very limits of endurance by its inertia and goaded on by the victorious army which was clamoring for power and privileges, he disclosed and gave full expression to his hidden, but profound tendencies.

At first Cromwell checked the violent attacks against Parliament on the part of the officers, who in January 1652 demanded its dissolution without delay. To one of his friends he complained of being pushed from two sides to an act "the consideration of the issue whereof made his hair to stand on end". But in the end he had to make his decision and this decision he carried out, as we know, with

utter ruthlessness. The burst of wrath and of moral indignation on his part which occurred during the scene of the
dissolution of the Long Parliament is extremely characteristic of the awakening dictator now gathering strength. At
first he addressed Parliament, commending its work and
solicitude for the common weal. He then changed his tune
and began to reproach the members for their iniquity,
selfishness and other sins. Carried away by anger and leaving
his seat, he started to pace up and down the hall, violently
upbraiding individual members, pointing at them with his
finger, citing instances of their wickedness and immorality
in both private and public life. "You probably think," he
shouted, "that I am not speaking to you in parliamentary
manner. I agree. But you cannot expect a different talk from
me. You are not a Parliament." Whereupon he ordered the
musketeers to enter and forcibly remove the speaker. Fling-
ing an appropriately contemptuous epithet at the mace, the
symbol of the speaker's office, he ordered it removed as well.

The limitation, or rather the destruction, of the rights of
the House of Commons, which if permitted to exist would
have perforce threatened his own rights, the application
of force and the display of violence—all these impulsive
actions, draped in a mantle of offended morality—afforded
at the same time gratification to the aggressive superego of
the neurotic sinner, who was perpetually performing the
mission of a militant prophet. At the moment when the
members, yielding to force, were leaving the hall he shouted
in their wake a characteristic statement which again was
intended to absolve him and show his pure intentions: "It
is you that have forced me to this, for I have sought the
Lord night and day, that He would rather slay me than
put me upon the doing this work."

After the civil war, the regicide, and the destruction of
Parliament, the need for a strong government was generally
felt. Cromwell's favorite delusion was that he was straining

every effort to preserve Parliament. This is evident from a
conversation between him and Whitelock, which took place
long before the second coup d'état (dissolution of the Long
Parliament—April 1653). Cromwell complained of Parliament and pointed to the need of a strong authority, which
would be able to curb the encroachments of a body seeking
the supreme power, but incapable of governing. Whitelock
expressed the hope that Parliament would mend its ways
and remarked that it would be difficult to create such an
authority. To which Cromwell replied: "What if a man
should take upon him to be a king?"

Our last observations point plainly to the double background of collective and individual mentality which favored
the formation of Protectorship or, in other words, of Cromwell's dictatorship. The relationship of the dictator to the
subsequent Parliaments was but a consistent evolution of
the tendencies we have just indicated. His feeling that he
was the chosen person, his inability to brook any opposition, his desire to make subservient tools of the elected
members were steadily growing.

This became clear even in the first salutatory allocution
delivered by the Lord Protector to his Parliament (September 1654). He greeted it with all due gravity and consciousness of his mission and superiority. When the members, however, referred to the tradition of the English
constitution which guaranteed the unalienable prerogatives
of Parliament, he did not hesitate to remind them of the
unqualifiedly divine right of his leadership and of the fact
that it was he and he alone who was the fount of their
power, which therefore could last only as long as they
recognized the supreme authority of the leader. We have
heard words like these before. Charles Stuart did not reason
any differently during his struggles with the House of
Commons. On the contrary, he conceded certain rights to
the House of Commons but insisted that the fount of these

rights was he himself. Not only Cromwell's manner of thinking, but all his behavior with regard to Parliament became increasingly reminiscent of the methods applied in a manner far worse, because less forcefully and less successfully, by the crowned ruler.

Lambert, one of the dictator's most zealous adherents inquired of Ludlow who was one of the leaders of the opposition, why he refused to recognize the Protectorship regime? Answered Ludlow: "Because it seems to be in substance a re-establishment of that which we all engaged against and had with great expense of blood and treasure abolished." And Stirling Taylor commented: *"If one observes closely, it will be seen that Cromwell learned most of his methods from Charles."*

Even in a matter as characteristic as the right of levying taxes, which at one time constituted one of the chief stumbling blocks between the King and Parliament, Cromwell struck a note which was well-nigh an echo of Charles Stuart's manner of thinking. "Though some may think that it is a hard thing to raise money without Parliamentary authority upon this nation, I have another argument to the good people of this nation, whether they prefer their will, though it be their destruction, rather than to comply with things of necessity." Here we have clearly expressed the principles of absolutism pure and simple.

His own lust for power, combined with the consciousness of being the man chosen by divine sanction, made Cromwell—in this respect a prototype of modern dictators—think that his rule was a blessing for the people and that it existed by the grace of God. For this reason he was determined to help divine grace along, in other words to uphold his rule by force. "The willful throwing away of this Government so owned by God, so approved by men—I can sooner be willing to be rolled into my grave and buried with infamy, than I can give my consent unto."

Thus spoke the new Anointed of the Lord. In a similar vein spoke Charles on the eve of his doom. His murderer became the echo of the victim's very own words and very own thoughts. The prerogatives and the authority of the executed parent passed by way of a mysterious introjection and merger of identities into the victorious son who, by the force of fatal laws, himself changed from a protector of liberty into a tyrant, an object of conspiracies and hatred. When after the truly regal ceremony of the Protector's inauguration, Cromwell, now the Lord-Protector, returned to the palace, his progress was accompanied by shouts of acclamation from the troops and by a half-mocking curiosity on the part of the populace.

Characteristic of the position of the dictatorship in the body social and in the collective mind at that time is the fact that both the royalists and the forerunners of communism, the "Levellers", conspired against the dictatorship's tyranny. The erstwhile extremists, the champions of liberty in the heroic period of the revolution, rose against the new tyrant. One of their number, a man by the name of Wildman was seized at the moment when he was composing "a declaration of the free and well-affected people of England in arms against the tyrant Oliver Cromwell, Esquire".

The Protectorship's second Parliament was subjected to a severe purge. Only those members were seated who signed the declaration of allegiance and these received special cards of admission. The excluded members, ninety-three in number, drew up a protest, a perfect counterpart of the protests made once upon a time against the King. In sharp and vehement language they condemned the tyrant's practice, "to use the name of God and religion and formal fasts and prayer to color the blackness of the fact".

However, neither the dictator's authority, nor his promises, nor his actual achievements were able to impose themselves upon the collective soul, to assume the topmost rung in its psychic hierarchy, in other words to take the place of the collective ego ideal. The feeling of this shortcoming and the desire to hold intact his limitless power were bound to intensify Cromwell's despotism and lead in the end to the institution of major-generals, a veritable military dictatorship, execrated by all of England. While protecting the regime against conspirators, these major-generals at the same time supervised the enforcement of all the laws regulating public morality.

Their punctilious and ruthless austerity was but a reflection of the ever-increasing austerity of Cromwell himself, whose general attitude in that period may be briefly characterized as an ever-stronger tightening of the noose by his aggressive superego. By way of illustration let us quote a passage from his allocution to the "Parliament of Saints": "If it lives in us, I say, if it be in the general heart, it is a thing I am confident our liberty and prosperity depend upon—reformation of manners. . . . Truly these things do respect the souls of men and the spirits—which are the men. The mind is the man. If that be kept pure, a man signifies somewhat, if not I would make very fain see what difference there is between him and a beast."

Such austerity put its imprint even upon the most tender and intimate of bonds. Here is an example, a fragment from a letter to his consort, in which he speaks of his daughter and son-in-law: "I earnestly and frequently pray for her and for him. Truly they are dear to me, very dear, and I am in fear lest Satan should deceive them, knowing how weak our hearts are, and how subtle the Adversary is, and what way the deceitfulness of our hearts and the vain world make for his temptations."

The fear of Satan's wiles in the realm of morals gave additional impetus to the despotism of the dictator and of his major-generals in matters political. How easy was it for an attempt at opposition to become the work of Satan when one's own regime was God-given and one was God's vicar by Him chosen? Accordingly, public opinion was gagged to such an extent that in the capital itself the press was limited to one publication issued twice a week under two different captions.

Puritanism as a movement had reached its peak at that time. It was inspired not only by the hatred for the Stuart monarchy and for Catholicism, but also by the powerful trend towards suppression of untrammelled instinctual life. This tendency led Cromwell ever further away from life and made of him an enemy of laughter and joy. After drawing an analogy between the fanaticism of Pythagoras, of Mohammed and of Cromwell, Spengler came to the conclusion that not only western Puritanism, but also the Puritanism of other cultures, was devoid of "the smile that brightened all the religions of early periods. A death-like gravity hovers above the Jansenists of Port-Royal and over the assemblies of blackclad Roundheads, who in the space of a few years managed to destroy Shakespeare's Merry Old England, also a Sybaris after a fashion". Thus in the community life, though to be sure, only in the community life of the ruling clique, the aggressive, actively suppressive superego reigned supreme.

The discontent caused by the regime of military dictatorship was so great and produced such a ferment in the body social, that Cromwell's keen sense of the realities, as well as his conscience, prompted him at last to abolish the institution of major-generals and to appeal once again to Parliament. His understanding of badly applied force which, contrary to Cromwell's *conscious* intentions, failed to bring happiness to the people at large, made him—in an address delivered to the "Parliament of Saints"—renounce the regime of military dictatorship and to abstain from any and all force and violence: "Yet the very thinking an act of violence was to them worse, he declared, than any battle that ever they were in, or that could be, to the utmost hazard of their lives. They felt how binding it was upon them not to grasp at power for themselves, but to divert the sword of all power in the civil administration."

Now the "Parliament of Saints" again had to put God's work into practical operation, Christ's might was to inspire the endeavors of holy men and lead them towards the creation of a veritable Kingdom of God. Happy indeed the people, happy the English lands that were to see this miracle come to pass.

Thus Cromwell's soul oscillated between the pure aggressiveness of austere despotism and glowing emotional faith in the automatic workings of ideal forces. His failure in the one direction increased the psychic tension in the other.

But opposition movements and even conspiracies—stifled by force and ending with executions—occurred within the army itself. Hence the history of the Protectorship is but the history of the growing supremacy of Cromwell who gradually emancipated himself from the political influence of the army which had elevated him to power until at last he became a full-fledged autocrat. In this he was helped along not only by his powerful personality which it was hard to oppose, but also by the general attitude of the body social upon which military rule weighed heavily and which still yearned for a government of laws under the sway of a strong, but just father.

Just as the intensely intimate fusion of realistic tendencies with religious zeal constitutes a characteristic trait of Cromwell's entire personality, so did the prophet and apostle of the true faith blaze the trail for the consummate statesman in his foreign policy. The solicitude for the salvation of not only his own soul and that of every Englishman, but also of the souls of all the people of Europe and other parts of the world, imperceptibly became a solicitude for the trade routes and the might of the United Kingdom.

The Lord-Protector, the great fore-runner of modern imperialism, was anxious to secure for his country new markets and maritime supremacy on all the seas. But at the same time he wanted to assure the victory in Europe of the cause of God, that is of Puritanism, by forming a great Protestant alliance against the alleged machinations of aggressive Papacy. In the dictator's mind there was taking shape a vast paranoid idea—perhaps the first figment of the persecution mania in modern history—centering around the Catholic menace. This idea obscured the horizon of the great man and completely distorted the political situation of contemporary Europe in his eyes. Spain was "England's enemy by disposition of God himself" and the great plunderer, Charles X, King of Sweden, was in his eyes "a poor prince, indeed poor . . . and a man that hath adventured his all against the Popish interest in Poland and made his acquisition still good for the Protestant religion". These words referred to the great wars of conquest waged by the Swedish monarch, who attacked Poland, occupied West Prussia, the estuaries of the Oder, the Elbe and the Weser, Livonia, and the archbishoprics of Bremen and Verden . . . Poor Tartuffe!

In Cromwell's imagination the great powers of Continental Europe were getting ready to attack virtuous England and the best means of defense was an attack . . . Sweden's seizure of the archbishoprics was to form—so reasoned Cromwell—a perfect basis for aggression against the Catholic states of Germany since, as he tried to convince Parliament, Catholic Europe was seeking "everywhere Protestants to devour".

"Popish plot," he inveighed, "it is a design against your very being, this artifice and this complex design against the Protestant interest wherein so many Protestants are not so right as were to be wished. If they can shut us out of the Baltic Sea and make themselves masters of that, where is your trade?"

Thus the fanatical aggressiveness of the superego plus the rapacity of imperialistic tendencies were woven together into one coherent whole, and became the source of an immense scheme representing a paranoid political idea. Its scale was vast, commensurate with the dictator's stature, with the purview of his ambition and with the tension of his violent desires. The one who fought sword in hand and burned with the fire of fanaticism saw himself all of a sudden surrounded by enemies, his country and the holy faith imperiled by the ruthlessness of the foe.

Eminently successful as Cromwell was both in his internal and foreign policy, immense as was his prestige which shed glory upon the entire United Kingdom, still the discontent and uneasiness among the people kept on growing. It seemed that by refusing the crown which was offered to him, he only strengthened his position, the more so as he succeeded in making his power hereditary and in thus establishing a dynasty. All of these successes, however, were illusory as new conspiracies broke out more and more often and strong opposition movements multiplied. The very soul of the English nation defended itself against the new despotism and, on the other hand, far from having forsaken its traditions of royalty, longed for the old form and symbols. As the hopes placed in the new father of the country gradually proved vain, the memory of the country's erstwhile father became idealized in an ever higher degree.

Small wonder that, with matters going as they did, Cromwell felt more and more lonely and isolated. Moreover, his iron physical constitution began to fail him. The shadow of death reached out to envelop the Lord-Protector. One of his last conversations before he passed away, reveals the earliest cares and anxieties of his tormented soul. "What do you think," he asked of one of those nearest to him, "if one once experienced the grace of God could he lose it again?" "No," was the answer. To which Cromwell replied with a sigh of relief: "Then I may rest peacefully as I once experienced it." Thus his old phobias returned before death and were assuaged. After examining his conscience and taking stock of his deeds Cromwell decided that the capital of his morality and religion was sufficient to redeem his sins. He spoke of having always labored for the good of God-fearing people, for God's cause, for England. He was well aware of the fact that while some people extolled him far too high, others hated him beyond his deserts.

While the Lord-Protector lived, his power kept oppositional tendencies in check, but as soon as he died, the Restoration quickly approached.

In December, 1659, the Long Parliament was reconvened and though it had been contemptuously called the "Rump Parliament", still in the eyes of the people it represented the remnants of the British constitution and won a greater measure of affection than the obnoxious military regime. Worn out by experiments, by the oppressive new despotism and the rule of the mailed fist, the English nation yearned for the old, traditional forms of life. General Monk who, while still in Scotland, had declared in favor of reconvening Parliament, marched into England at the head of six thousand troops. With his assistance a new, free Parliament was convened in keeping with the explicit wishes of the people, as expressed by numerous petitions. Thanks to Monk, the transition from the rule of an armed minority to a government by the majority of the people was accomplished peaceably and without bloodshed. The Puritan regime, established by force and supported by force, collapsed without force having to be applied. At last on May 29, Charles II, the new monarch, made a triumphal entry into his capital. "With a triumph of above twenty thousand horse and foot, brandishing their swords, and shouting with inexpressible joy, the ways strewed with flowers, the bells ringing, the streets hung with tapestry, the fountains running with wine."

"Galilean, thou hast won", the dead regicide could have said, had he lived to witness the turn of events.

The destructive violence of the King's murder rebounded against the revolution itself and in so doing did not spare even the mortal remains of the revolutionary leaders. As a gesture of atonement and expiation for the crime committed, as well as an act of vengeance for all the wrongs inflicted by the civil war and the military despotism, the corpses of Cromwell and Ireton were dragged forth from their sepulchres in Westminster Abbey and on the twelfth anniversary of Charles' execution conveyed on a sleigh to Tyburn, there to be dealt with in a gruesome way, the crowds howling maledictions and curses at them. As far as the collective psyche was concerned, the image of the old traditionally revered Father of the Country gained the upper hand, the monarchy came alive again, but its new shape preserved the marks left by the struggle that had been fought. The attachment to the image of the country's Father remained alive in the nation's mind which for centuries on end remained true to the tradition of royalty, but the negative reactions against the tyranny of the kingly father and against its other edition as embodied in the despotism of the Protector, became an imperishable component part of that national mind and of the British constitution as well. Neither of them tolerates subservience to a despot and it is doubtful whether any dictatorship could ever thrive in England.

In conclusion, we shall attempt to make a psychoanalytic synthesis of Cromwell and his destiny. Because of the extremely complex nature of Cromwell's personality this task appears so difficult, that we would much rather content ourselves with the material as presented, the more so as our main problem, to wit, the relationship between the masses and the dictator appears quite clearly outlined against the background of this material. The searching mind, however, seeks a synthesis and we would be loath to part from our hero without having found a proper niche for him.

Knowing nothing of the basic conflicts of his childhood days we can at best imagine them. In a boy of a violent disposition, nurtured in an atmosphere of puritan constraint and austerity, processes of forcible and yet insufficient repression of the oedipus complex must have undoubtedly occurred. Such forceful repression of "wicked" tendencies left behind a visible trace in the shape of a sense of sinfulness and guilt, as well as a recurring fear of death. The latter is undoubtedly linked up with the impulses of an early sexualism. The youthful "sinner" seems to have reached out for salvation. Some of the letters he wrote later in life give the impression of "a cry from the depths".

Another vestige of his childhood experiences was his consuming ambition, the desire for preferment—restrained though it had been by a sense of guilt—his craving for power and domination constituting an additional derivative of sadistic tendencies. The austere superego contains substantial amounts of repressed aggressiveness and keeps in check fermenting impulses, all the while, however, instilling into his ego the never-satiated longing for ideals and for harmonizing his actions with the exigencies of severe, Puritan piety. The deep sense of sin exacts ever-new deeds to atone for old transgressions.

His entire personality carries the imprint of a strong ambivalence. Its organic, biological elements are most likely connected with the violence of his temperament, the acquired structure of his personality, however, is unquestionably very complex.

On the one hand a powerful current of the libido strove

to tie Cromwell to his environment. This is quite plainly evidenced by the affection for his family, the strong attachment he felt for his soldiers and collaborators as well as by the sentiments he in turn inspired in them. The frequent reflexes of sympathy, kindness and compassion, the tendencies toward tolerance and forbearance constitute additional evidence.

His libidinal impulses are closely welded with aggressive tendencies. His affection is rather domineering, his friendship possessive and despotic, his readiness to help combined with the desire to impose his own principles and to gain control. Woe to the weak who refuse the price demanded for affection and protection. Cromwell immediately sees resistance, but since he brooks no resistance, that resistance must be broken. One may love his fellow-men, but at the same time one should uplift, judge and educate them. In this connection we see the aggressive impulses serving the despotic superego. In the desire to repair injustice his fanatical aggressiveness easily gains the upper hand over kindness and sympathy. The object of affection which refuses to be completely absorbed and mastered becomes a symbol of hostile reality and as such must be destroyed. This happens particularly whenever religious interests, dictated by commands of the superego, are involved. At such times the gratification of his own aggressiveness signifies not only complete control over the object, but also doing justice to the severe ideal, uplifting his own sense of worth and, last but not least, the appeasement of the ever-ready-to-erupt sense of guilt. From this stemmed the fanatical moralizing and proselytizing practiced not only on the groups of obedient adherents close to him, but on the country at large. At such times his sense of power was endowed with the sanction of a high mission.

Rationalization of his own desires by endowing them with a sanction of predestination and a divine mission was a characteristic technique of Cromwell the general and Cromwell the dictator. A critical appraisal of the factual data at our disposal does not justify us in interpreting this phenomenon as hypocrisy. In this instance the sincerity of Cromwell's conviction was complete and it sprang from the deep well of his personality which evolved from the doctrine of Calvin and the teachings of Dr. Beard.

Operating against these dynamic elements of Cromwell's mind were, as we have seen, mighty dams of inhibitions. Special circumstances, as well as increased tension in the sphere of impulses, time and again overthrew these restraints whereupon the dictator displayed violent and elemental fits of wilfulness. It is obvious that with such strong inhibitions Cromwell could never have played his part in history, had it not been for the specific situation in the socio-historical evolution which he faced. Due to this situation Cromwell took the lead in the struggle against the monarch and eventually guided the axe that cut off the head of the Stuart King. To this high tension in the historical situation Cromwell owed his opportunity for putting into effect on a vast scale the aggressive components of his oedipus complex. And he is one of the few mortals who ever achieved this.

The moment he did it, there were laid in the collective mind the foundations for the future Restoration, in other words for the turning-back. As for himself, the powerful discharge led rather to an increase in the sense of guilt which he sought to compensate inwardly by identifying himself more and more with the murdered King-father, as well as by striving more and more severely towards an ideal regime that would reconcile all contradictions and gratify all tendencies.

He himself was not only to become ruler and father of the country and people, but a better ruler and father than the King, that is the most recent incarnation of that idea,

had been. If the King had to be put out of the way because
of his transgressions, and because of his opposition to divine
commands and to the true faith (as the reformed understood it), then the King's successor should strive to govern
and organize the state in a more perfect manner, so as to
carry out the Lord's will and atone for his own sins as
scrupulously as possible. Cromwell's mind seems to have
been possessed by the great dynamic idea of creating an
ideal, model Kingdom of God, of transforming the existing
state by lifting the people to the highest moral level, by
elevating them to ideal standards such as obtained in his
own group of God's people, in other words, in the small
Puritan clique. The images into which these dreams of
Cromwell crystallized contained, quite in keeping with his
education and reading, elements from the Old Testament,
whereas he himself, as we have seen, grew in these images
to the proportions of a prophet, almost a Messiah.

After having fought Parliament tooth and nail, he would
address it again as an assembly of chosen, godly men. At
such times his idealistic attitude hid reality from his sight
and drew it for him in a sublimated, ideal shape. And he
extolled the lucky members of Parliament whom Providence
had chosen to be the executors of Its great dispensations.

These idealistic attitudes were so closely intertwined with
aggressiveness, that as Britain's power increased, Cromwell
dreamed of spreading the same idealistic patterns over other
countries as well, perhaps over all of Europe. This meant
establishing, in cooperation with similarly thinking allies,
the true faith and the kingdom of God far beyond the
confines of his own mother-country.

The close union between such idealistic desires and aggression manifested itself in other symptoms, too. Whenever
experience (and his sense of reality) convinced him of the
distance separating his dreams from stark actuality and
whenever it turned out once again that not all the people

were willing to be the submissive tools of his lofty designs, he flew into fits of rage and indignation. At such moments he was seized by an irresistible desire to remove all obstacles and to destroy his opponents.

Cromwell's famous saying that he, who knows not whither he is going, goes highest, was most closely related to his customary method of searching—at times—very slowly—for God's designs and intentions in events as they occurred and of drawing from them guidance for his further actions. The deeper sense of this statement is quite clear. To reach the topmost gratification of one's own ambitions it is necessary to hide them from one's own self and not become conscious of them. Then and only then, will the Almighty Father himself permit such preferment, will modesty and unconditional submission to His will be magnificently rewarded.

While serving his own ambitions and desires Cromwell never ceased to serve the commands of his highest ideals as well. The measure of his satisfaction was the feeling of being in harmony with that high authority and perhaps also the feeling of sin atoned for. As we have mentioned before, there is a deep sense in his asking about the grace of God in the last moment of his life. It is clear that eagerness for and worry over God's grace penetrated him to his very depths.

We do not know whether or not Cromwell originally had a conscious desire to be a leader and a dictator (it is reported that as a child he once dreamed of being king), but it is certain that he had to become one, impelled as he was by his own genius, by the dynamic force of his own impulses and unconscious desires, and by the imperative of events, as well as by the fatalism of his own transgressions, transgressions of a youthful Oedipus and an adult regicide.

ROBESPIERRE AND THE TERROR *

To the student of social psychology the French Revolution offers an invaluable object of study. This great historic upheaval can help us understand many aspects of the inter-relationship between leading individuals and society at large. The great Jaurès himself insisted that the psychological point of view supplement the dialectical materialist inter-pretation which orthodox Marxists consider sufficient.

How did the dictatorship of the Terror arise and what were its psychological implications? Some historians con-sider the Terror an unavoidable consequence of revolu-tionary activity. "It seems," says Le Bon, "that one cannot be an apostle without experiencing the need to massacre someone or something. This is an almost universal psy-chological law." He goes on to say that "the Terror should be considered a general procedure of destruction, not a mere expedient of defense". (1)

This view is opposed by the apologists of the Revolution, headed by Aulard. In their opinion, the Terror was a neces-sary measure of defense against powerful enemies, external as well as internal, and the leaders of the Terror and the dictatorship submitted to this necessity against their will and at times very much to their regret.

When we consider the various factors that led to the Revolution, we can single out two as essential from a psy-chological standpoint. These two factors are the rapid growth of deep discontent with existing conditions and the break-down of universally accepted institutions and standards.

The general discontent was due to a variety of causes.

* Reprinted from *The Journal of Clinical Psychopathology*, vol. 7, no. 3, January, 1946.

Foremost among these were the famine from which the
poorer classes suffered most and the resentment felt by the
bourgeoisie, whose social status had remained dispropor-
tionately low in consideration of the vast increase in their
wealth and their actual importance in the life of the nation.
The aristocracy became the common enemy of the lower and
middle classes, whose hatred of it swelled into a mighty
flood.

French foreign policy contributed to the psychological
tension of the masses. Violent hatred of the existing powers,
mingled with longing for better conditions of life, mounted
in intensity and sought an outlet.

The educated people of the time were greatly influenced
by the teachings of the philosophers of the Enlightenment,
who contrasted the corruption and decadence of civilization with a supposedly innocent natural state of man. The
universal restlessness became more and more intense with
the result that the people felt a need for a sudden and
violent change.

The feeling of protest against oppressive reality provoked
a craving for destruction. This situation is strikingly similar to the condition of some psychopathic criminals, notably
pyromaniacs. As I have shown elsewhere, such individuals,
unable to endure the reality that confronts them, try to
destroy it in some symbolic way, since they are unable to
transform it in accordance with their wishes. (2)

The second of our two factors, the weakening of the old
ideals, can be defined psychologically as the breakdown
of the collective superego. The authority of the King, the
church, and the nobility had gradually lost its awe-inspiring
character. The disintegration of the superego released repressed tendencies. Resentment, envy, and other primitive
aggressive drives began to manifest themselves in the attempt to destroy the existing order. Those institutions that
had always symbolized repression and whose images had

formed the important elements of the collective superego were the main targets against which the destructive tendencies were directed.

The external struggle—that is, the struggle between the collective ego and social institutions—paralleled the internal struggle between the ego and the superego. But the overthrow of the monarchy, the church, and the nobility proved in some respects easier to accomplish than the corresponding internal liberation.

The constructive activity of the people and of its leaders was manifested in the work of the Constituent Assembly. There, a center of legislative action, inspired by prominent personalities who represented the aspirations of the oppressed classes, was set up against the currents of anarchy and destruction.

Even a cursory study of the initial period of the French Revolution reveals that the violent outbursts of collective passion and the brutal excesses that characterize this period served as an outlet for the vast load of accumulated hatred. At the same time, they constituted a reaction against the powers entrenched in public offices.

Necker's return to office and the convening of the States General meant the first victory of the French people over the absolutist regime. But the aristocracy then attempted to deprive the States General of all real power to enact reforms, hoping to reduce its status to that of a merely advisory body.

"Never did execration more suddenly replace enthusiasm," an eye-witness relates. "I saw the very same Parliament hailed in triumph on June 22, because it had convened the States General, and covered with contumely on June 25, because it tried to impose on this body the character it had in 1614."

The National Assembly that met in the royal tennis court abolished the prerogatives of the nobility. On the way to the session which the King was to attend, the Keeper of the Seals and the Archbishop of Paris were set upon by a mob that derided them, spat at them, and so brutally insulted them that the King's secretary, who was escorting the Keeper of the Seals, dropped dead of mortification.

Religion, seemingly the strongest of all the established institutions, was one of the first targets of mass fury. The church and its personnel were the objects of the most violent persecution. Religious ceremonies were ridiculed; the religious elements of the collective ego ideal were now subjected to unrestrained blasphemy. Even clergymen participated in sacrilegious practices, some of them declaring in plain terms that the holy guillotine, not the cross, would save the world. The bloody symbol of the Revolution did in fact replace the crucifix. Miniature metal replicas of the guillotine were worn suspended from necklaces.

In the minds of the people, the power of the church was closely associated with the power of the King. For that reason, the royal tombs which had been revered as symbols of religious as well as political authority were the target of an aggressive reaction. The sacred and historic temple of St. Denis, containing the tombs of the Valois and Bourbon monarchs, was broken open and despoiled. Even the coffin of Henry IV was taken from its vault; the corpse was placed upright on a stone, and desecrated by the ferocious rabble until finally a drunken woman knocked it down with a blow in the face.

This macabre act of aggression indicates the intensity of the emotion with which the symbols of royal power were invested. The fact that entire sections of the population, including a part of the aristocracy, participated in royalist plots is still another proof of the violence of the emotions aroused by the images of authority. Such plots, of course, intensified the severity of the revolutionary counter-measures. Thus the intrapsychic struggle against old ideals was reflected in collective movements and demonstrations directed against the external symbols of those ideals.

There is another important problem to be considered with regard to the psychological background of the class struggle. The ancient feudal structure of France began to crumble long before the Revolution took place. The nobility had already lost much of its prestige; the so-called Third Estate (the bourgeoisie) had gained in importance as its educational standards rose and its wealth increased, but it was still overshadowed in many ways by the privileged aristocracy. The Third Estate, aspiring to legal and social power commensurate with its economic power, inevitably clashed with the aristocracy, which was unwilling to relinquish, in the form of its privileges, the only means of domination that still remained to it. In its eagerness to attain its goal the bourgeoisie subverted the inner framework of the old ego ideal which was based on the long accepted social structure, and thus prepared the eruption of destructive impulses.

To be sure, the King and the aristocrats were incapable of giving up either their principles or their privileges, to which they clung with narcissistic tenacity. The lower classes were bound to develop an ever increasing hatred for those in whom they saw the cause of their present distress as well as the enemy of their future happiness. Frustrated in their desire for social power, the bourgeoisie shared this mass hatred with the poor of towns and villages, whose aspirations were usually limited to obtaining the daily bread that they were denied.

Hatred always unleashes destructive impulses, sadism and aggression. In individual situations, hatred is to a certain extent controllable, but mass hatred is unmanageable. Historical records and personal reports contain ample illustrations of destructive and often clearly criminal acts perpetrated during that period.

These primitive impulses were so strong, produced as they were by the constant fear of internal and external enemies, that the revolutionary struggle did not suffice to absorb them in full. When the old social barriers had been broken down, new forms of authority were created to replace those that had been destroyed. New ideals and allegiances developed out of the common struggle. Nevertheless, hatreds, far from being assuaged, were focused against the new institutions and continued to disrupt the social order. The Constituent Assembly was too weak to resist these forces and had to give way to the Terror, which in its turn failed to put an end to factional strife. Records of that era clearly show that the Gironde was no less bloodthirsty than the Mountain. In fact it was the first to declare, through Pétion, its spokesman, that opposition parties should be suppressed by force. It also tried to justify the September massacres. In this way it helped prepare the ground for the method of government that Robespierre most clearly formulated when he said that the defense of the Republic required the destruction of all opposition.

The foundation of the new society on the basis of equality did away with the last vestiges of the feudal structure. At the same time it gave full opportunity for the expression of resentment and hatred. "The concept of equality," says Le Bon, "frequently covers feelings that are entirely contrary to its true meaning. In such cases it actually represents an imperious need to know that nobody is above us and a desire, no less intense, to feel that somebody is below us." (1)

When new elements of the collective ego ideal began to replace those that had been broken up and destroyed, the tendencies toward domination and submission, toward self-aggrandizement and adulation, that had been momentarily frustrated by the leveling of the old society, now found other channels of expression. Generals and dictators were able

to satisfy their aggressive and sadistic impulses by imposing
their will on others, and masochistic individuals could find
gratification in submitting to their leaders. Such primitive
instincts were rampant in the national assemblies as well
as in party factions.

All the national assemblies, and particularly that of the
Convention, were slavishly submissive to their leaders, with
the result that a dictatorship rapidly developed. The Convention became an instrument in the hands of either the
Jacobin Club where Robespierre ruled, or the Committee
of Public Safety. The rank-and-file of the Convention, referred to as "La Plaine", were noted for their abject obedience. Their leaders encountered little opposition in forcing on them their ever-changing and often contradictory
decisions.

Whatever aggressive impulses most of the members of
the Convention may have had, they apparently found sufficient satisfaction in the work of destroying the last remnants of the old regime and in fighting against real or
fancied enemies. In their relations to their leaders they
acted as a passively obedient mass.

The new elements of the collective ego ideal soon took
definite form. The reverence that had been attached to the
old forms of government, the devotion to the King and his
deputies, were transferred to new idols. The new government, the popular leaders, the revolutionary ideals, the
nation, the people, now became, along with the ultimate
generalization—welfare of humanity—objects of veneration.
An attempt was even made to replace the prevailing religious ideals with those of a new cult, made to order. An
enlightened religion free from superstitions was proposed.
Equality, freedom, patriotism became the ideals of the day,
developing, in the course of the Revolution, partly as an
expression of reaction against oppressive authority and
partly as a basis for defending the Revolution against its

enemies. When the monarchies of Europe threatened the French Republic from all sides, the ideal of national independence became inseparably connected with that of personal liberty. The fear of foreign enemies thus intensified the patriotic fervor of the French people and at the same time increased their distrust and hatred of the nobility who were regarded as allies of the foreign governments.

This sense of being menaced appeared in other connections besides that of national defense; fear came to be one of the main elements of the Terror and the dictatorship.

With the release of aggressive impulses from the restraints imposed on them by oppressive institutions, the danger of anarchy was always present. Rebellious movements were a constant threat to the government. Anyone and everyone was a potential ruler. A Hobbesian state of war of all against all threatened to develop. Against such tendencies, even though they themselves often shared them, the leaders of the Terror erected defensive barriers by resorting to measures as violently fanatical as the acts of those against whom they were directed.

Since the aggressive acts of the leadership equalled in violence those of the people who tried to capture power, anyone who took part in the political struggle had reason to fear repressive measures on the part of his competitors. Moreover, the unrestrained behavior of leading personalities had the effect on the masses of increasing their tendency toward anarchy and of producing in them a strong tendency toward projection.

In this general atmosphere of unrestrained aggression, incidents occurred that vividly illustrate the extraordinary sadism of the period. The individuals involved in such incidents probably had a predisposition for cruelty and took advantage of the absence of effective social controls to give free rein to their criminal impulses under the guise of defending France and the Revolution.

The trial of Lebon, an ex-priest, who as a close collaborator of Robespierre had brought about the deaths of many people at Arras and Cambrai, has been recorded in a two-volume work. The trial revealed acts of fantastic cruelty. "This book is a nightmare," a historian declares, "it is a product of the Marquis de Sade, transformed into an epic."

But manifestations of primitive criminality by hangmen who carried out orders from above were perhaps to be expected. The sadism of the leaders was a different matter again. In the latter case the psychic structure involved was more complex and the veil of rationalization less transparent.

Fear was the dominant emotion in the members of the Convention and the Committee of Public Safety who conducted the reign of terror under the leadership of Robespierre. Afraid for their own lives, they were willing to pay any price for their personal security.

Many years later, when one of these men was asked how he had felt about his role in the execution of hundreds of persons, he replied: "We were simply trying to preserve our own lives."

The ego drives, kept thus in a state of permanent tension, were distorted to the point where the individual's energies were concentrated exclusively on the problem of his personal survival. The extermination of his fellowmen ceased to be a matter of great concern to the individual if it was the only means of protecting himself. Like men on a sinking ship who, crazed with fear, push their comrades into the sea in a frantic effort to reach the life-boats, the dictator's subordinates tried to protect themselves by sending others to the guillotine.

However, as we examine the upper strata of the party hierarchy and the executive body of the Terror, we find that the psychic structures of the individuals involved were more complex, and the motives for their acts cannot be as simply stated.

The desire to remain in power may be regarded as a simple motive. Sorel is indisputably right in stating that, "the Terrorists of the Revolution resorted to their terrorism because it was their only means of maintaining themselves in power, justifying these same methods by claiming that their purpose was to safeguard the state". (3)

Ideological factors are not the least important element of the psychic structure. If the new regime was to entrench itself securely, the ideals and social objectives that had replaced the old values in the collective psyche had to be supported at any cost. However, these ideals were constantly under attack by people who remained loyal to the old regime, and the fear and mistrust engendered in the masses served also to weaken their fidelity to the new principles. The danger was always present that their former beliefs, which still remained extant in the form of unconscious fixations, might eventually be re-established in power. The fact that the King had been murdered did not prevent his image from continuing to be a powerful psychic force, nor were the people willing to accept all the substitute objects of veneration that were offered in place of the royal symbol. The past has a powerful charm for the unconscious. To free oneself from it completely, one must break forcibly with the past, especially if everyone else is equally under its influence.

The new values that had come into being, catalytically aided by an immense charge of impulse and emotion, only partially reflected an aggressive attitude toward the former symbols of power and the social forces they designated; these values also expressed a deep yearning for a new society, for prosperous conditions and great achievements, and a desire to rebuild in a new form the social edifice that had been demolished. So glorious did these ideals seem to the masses and to their leaders that they were considered the essential purpose of human existence. Whoever failed to profess them was ipso facto denounced as an enemy of the French people and of everything else that was held dear: the Republic, national independence, personal liberty, the welfare of mankind, and so forth. Politicians identified their personal interests with the defense of such ideals and consequently claimed the right to destroy their rivals in the name of the Revolution.

"We shall make a graveyard of France rather than fail to regenerate her in our own way," declared Carrier.

Sadistic destruction was given supreme sanction. Supposedly only evil was destroyed so that it might be replaced by good, but actually destruction became an end in itself, pursued by those who could not resist the gratifications it seemed to offer.

The method of painting everything pure white or pure black, which is characteristic of fanaticism, was often employed. Any expedient, any crime that served the interests of the rulers became absolutely good. Any kind of opposition to them was regarded as absolutely evil. Whoever dared to think differently or to maintain a suspect aloofness was included among the forces of darkness.

Like the agents of the Holy Inquisition, the delegates to the Convention showed no pity toward their victims. No legal restraints could be imposed on them, since they themselves had destroyed one legal system and were in the act of creating another. They permitted no interference with their plans for the new society, forcing their measures on the people in the name of the people's welfare. They seemed determined to reform France whether France liked it or not.

This fanatical attitude was most clearly illustrated by the policy followed by the Incorruptible and his collaborator, the arch-criminal Lebon. Lebon carried out Robespierre's orders with blind obedience, placing the desires of his leader above all other considerations. Robespierre, under the fanatical conviction that he alone represented absolute truth and absolute virtue, regarded everything as a possible means to his sacred ends and considered any act justifiable provided that it served his purposes.

It may be of value to inquire into Robespierre's personal life in order to determine the relation between his character as an individual and his historical role. It may also be of value to investigate the specific conditions under which he became Dictator of France.

Robespierre's mother died when he was seven. His father, a shiftless, erratic man, became completely helpless after the death of his wife, to whom he had been deeply devoted, and had to be assisted by relatives. When Maximilien was fourteen, his father left home one day and never returned, leaving his three children behind. Their relatives took care of them. Maximilien Robespierre endured his misfortunes and his poverty with proud defiance. His sister Charlotte writes of him in her memoirs:

"It is difficult to realize how deep was the effect on Maximilien when we were left orphans. A complete change took place in him. When he suddenly found himself head of a family, he became sedate, thoughtful and diligent." (4)

As a student at the lycée he was proud, taciturn and industrious. He worked hard but seldom mixed with other people. Abbé Proyart, his teacher, said of him:

"Pride, the only guide of his actions, made him apply himself to his studies at the College of Arras; it soon became clear that he was, if not a genius, at least a skillful and patient worker. The poverty from which he suffered penetrated his soul and the very idea of it was repellent to him."

Robespierre seemed to feel that his father's poor reputation reflected on himself and that fate had been unfair to him. This deep wound to his pride effected significant changes in his personality.

His diligence and asceticism indicated that he had resolved to redeem the tarnished reputation of his family and, as his sister Charlotte justly remarked, to become the respectable head of a household.

The intensity of the psychic trauma that Maximilien suffered when his father abandoned him is revealed by his significant confession:

"Such souls (those whose parents have disgraced them) find within themselves only the bitter sense of injustice, the injustice of which they are the victims. Their minds, dominated by the awareness of the inhuman treatment they have suffered, can conceive only sinister ideas and cruel projects. To fill the cup of horror it only remains to see them one day themselves lying beneath the sword of justice." (5)

Thus the reaction produced by the injury that his pride received in his early childhood still motivated him as an adult. All the evidence tends to show that his bitter experiences in that period of his life had considerable importance in determining his future.

When he was elected to the Academy of Arras, Robespierre made a speech. Instead of devoting it to the praise of his predecessor, as tradition required, he made use of this opportunity to denounce the unjust prejudices of people who attach the censure incurred by a wrongdoer to his entire family. Shortly afterward he published an essay on the same subject. (Royal Society of Arts and Sciences in Metz, 1784.)

The essay in question contains a sort of daydream in which the King bestows a signal honor on a man who is generally despised because another member of his family behaved badly. This man, obviously a substitute for Robespierre himself, finds recognition of his merits in the understanding King-father. Wronged and despised until then, he is at last rewarded for his virtue. In actuality, Robespierre eventually became not only the one who was rewarded but the King-father as well, dispensing rewards to the virtuous and punishment to the wicked. He could then have the satisfaction of regarding himself as the supreme judge of good and evil, rather than an object of contempt and pity.

Robespierre became acutely aware of the unjust nature of a society whose institutions were based on prejudices. He decided to study law in order "to defend the oppressed against their oppressors, to plead for the weak against the strong who exploit and crush him, this being the duty of every man whose heart has not been corrupted by selfishness. It shall be my life's task to help those who suffer and to castigate with vindictive words those who, having no pity for their fellowmen, revel in the sufferings of others."

Robespierre's deep sensitivity to the sufferings of his fellowmen led him to identify his own wrongs with those of humanity, and deepened his resentment toward the people who were responsible for those wrongs. Charlotte recalls how upset he was by an injury to a pigeon that was under her care. Records of his early life show that the idea of causing the death of another creature was terrifying to him. He was a judge at a trial in Arras, on March 9, 1782, where a murderer was condemned to death. For two days following Robespierre was unable to eat, so intense was his grief. "I know well," he said, "that the man was guilty, that he is a criminal, but to condemn a man to death . . . !" He finally resigned his judgeship, unwilling any longer to discharge such painful duties.

Unquestionably Robespierre felt great sympathy for the oppressed and had a sincere desire to help them. In the works of Rousseau he found the political and philosophical expression of his values. He not only accepted Rousseau's ideas, but came to admire that philosopher so deeply that he began to identify himself with him. Like Rousseau, Robespierre held to the conviction that man is virtuous by nature but corrupted by an unjust social system. His future task was to restore man to his natural state of innocence by cleansing him of the faults engendered in him by the society in which he lived.

Robespierre's faith was the faith of Rousseau's *Curé de Savoie*. He often referred to the injustices and the persecution of which the author of *Emile* had been the victim in spite of (or rather, because of) his virtuous conduct. Such statements of Robespierre indicate clearly his identification with his idol. A report which he submitted to his constituents after the dissolution of the Constituent Assembly contained a dedication to Rousseau that read:

"The knowledge that he has contributed to the welfare of his fellowmen is the reward of a virtuous man. The gratitude of posterity, who surround his memory with honors, bestows on him the due that his contemporaries denied him. Like you I would purchase such a prize at the cost of a laborious life and even of a premature death."

When Robespierre was elected to the Constituent Assembly he at last had the opportunity to put his ideals in practical operation and at the same time satisfy his ambitions. He was extremely active and industrious, devoting himself completely to his work. It was evident that he had finally found his true calling. What was merely politics for others, became for Robespierre the essence and the religion of his life.

Rousseau's life and his ideas deeply affected Robespierre. He began to think of himself as a crusader surrounded by pagan hordes. In this way he symbolized his role as the defender of the poor and the oppressed against the forces of evil. His view of the universe became deeply spiritual. "Vice and virtue," he said, "control the destiny of the world. Nature shows us that man is born free and the experience of the centuries shows us man enslaved. His rights are written in his heart and his humiliation is written in history."

One can detect, even in this first period of his political activity, the direction of his psychological development and its subsequent stages, down to the fatal end.

It became clear that he classified all men as either virtuous or corrupt. "There are but two kinds of men," he said, "the kind that is corrupt and the kind that is virtuous. Do not classify men according to their wealth or their social status, but only according to their character." By the virtuous he meant those who thought as he did, since he was already quite advanced in the process of identifying himself with his ideals. His main criterion for judging the morals of others became the extent to which they agreed with his ideas. The ideals of justice and liberty were gradually becoming indistinguishable from the judgments of Robespierre. But as one historian judiciously remarked: "If Liberty and Robespierre become identical, then Liberty becomes Tyranny."

Thus began the process, typical of fanaticism, of conceiving the world as the scene of a struggle between the forces of light and those of darkness. On the one side was everything that conformed to Robespierre's way of thinking. He was Ormuzd, the spirit of light and purity. On the other side was all that he opposed and regarded as hostile to him. That was Ahriman, the spirit of evil, depravity, and darkness.

It followed that, in order to strengthen the rule of virtue, evil had to be destroyed. But although the destruction of evil was only the negative side of the process and therefore but a means to the end of upholding virtue, it soon acquired the main emphasis.

Robespierre was gradually becoming a stern censor of men. He stressed the existence of evil, opposition, and danger to such an extent that all attention was diverted from the importance of virtue, cooperation, and belief in humanity. He developed the sinister habit of noting down the names of people who for one reason or another incurred his censure. These lists of names furnished him with the material for future executions. The lists grew longer as his judgments of people became increasingly caustic and intolerant.

Robespierre considered himself a paragon of virtue and he never forgave others for the shortcomings he found in them. It was never difficult for him to find justification for acts of violence committed in the name of virtue and liberty. On the other hand, he condoned the most ruthless behavior as long as those guilty of it remained loyal to him.

At the same time, he began to sense that danger threatened him and the Republic. He constantly imagined that plots were formed against him and the ideals he represented. After twelve months of his rule, these fears of his became so manifest and his measures for suppressing the fancied conspiracies so despotic that Marat was provoked to remark that Robespierre was following the road of the Inquisition.

I might note at this point that illusions of persecution were very common in that political atmosphere. For instance, Barère declares in his memoirs that "Marat was a secret agent for Pitt and the Count of Provence—and Danton was active on behalf of the Commune under the influence of a powerful party located first in Germany and later on in London". (6)

Let us examine Robespierre's concept of "the people". This term was constantly on his lips and together with the word "virtue" represented to him the meaning of his life. A peculiar combination of personal feelings and general ideas is here involved.

In Rousseau's conception, "the people" meant primarily the oppressed classes—those who were deprived of rights as well as wealth. In another sense the people were an aggregation of ordinary human beings, least spoiled by civilization and therefore least removed from the primitive state of innocence that every individual, according to Rousseau, enjoys at birth. Family customs and social institutions draw the people away from this state of innocence. It was imperative to break down these barriers to natural virtue which had been created by the ruling classes for the purpose of maintaining power over the people.

Memories of his personal experiences gave an emotional depth to Robespierre's social theories. He himself had suffered from the injustices that always oppressed the people. The hereditary privileges of the aristocrats made it possible for them to despise men who were superior to them in intellect and virtue. Thus the enemies of the people were also Robespierre's personal enemies. As the champion of the people he would revenge his own wrongs as well as theirs. He thought of the oppressed classes as a kind of Cinderella and of himself as the Prince Charming who had come to their rescue. He felt entitled to this role since despite the disgrace into which his family had fallen because of his father's behavior, his own actions had always been irreproachable and his character was far above that of many who had treated him with contempt. The people were the personification of virtue in contrast to the corrupt upper classes, and he was the personification of the people.

Wealth was for him the symbol of the privileged classes and also the symbol of evil. For Robespierre, virtue was inseparably connected with poverty—or at least with the absence of luxury. This attitude expressed strong ascetic and masochistic tendencies that impelled him to shun all pleasures, to refuse to seek any so-called personal happiness and to see in suffering only purity and virtue. "I, too," he said, "could have battered my soul for wealth. But wealth is not only the reward of crime, it is also the greatest punishment. I prefer to be poor so as not to be unhappy."

In the successive Constituent Assemblies, Robespierre fought for the people's rights and for the enforcement of the revolutionary principles. His prestige and influence constantly increased and with them his self-confidence and the complete conviction that his ideas were just and his judgments infallible. He was now developing into a tyrannical dictator, eliminating comrades as well as adversaries in the attempt to hold absolute power.

He became more ruthless as the Revolution became more ruthless. He was the leading spirit of the Revolution, its guardian and its guide. Certain phases of the evolution of his ideas and his personality merit special attention. As he fought for the rights of the common people and for the consolidation of the Revolution's achievements, Robespierre recognized only three categories of men—antagonists, supporters, and indifferents. He manifested increasing hatred toward those whom he regarded as his antagonists and he continually added more names to this category. He tried to arouse the indifferents from their lethargy and persuade them to take his side. His elaborately prepared speeches afford evidence of the efforts he exerted to win new supporters.

He regarded as his friends those of his collaborators who thought and felt as he did. Their power increased with his, and it was these colleagues in the Jacobin Club and the Committee of Public Safety who constituted the real governmental power that ruled over the Convention and over France.

Led by Robespierre, these men defended the revolutionary principles that Robespierre was accustomed to designate by the term "virtue". As time went on, it appeared that only they (and eventually, only Robespierre himself) knew what true virtue was. In defending the state against its real and imagined enemies, they gradually acquired for themselves all the privileges that they claimed for the people. Only they understood what the people required for their happiness, and by what means it could be attained. If the people failed to agree with Robespierre and his followers as to what constituted their real welfare, then it would have to be imposed on them by force.

The power that had been wrested from the monarchy and the old social institutions was thus concentrated in the hands of a new ruling group that surpassed its predecessors in despotism and ruthlessness. Former class distinctions were replaced by new distinctions despite the ideological emphasis on equality. The formalities of democratic parliamentarianism were preserved in the Convention, but the real decisions were made by a few men who controlled it.

All power and authority was concentrated in the person of Robespierre. It is true that consciously he regarded power only as a means of realizing his revolutionary aims. But unconsciously he played the role of a high priest enforcing the worship of a new deity. This deity was represented in his ego ideal as "virtue".

As a child Robespierre had played at building shrines. Now he was seriously undertaking the creation of a new religion, based on the notions of virtue and pure reason. The established religion which he had helped to overthrow was now to be replaced by an even stronger ideological structure. This was made necessary by his desire to obtain sanction for his own acts and to strengthen popular belief in the new society. He required a means of justifying himself to the people as well as a means of holding in check the anarchistic impulses of the revolutionary masses, from which he himself was not entirely free. The deep sense of guilt that he must have experienced as a result of his despotic acts could only be successfully assuaged if he represented them as steps towards the realization of a universally accepted ideal. In this connection it is significant that the religious ceremony of the Feast of the Supreme Being was Robespierre's first offering to the French people after the bloody executions.

He became the high priest of the new religion that he established. He was the representative on earth of the new deity. In this way his narcissism was gratified and the demands of his ego ideal were fulfilled. The old image of the Divine Father was replaced by an image that was a projection of Robespierre himself, and the fact that he had created this image was ample reward for his pains.

It is clear that Robespierre's next step in this direction would have been to proclaim himself a god. Had he been completely paranoiac or paraphrenic, he would have taken this step. But he preserved a strong sense of reality and great self-control. Furthermore, the enlightened and skeptical spirit of his era did much to restrain such excesses. Robespierre remained the secular representative of virtue, rather than its divine incarnation. Nevertheless, as he entered the temple during the ceremony and approached the altar of the Supreme Being, he seemed to experience a religious ecstasy.

His rivals among the deputies were unwilling to accept such a state of affairs. They resented the way in which Robespierre assumed the leading role in the religious ceremony and protested that he was using it as a means to achieving absolute power.

Claiming that the Supreme Being "had decreed the Republic since the beginning of time", Robespierre identified his own ideas with the will of God. The Jacobin Club, serving Robespierre as an advisory council, assisted him in proclaiming the glory of God who protects the innocent and chastises the wicked. It is not difficult to perceive that the deity to whom they were referring was in reality a projection of the Incorruptible himself, a creation of his idealistic megalomania and his narcissistic superego.

From this time on, Robespierre's political activity assumed an ethico-religious character and he became the apostle of virtue, the militant prophet of the Republic. As the Terror intensified, he referred to his political opponents as vicious criminals and in his public addresses moral epithets more and more replaced political analyses. In fact, after 1793 such terms of abuse as felon, criminal, monster almost universally supplanted political terminology.

The rational character of the new ideology was subordinated to emotional needs. The circle of those who were accepted as true representatives of the revolutionary ideals grew constantly narrower. The only men who merited this distinction were those who, accepting without question the ideas and judgments of Robespierre, provided him with an inexhaustible source of narcissistic gratification.

He found an even greater source of gratification in his personal relations. Madame Duplay, in whose home he lived, took the place of his mother in her relation to him, treating him with loving care and almost worshipping him as a god. Robespierre submitted gladly to her maternal authority and remained with the Duplays against the wishes of his tender-hearted but jealous sister Charlotte. Records of the time contain a description of a visit to Robespierre by a Deputy named Barbaroux. While he waited for Robespierre in the drawing room of the Duplay home, Barbaroux looked around him and saw on all sides only paintings, busts, etchings and woodcuts of the Incorruptible. He felt as if he were in a sanctuary dedicated to a god named Maximilien Robespierre.

To his contemporaries Robespierre presented a very complex personality. Religious ideals were mingled in him with a sharp critical faculty and a capacity for deep hatred. The cult that surrounded him in both his public and private life gave further stimulation to his intense narcissism.

When he became ill, the people waited restlessly and fearfully for news about the condition of their leader and protector, who they felt was alone capable of defending France from her enemies. A police report contains the following description of the effect Robespierre's illness had on the masses:

"Near the Jardin des Plantes a great crowd assembled to discuss Robespierre's condition. The people appear to be deeply moved by the danger to Robespierre. They say that if he dies, all will be lost. It is Robespierre who detects the conspiracies of the enemies of the Republic. May God preserve the life of this incorruptible patriot."

Only a few weeks prior to his downfall an old soldier wrote to him: "I regard you, citizen, as the Messiah who The Supreme Being promised would come to reform the world."

The cadets of St. Cyr, the famous French military school, were called Robespierre's pages. Aimée Cécile Reynault was regarded as a parricide when she was convicted of attempting to assassinate the dictator.

All these facts serve to indicate that the Incorruptible was endowed, in the collective mind of the French people, with all the attributes of a father of the nation.

He exerted an almost incredible fascination over the masses. He was a mediocre speaker, his orations were lengthy, elaborate, highly emotional, his voice lacked resonance and the fiery eloquence of the most effective orators was missing in him. And yet he held his listeners spellbound. People flocked to hear him, crowding into the halls where he spoke; women often sobbed in an ecstasy of emotion as they listened to his words. A letter of Camille Desmoulins contains a description of one of Robespierre's speeches. "You could not possibly picture to yourself," he writes, "with what naturalness and with what emotion he expressed himself. Not only the women in the galleries were moved to tears, but most of the assembly as well."

A study of Robespierre's public addresses, with their powerful enthusiasm and lofty idealism, fully consonant with the greatness of the events that were transforming France, reveals the intensity of his faith in the sacred mission that the French people were to perform by means of the Revolution.

In his second speech on Louis Capet, Robespierre declared: "Citizens, the outcome of our struggle will decide whether we are rebellious enemies or benefactors of mankind, and it is the nobility of your character that will decide the outcome." (7)

In his address on the Constitution, delivered May 10, 1792, he proclaimed the new gospel as follows:

"Man is born to happiness and liberty, yet everywhere he is enslaved and in misery. The function of human society is to protect the rights of man and to develop his natural abilities, and yet everywhere society oppresses and degrades him." (8)

When he spoke of the people he was able to extol them in the most glowing terms because he transformed them into an ethical abstraction. For example:

"First of all establish the incontrovertible axiom that the people are good but their delegates are corruptible. The virtue and sovereignty of the people are the only safeguards against wicked and despotic government . . . I can recognize only one champion of the people and that is the people itself."

He bestowed equal praise on the Revolution:

"Furthermore, though all of Europe should unite against you, you are stronger than all Europe. The French Republic is as invincible as reason, as immortal as truth." (From his report on the political situation, November 18, 1793.)

He expressed his absolute certainty of ultimate victory by declaring:

"Whatever be the destiny that awaits you personally, your triumph is assured. For the founders of Liberty, is not even death a kind of triumph?"

Despite his success as an orator, Robespierre felt uneasy before every speech he made. Each time, as he began to speak, his hands would shake and his voice would falter. But he would soon become so enthusiastic that his self-confidence would return and he would speak without further difficulty. His deep faith in himself and his cause made it possible for him to overcome his timidity.

The reasons for his effectiveness as a speaker are not difficult to perceive. The inflexibility of his principles, the directness and intransigeance with which he pursued his objectives, the unusual fervor and strength of his convictions made a great impression on the people at a time when long established institutions were collapsing and all values were questioned. His personal merits alone were not sufficient to account for his powerful hold on the masses, if we do not take into consideration the affinity that existed between the character of this leader and the emotional state of the masses.

In his personal relations Robespierre was coldly formal, mistrustful, and extremely timid. He disliked and feared the informal ease with which other men behaved toward him. He would tremble when some friend would greet him unexpectedly with a slap on the back. When he had to kiss an opponent in the Jacobin Club as a token of reconciliation, he did it blushing deeply and with an expression of disgust. Danton said of him that he looked at that moment like a cat that had just tasted vinegar.

He was equally reserved with women. Although he was willing to receive their adulation from a distance, he refrained from any form of familiarity and treated them with cold politeness. The only woman toward whom he displayed any personal emotion was the maternal and imperious Madame Duplay. Her daughter was thought to have been Robespierre's fiancée, but there is no evidence of any deep emotional relationship between Robespierre and Mlle. Duplay.

Robespierre's stature and physiognomy did not give the

impression of great virility. He seemed timid, delicate, and unsure of himself. But on the speaker's platform in the Convention or the Jacobin Club his personality changed and he became strong, intense, and self-confident.

It may be of interest to trace the process by which Robespierre's feelings of hatred deepened to the point where he began to exterminate friends and enemies indiscriminately. At the trial of the King he had spoken in the name of the people, demanding on their behalf the destruction of the old regime. He insisted with striking impetuosity that the King be sentenced to death. In the second of his two famous orations on this question he protested vehemently against the motion submitted by one of the deputies that the verdict be ratified by the National Assembly. In that speech he made a characteristic confession, the ominous meaning of which was made clear by subsequent events:

"Inexorable as I am when it comes to determining in an abstract manner the degree of severity that legal justice must show to the enemies of mankind, I felt the republican virtue in my heart waver in the presence of the culprit standing humiliated before the sovereign power. . . . But citizens, the supreme proof of the devotion that the representatives of the people owe their country is given when they sacrifice the initial stirrings of natural sympathy in order to insure the salvation of a great people and of oppressed humanity."

As the political struggle intensified, Robespierre's hatred revealed itself more clearly. It could be concealed under the cloak of political necessity during the purge of the Hebertists, but the execution of Danton can be explained on no other grounds than those of personal animosity.

Danton was one of the first leaders of the Revolution, a close friend and comrade of Robespierre. When Danton's wife died Robespierre wrote him: "I love you more than ever now and shall love you unto death. At this moment I am your own self. Let us weep together, my friend, and may we soon make the effects of our profound sorrow felt by the tyrants who are the cause of our public misfortunes and our private griefs."

Such a sense of identification with another person would seem to provide the basis for an enduring friendship. However, the last sentence of the above quotation reveals the ruthless attitude of which Danton eventually became a victim. Robespierre wished to make the "tyrants" responsible for all personal as well as general misfortunes; the difference between public and private grievances no longer existed as far as he was concerned. By the term "misfortune" Robespierre apparently meant not only real injuries, but anything that irritated him, anything that caused him psychic pain, and he seemed to claim the right to identify the cause of his misfortunes with anyone he pleased. It is possible that Robespierre was unconsciously passing judgment on Danton at the very moment he wrote that letter. Filled with concealed irritation and mistrust, he begrudged his friend the happiness, success, and vitality that he felt he himself lacked.

Attention has often been called to the antagonism that results from the conflict of contrary psychophysical constitutions. In this particular case we have, on the one hand, the asthenic schizoidism of Robespierre and on the other, the superb cyclothymia of Danton. However, we must bear in mind that this conflict of personalities was not the only factor involved in the execution of Danton by Robespierre and his followers. No murder was ever committed simply because of a disparity in psychophysical constitutions.

The death of Danton was prepared carefully by his perfidious colleagues. Billaud-Varenne was employed to bring the first charges against Danton. The Committee of Public Safety expressed great indignation and Robespierre even defended

Danton—only, as Legendre points out, to be able to execute him more easily at a later moment.

After the execution of Hebert, Robespierre broke openly with Danton. He secretly supplied St. Just with memoranda full of lies that were to serve as material for the terrible accusation. These memoranda were pure fabrications, made use of in the absence of any real evidence against Danton. In the fear that if allowed to defend himself Danton might succeed in proving his innocence, Robespierre endeavored to persuade the Assembly to sentence him without a hearing. When the Assembly manifested horror at the idea of sending the hero of August Tenth to the scaffold without giving him a chance to defend himself, the Incorruptible delivered his fatal address.

The burning hatred that Robespierre expressed in this speech must have had a more personal cause than the political reasons he gave for the execution of his former friend. The ideological superstructure of his mind was essentially the rationalization of acts that were motivated by impulses of hatred and destruction.

In this case jealousy must have played an important, if not the chief part, just as it did in the case of Desmoulins, whose literary talents were envied by Robespierre. Danton was an unusually gifted orator and might have displaced Robespierre in the affections of the people. In his jealous fury, Robespierre destroyed the rival who personified the qualities of virility, optimism, and audacity, apparently wishing to take revenge on Danton for all the grievances he held against anyone, for whatever wrongs he had suffered in the past, for the deep inferiority complex that plagued him, and for the weaknesses that he could not overcome.

In his speech of indictment he asserted, through the mouth of St. Just, that the Revolution should by no means devour its children, but that it should "devour to the last the allies of tyranny, and not one true patriot will perish for the cause of justice." Whatever good faith he may have had in making this declaration, it was able to serve as a justification for any crime. Whomever one decided to kill one could denounce as an ally of tyranny. Whomever one retained as a friend one could praise as a true patriot.

For Robespierre the people were infallible, but only he knew what the people wanted; therefore he was infallible. Thus he would not admit the possibility of error, and he indignantly rejected the pleas of the wives of men whom he had arrested, replying to their requests that he release their husbands: "Does the people's justice attempt to punish the innocent?" Anyone who asserted that a victim of the Terror could be innocent was guilty of blasphemy.

Two fundamental mental disorders were developing in Robespierre. One was the absolute identification of himself with the Revolution, France, Justice, Virtue and The People. The other was the division of reality into absolute good and absolute evil. The realm of the good became smaller and smaller until it included only himself and a few close friends, while the realm of evil grew until it encompassed the entire world.

Fear, hatred, and mistrust made him see enemies everywhere. He scrutinized minutely the men whom he particularly suspected of conspiring against him and, as I have already pointed out, he kept a notebook in which he recorded every day the names and suspicious acts of anyone unfortunate enough to incur his enmity.

He kept a diary in which he recorded no self-criticisms, since he could perceive nothing in himself but perfection.

The extermination of his enemies was a process of cleansing, through which he hoped to achieve moral perfection—if not of the people as a whole, at least in the Convention, and if not there, at least in the Committee of Public Safety. He began to formulate plans for future purges, a practice lately improved upon by the Bolsheviks. "The Terror," declared Robespierre, "is nothing but Justice, prompt, severe and inflexible. It is, therefore, the incarnation of virtue." (February 6, 1794.)

The sincere protagonists of the Terror aimed at purging France of her enemies so as to make future tyranny unnecessary and impossible and to clear the way for a democratic and equalitarian society. The ghastly cruelties perpetrated by the Terror were expected to prevent any future crimes. If cruelty can be justified, there is no better justification than this. And yet Robespierre himself had warned against the fanatical abuse of power when in an earlier speech he had said: "Woe to the man who should dare to use the Terror against the people. It should strike only the people's enemies!"

Robespierre's love of France, liberty and the Revolution was contaminated by hatred for all that he imagined stood in his way. His attitude was most vividly described by the ominous words of St. Just:

"There is something terrible in the sacred love of one's country. It is so exclusive that it sacrifices everything without pity, without fear, without humane consideration for the public interest." (Report of the 11 Germinal.) (9)

Absolute rigidity of ideas supercharged with emotions was a result of the character of the times and the struggle that was taking place. In an essay for which as a student he had won a prize at the Academy of Metz, Robespierre gave a philosophical definition of honor that reveals the absolutism of his ideas even at that early date. He defined honor by stating that it "has reason for its basis and merges with duty. It would exist even when far from the eyes of men, with no witness other than heaven, and no judge other than conscience". It is important to note that this philosophical absolutism was a reflection of the absolute authority exerted by the superego.

By a similar process of hypostatization Robespierre identified the ideals of Rousseau that he had adopted in his youth with the very essence of reality. When he could no longer fail to see that these ideals were not realities but only creations of his imagination, he turned the full force of his indignation and hatred against all those who in his eyes were responsible for such a state of affairs. Man is born good, as Rousseau, Robespierre's master, said, and only civilization makes him evil.

Nothing is more characteristic in this respect than the apotheosis of the Revolution in the decree of the 18 of Floreal on "the Supreme Being and feasts in His honor". Robespierre, exulting over the Revolutionary deeds of the French people and confident of approval by the heavenly powers, exclaimed:

"Being of beings, could the day when the universe came forth from Thy almighty hands have shone with light more pleasing to Thine eyes than this day when, having shattered the yoke of crime and terror, we appear before Thee, worthy of Thy consideration and concern for our destinies?"

But just as Satan once upon a time disturbed the paradisiacal bliss of our forebears, this modern idyll could not last because of the machinations and intrigues of the enemies of the Revolution. "The charlatans became active again. Faith and sublime unification of the first people in the world having come to pass, who would have thought that crime could still exist on earth?"

In this way the hymn in honor of the Supreme Being was at the same time used as an accusation against the enemies of the people—or, more accurately, the enemies of Robespierre.

It was these "charlatans" who accused him of being a tyrant. They had caused the indictment of Danton and now, in an attempt to overthrow the Incorruptible, they were reproaching him with Danton's death! Robespierre, as the high priest of the Supreme Being, ended his hymn with this portentous statement:

"I was made to fight and not to rule. The time has not yet come when a man of merit can serve his country with impunity; the defenders of liberty will remain outlaws as long as scoundrels hold power."

Thus the high priest was also prosecutor, judge, policeman and executioner, all in one.

The culmination of the process that has here been outlined was the law of Prairial that did away with legal justice by depriving the accused of the right to defend himself. This law was based on the theory developed by Robespierre that the people's judges were at the same time the best friends and defenders of the accused, since as the representatives of absolute virtue they were incapable of mistaking innocence for guilt.

The more victims Robespierre sacrificed at the altar of absolute virtue, the more intense his sense of guilt became and the greater his need to justify his acts in terms of his sacred mission. It was no coincidence that directly following the mass executions and the murder of Danton, Robespierre arranged the celebration in honor of the Supreme Being. It was a final attempt to exonerate himself.

One evening at the home of the Duplays, Robespierre read his favorite dialogue between Sulla and Eucrates from the works of Montesquieu before an assemblage of guests. After some time his listeners noticed that he was not looking at the book. It was not necessary for him to consult the text, so deeply engraved in his memory were the words that he connected with his own political career:

"It was precisely the shedding of all this blood that enabled me to accomplish my greatest deeds. If I had ruled the Romans mercifully I might well have been induced to abdicate my office through vexation, disgust or caprice. But I laid down my dictatorship at a time when there was no one in the world who did not believe that dictatorship was my only means to safety. I appeared before the Romans as a citizen among fellow citizens and dared say to them, 'I am ready to answer for all those who come to plead for a father, a son or a brother.' All the Romans were silent before me."

The conviction that he was absolutely right was Robespierre's only defense against his deepening sense of guilt. He became more and more detached from reality, focusing his gaze on his ideal objectives in order to escape from the awareness of the brutal character of his practical measures.

His ethical ideas became more unreal and absolute. They absorbed practically all his libido. As a result of this fixed concentration on absolute notions, he lost sight of the distinction between the interests of the people and his own. He could perform acts that were motivated by hatred or injured pride and believe that he was only doing what was necessary for the defense of the Republic.

Robespierre's main objective was to rebuild France according to his own ideas. The dictatorship was only a necessary means to that end. His colleagues were aware of the sincerity of his ideals, but some of them began to realize the dangers involved in his identification of himself with absolute standards of judgment. After having listened to many of Robespierre's speeches to the Committee of Public Safety, one of his friends wrote him a letter in which with rare perspicacity he warned Robespierre of the consequences of such a course. "After attending several sessions," he wrote, "I became aware of the fact that you were holding the association spellbound, that the galleries were also on your side. But to speak always of oneself, one's virtue, one's principles, and of the sacrifices one makes for liberty and the dangers by which one is surrounded is simply a demagogic means of getting votes." The letter closed with a personal warning: "You are far above entertaining views so destructive to liberty, but how can you be assured that some nefarious influence will not push you in that direction by imperceptible degrees?"

But the Incorruptible's belief in himself was so strong, the rationalization of his acts so convincing, that to the very last he considered himself innocent of any crimes. Thus his final speech, in which with deep indignation and grief he accused his enemies instead of attempting to justify himself, was a sincere expression of his conviction that any injustices that might have been committed could not be charged to him.

"What am I," exclaimed the doomed hero of the Revolution, "but an unfortunate slave of liberty!" He represented himself to the hostile assembly as a victim of intrigue and blamed the enemies of the Revolution for all the crimes of which the Terror was accused. There seems to have been no note of hypocrisy in what he said, but it is clear that he was as much a victim of paranoiac delusions as of the machinations of his enemies.

The major problem of this study is to determine to what extent Robespierre's character and actions were responsible for the Terror of which he was the guiding spirit.

It should be understood that to separate the acts of Robespierre from the general context of the revolutionary period is not a fair way of arriving at a judgment of the man. He was swept along by events and by the passions of the people around him and in a sense he was himself a victim of the Revolution. The Committee of Public Safety which was the chief stage for his activities in the last years of his public career was organized not by him but by Danton and Inard, the Girondist. It was created in April, 1792, when Dumouriez' treachery had brought closer the danger of an invasion by foreign powers, the people were evacuating Paris and the parliament was hopelessly divided. At that moment the Committee of Public Safety came into existence in order to establish centralized control of the revolutionary movement. Although at first Robespierre had no connection with the Committee, it later became his chief instrument of domination.

The masses, divided into conflicting groups and in a state of panic, needed a strong leader who would serve as the personification of their ideals, the instrument of their collective will. Whoever was to lead the Revolution to victory would have to share their basic impulses. He would have to be a man who had joined the Revolution because of a burning desire to overthrow the oppressors of the people and establish justice for all men. Robespierre fulfilled all these requirements.

He was able to eliminate Danton as a rival and to remain in power because his convictions were deeper, because he was less inclined to doubt himself, and because his temperament and ideals coincided more than those of his rival with the collective spirit of the people. In the ideas of Rousseau he had discovered a convenient idealization of his emotions and prejudices. His personal grievances became a nucleus around which the desires and anxieties of the revolutionary masses were crystallized.

As we have already seen Robespierre began to identify his personal needs with those of France and the Revolution. He believed in the sacred nature of his historic role with an intensity that bordered on complete megalomania. His personal greatness represented to him the greatness of the French people. In his fanatical delusions of grandeur the entire nation was fulfilling its noble destiny in the acts that he performed. France would become great through him, the French people would return to their natural state of purity by means of his efforts on their behalf. The false glory of the old regime would be supplanted by the true glory of the Robespierrian Republic. The blood he shed and the suffering he caused were the necessary steps toward realizing a Kingdom of God on earth. Robespierre proclaimed as a main objective of the Revolution, "the substitution of the charms of happiness for the boredom of luxury, the substitution of the greatness of man for the smallness of this earth". Happiness and greatness were to be made accessible to all who merited them; in other words, to all who reflected his own moral perfection.

When reality presented obstacles to the realization of his ideals, Robespierre reacted by closing his eyes to reality. Unwilling to face the problems that he feared he might not be able to solve, he blamed his opponents whom he characterized as "charlatans" for his own mistakes and failures. Under Robespierre's influence the persons whom he singled out for blame were regarded by the masses as enemies of the Republic.

Thus when he came to see himself as a victim of criminals and "charlatans" he felt that the French people were victims with him. His last speech, made on the 8 of Thermidor, the eve of his downfall, was a justification of himself and at the same time a justification of his unfortunate people.

Robespierre was not altogether mistaken or deluded. It was true to some extent that the Revolution was threatened by enemies. Not all the conspiracies that he suspected were figments of his imagination. But once his hatred was set in motion against the real enemies with whom he struggled, it descended like an avalanche on friend and enemy alike, burying under it many of the best revolutionary leaders.

In the Committee of Public Safety, fear and hatred were as active as friendship and loyalty. Sorel described the psychic structure of that organization and that of the Convention as follows:

"Great as the villainy of his colleagues toward him may have been, it was nevertheless exceeded by his mistrust of them. The servility of Robespierre's followers in the Convention was not at all based on sentiments of sympathy. His dictatorship inspired a deep fear in them and the outward signs of admiration and enthusiasm which fear compelled them to manifest toward him concealed an intense hatred." (3)

Robespierre's destructive impulses were turned against anyone who disagreed with him. Any deviation from his way of thinking constituted a threat to the Republic as far as he was concerned. Such deviations had to be treated with complete ruthlessness. We have seen how he expressed this attitude: "Terror is nothing else but justice, prompt, severe and inflexible; it is therefore the incarnation of virtue."

In destroying all whom he considered enemies of the Revolution he destroyed the Revolution itself. Faith in their ideals and in their ultimate victory diminished in the masses with each succeeding execution. How could new leaders develop among the French people when Samson, the official executioner of the Revolution, constantly showed them the severed heads of trusted revolutionaries who had been sent to the guillotine, with a warning that they should mistrust everybody, so as not to be duped again?

The new collective ego-ideal that had been created by the Revolution was destroyed by the Terror. Robespierre's downfall was the tragic result of the weariness and hatred that he had helped to engender in the masses. But Robespierre never lost faith in himself, even when he fell from power. As he was taken to prison he pointed to a tablet on which the declaration of the rights of man was inscribed, and said: "And yet it was I who made that possible." When face to face with his own death, he expressed his sublimated narcissism by representing himself as the apostle of virtue and liberty. His highest ideals remained strong, while the vindictive elements of his superego were purged by the approach of death. However, the effect of his execution on the people was the very reverse; their revolutionary ideals, already weakened by the Terror, now lost all vitality. The victory of the Reaction followed. "By the 10 of Thermidor," one of Robespierre's contemporaries wrote, "a metamorphosis could be perceived that never occurred in any other period or in any other people. It was a different France with a different heart, a different spirit—almost a different language. Even the expressions on people's faces seemed to have changed."

In view of the change that had already been taking place in the attitude of the people toward their revolutionary leaders, the behavior of the crowds during the execution was not surprising. The tyrannical leader, the exacting moralist, the man whom everyone feared could now be judged as he had judged others. The severity with which he had governed them had engendered in the people a deep hatred that found an outlet in the passion with which he was executed.

Robespierre had helped dig the grave of the Revolution, and when he perished, it perished with him. His dictatorship had prepared the ground for the subsequent forms of tyranny that culminated in the reign of Napoleon. The return of the monarchy was effected through a military dictatorship, liberty and equality were abolished, and a king again became the object of popular worship. The glamor of the court with its titles and decorations took hold of the people's consciousness once again under Napoleon and the revolutionary ideals of liberty and equality were forgotten.

The lethargy and fear that the Terror had provoked were responsible for the submissiveness with which the new dictatorship was accepted. After the death of Robespierre, who in the words of Hegel, "took virtue seriously and gave it the most important place in the ordering of policy", the masses, enervated and bewildered by the storm of revolutionary events, were unable to govern themselves and yielded the power to other tyrants. At the very time when Robespierre's execution took place, another dictator was starting on his road to power; one of the armies of the Revolution was commanded by Napoleon Bonaparte.

At this point it seems appropriate to draw a psychoanalytical portrait of Robespierre. In his psychic structure one can perceive strong narcissistic and aggressive drives, as well as imperative tendencies toward sublimation and repression, toward idealization and rationalization. Because of the weak personality of his father and the dominant influence of his mother, whose tenderness had a deep effect on Robespierre, it was difficult for him to establish an identification with his father, which would have been a necessary step to achieve full virility. On the other hand, he developed a strong fixation to his mother. Her early death intensified this fixation, since it created in him an unsatisfied craving for love.

The trauma that resulted from being abandoned by his father probably had an even more destructive effect on Robespierre's personality. The loss of parental authority must have impeded still further the natural process of identification with his father, with the consequence that he actually failed to attain full virility. The deep injury to his pride caused him to react by developing an ego ideal of perfect masculinity and virtue as a compensation for the crushing awareness of his father's weakness. He developed an insatiable desire for fame to compensate for the shame he felt at his family's disgrace.

Frustrated ambition as well as real and imaginary humiliations caused by the precarious social and financial position of his family engendered in him powerful feelings of hatred. People whom he regarded as evil, unjust, or tyrannical served as objects against whom this hatred could be directed. His great capacity for sublimation made it possible for him to express these tendencies in an ideological form that corresponded with the prevailing social and political ideas. Rousseau's ideas were the weapons with which he would overthrow the oppressors of the people. He found in the philosopher he so deeply admired the spiritual guidance that his father had failed to provide.

Because of his powerful inhibitions, his relations to women were always coldly formal. These inhibitions were the result of his fixation to his mother, his reaction against identification with his father, his sense of weakness and humiliation, and the aggressive impulses which his ego could only with great difficulty hold in restraint. As a result, he was never able to find release for his aggressive impulses in sexual relations. On the other hand, his mother fixation was transferred to the maternal figure of Madame Duplay.

This brief description indicates the existence in Robespierre of a great deal of latent homosexuality, which would account for his neurotic behavior toward other men as well as for his inhibitions with regard to relations with women. According to psychoanalytic theory his paranoia can be considered a defense of his ego against the impact of suppressed homoerotic libido. The fusion of homoeroticism with strong sadistic drives may account for the ruthlessness he manifested toward anyone whom he regarded as an enemy.

The revolutionary struggle provided an outlet for Robespierre's aggressiveness and a source of gratification for his narcissism. He enjoyed public recognition of his abilities and had power and opportunity to take revenge on anyone who had caused him personal injury. By presenting himself as the paragon of virtue he could make up for the opprobrium from which he had suffered in his childhood. The persons against whom his hatred was chiefly directed probably were unconsciously associated with his father, the cause of all his misfortunes and the prototype of immoral individuals. It is safe to assume that his moralistic severity was a reaction against the instability of his father's character.

The characteristic elements of Robespierre's superego were evolved in contrast to his father's personality. Although narcissism predominated, his superego was extremely aggressive and ruthlessly turned against the outside world. Robespierre's intense sadism and moral fanaticism indicate the vehemence of his repressed aggressive drives. These sought an outlet in activities that would be approved by the superego. He compensated for his feeling of inadequate masculinity by exerting overwhelming political power, and by pitilessly prosecuting all those who in his eyes deviated from his ideal of strict morality. His habit of systematically recording the shortcomings and errors of his fellow citizens was a way of justifying in advance the cruelty with which he exterminated his opponents. It also reflected his envy of those who were able to indulge in sensual pleasures.

He gratified his narcissism and compensated for his sense of inferiority by a deepening conviction that he was a great man and that he represented absolute truth. At the same time, his exacting superego compelled him to submit to high ethical standards. The certainty that he was acting in full accordance with these standards provided him with sufficient justification for the crimes committed during the Terror. While his craving for greatness led him to entertain megalomaniac delusions, the need to secure the sanction of the superego led him to establish the cult of the Supreme Being and to assume the role of high priest of the new religion. Thus the revolutionary iconoclast created a new church and a new god in the place of those which he had helped to destroy. This was undoubtedly the climax of his efforts to justify his aggressive behavior by means of elevating his own person.

The schizoid structure of his personality is revealed by

his tendency to conceive everything in terms of absolutes, by his intellectual inflexibility and his inability to perceive that many of his acts contradicted his own moral principles. The intensity of his repressions resulted in strong reaction formations. His marked ability to experience feelings of pity was undoubtedly a reaction of his ego to repressed aggressiveness. This aggressiveness, while usually sublimated in the revolutionary struggle and translated into despotic ideas, often expressed itself directly in the cruelties perpetrated by the Terror. Through these acts Robespierre's aggressive superego protested against his inability to attain normal happiness and at the same time attempted to eliminate any opposition to his complete identification with his fantastic ideals.

The harmony and cooperation between Robespierre and the French people during that momentous period of history may also be described in psychoanalytic terms. Such procedure may shed some light on an interesting problem: the coexistence in the French people and in their leader of a strong sense of justice and equally strong aggressive drives. Robespierre, unconsciously motivated by a dynamic protest against the wrongs he had personally suffered, raised the struggle for justice to the level of the highest ideal. While helping the people to destroy the old institutions and the repressions that they created in the collective superego, he did everything in his power to give the highest moral sanction to the new order that he had introduced. In this way he was able to satisfy both his own and the collective superego and to compensate for the sense of guilt that accompanied the overthrow of all established traditions, which culminated in the execution of the king.

Robespierre succeeded in giving the French people an unprecedented sense of their greatness and in raising their national ideals to the level of universal principles. Thanks to him, France could be regarded as the most progressive nation in the world. He saw himself as the leader of the French people in a great crusade against the oppressors of mankind, thus gratifying collective narcissism immensely. His belief in his own greatness was made possible by the psychic affinity that obtained between him and his people. Because he fully shared the aspirations and resentments of the masses he was able to pursue his objectives with confidence and energy; the thwarted desires of Robespierre and his fellow countrymen were sublimated in the idea of national greatness. In return for the ideals he gave them, the people gave Robespierre a major share in their own greatness. At the same time they fed his megalomania by, in turn, gratifying his narcissism with manifestations of obedience and worship.

Another bond that united Robespierre with his people was the hatred they had in common. He supplied a sublimated and rational expression of the primitive aggressions of the populace and sanctioned their behavior by invoking the patronage of the Supreme Being. The people on their part, supplied fuel for Robespierre's own repressed sadism by communicating to him the passion with which they fought for their rights.

Robespierre was unquestionably right when, in his last speech before his death, he disclaimed exclusive responsibility for the Terror. It is certainly true that the people shared this responsibility. Common was their struggle, common their ideal, and common their folly.

THE SPIRITUAL BACKGROUND OF HITLERISM *

An examination of the spiritual background of Hitlerism is essential to the understanding of Hitler's personality and the nature of his actions. This background cannot, however, be clearly defined without a preliminary analysis of the German mind. We must make clear to what extent national character was responsible first, for shaping Hitler's character, and then, for influencing the course of German history during the entire period of the Nazi regime.

Without going into a general discussion of the concept of national character, I shall deal with a few specific concepts that are relevant to the problem stated above. In my opinion, it is justifiable to speak of national character as a distinct psychic structure. By this term I mean a complex unity which, just as in the case of individuals, is determined by both innate and acquired characteristics, the latter denoting those that flow from environmental factors such as climate, forms of subsistence, propinquity to other nations.

This psychic structure is characterized primarily by a reciprocal relation to outside events, in that it affects them and in turn, is affected by them. The same holds true, of course, for the individual, although in the case of the single human being the components are simpler, and certain factors—such as the economic—play a less significant role.

The approach to the German national character delineated in the following pages, being based on historical studies and the conclusions of a small number of students, will by

* Reprinted from *The Journal of Clinical Psychopathology,* vol. 4, no. 4, October, 1945.

no means exhaust the subject. It is nevertheless possible that as a result of this study motives and inferences will assume a clearer and deeper meaning.

Nietzsche, whose insight into the German soul was unsurpassed, considered it a warring nest of inconsistencies. Elaborating Goethe's famous notion of the "two souls" of the Germans he declared: "Not two, but a hundred, a thousand and even more souls dwell in the German breast." (1)

The two epithets, "good-natured" and "wily", which cannot be applied simultaneously to any other nationality, can be applied with full justification to the Germans. "The German soul has passages and galleries; there are caves, hiding-places, and dungeons in it. The German is well acquainted with the by-paths of chaos . . . Finally, we should do honor to our name—we are not called the *Täusche Volk* (deceptive people) for nothing! And further, the German lets himself go, all the while gazing vacantly with his faithful blue German eyes. Other countries make the mistake of thinking that he is relaxing in his lounging robe." (1)

In considering the racial myths spread by Nazism, it seems advisable to mention Nietzsche's maxim, "to associate with no man who takes any part in the mendacious race swindle". (2) Accordingly, he refers ironically to the "purity" of the German race as "a people made up of a conglomeration of races in which pre-Aryan elements may even predominate, the Germans are more unaccountable, unpredictable, inconsistent, incomprehensible, impetuous and, finally, even more addicted to fear than any other race". (1) Nietzsche objects to any simple historical explanation of German psychology: "The smallness and baseness of the German soul were not and are not consequences of the system of small states . . ." (2)

The strongest and most important chapter of Fouillée's work, *Psychologie des peuples européens,* is devoted to the Germans. It should be borne in mind that this book was written shortly after the French defeat in 1871, and undoubtedly did not escape the influence of its period. Fouillée maintains that even the early Germans invoked the principle of *Lebensraum* to justify their invasions of foreign territory. "They asserted that they had a legal right to occupy any region that they needed. From the beginning of history the Germans had rights where other peoples had none." (3)

The Germans are notoriously inclined to disregard public agreements, but they recognize the validity of ties binding one individual to another. They place emphasis on warfare, even in their conceptions of a future life. "The German mind," says Fouillée, "responds and awakens slowly but lastingly. . . . This inner fervor has a negative aspect, for it goes hand in hand with hatred of those who oppose a good cause, a good race and a good fatherland. . . . All the old enemies, the Romans, the Gauls and the Slavs are regarded with malevolence, as if they were still attacking the frontier." (3)

The self-hatred that kept apart the German tribes—and later the small German states—found external targets after the unification of Germany had been accomplished. "After such a long period of mutual hatred within the state, the Germans have continued this custom until the present day. But now their hatred is directed with an unprecedented violence against the enemy outside their state." (3) Even Treitschke admits: "We are a race capable of the most intense hatred."

German unification resulted in a transitory upsurge of idealism, followed immediately by a retreat to the plane of realism and the extreme of aggressiveness and vainglorious chauvinism. In historical terms, one might say that Germany, while cradled in Western civilization, retains to this day a primarily feudal mentality.

Hegel makes an interesting observation about Germany's precarious transition from feudalism to political absolutism.

He asserts that the weakening of feudal relations between king and subject permitted the power to become centralized in the hands of the king. The vassals became independent princes and expended their strength in continual wars. Each state became a battlefield. But these aggressive, egoistic forces were checked by the strict discipline of the Middle Ages (church, state and monarchy). This brutality, however, carried the seeds of its own destruction. "Humanity has not been emancipated from slavery, but through slavery." (4)

Fouillée's conclusion that traces of feudalism, which Hegel calls "mutual dependence", still remain in the German mentality, seems more in accordance with historical reality than the theories expressed by Hegel's philosophical idealism. Fouillée says: "The German mind strives to broaden itself progressively but without success; it has preserved too much of its original character of national particularism." (3)

To form a complete picture of German imperialism, one need only consider the insatiable aggressiveness of princes and states within the Reich. After the unification of Germany, this aggressiveness was turned outward toward other nations. At the same time, the feelings of superiority and of their own importance which express the primitive narcissism of the composite German character, far from being suppressed, were made into conscious ideals of the people. The idealistic philosophy of this period created a convenient system of thought which was used by the imperialists for their own ends. The beautiful ideals expressed by the philosophers were made a justification for self-seeking passions and employed as a means of influencing the masses. With the aid of these philosophical concepts, medieval savagery disguised itself in attractive robes.

In 1922 a German psychologist, Müller-Freienfels, published a work which contributes much elucidation to this theory. (5) According to Müller-Freienfels, the irrational factor is dominant in the psychological make-up of the

Germans. Earlier, Madame de Staël had written that the Germans have ". . . *trop d'idées neuves, pas assez d'idées communes"*. The German soul matures slowly and becomes rational only with great effort. The German is diffuse and prolix in his thought. His expressions are unclear, his phraseology obscure and his speech full of synonyms and metaphors. His conceptions verge on the fantastic and they overwhelm a mind that lacks the discipline to control them. The German's sense impressions are unrefined, which may account for his great capacity to endure dissonance and ugliness in art.

The principle of voluntary action plays a large part in the German psyche, although the German's emphasis on activity, his will to action, has subjective and highly imaginative rather than rational motives. The German conceives of "will", particularly the "Will of the Universe", as aimless and infinite. German policies are formulated in terms of this boundless and purposeless will. In summation, Müller-Freienfels adds: "Germans have always surrendered themselves to fantastic ideas. How much blood has been spilled because of the Holy Roman Empire and the Crusades!"

These fantastic ideas are also utilized by political parties engaged in the struggle for state power. No party can hope to defeat its rivals unless it formulates its program in terms of such theories of expansion. This desire for the infinite, resulting in lack of restraint in political affairs, has already brought a great deal of misfortune to the German people. During the periods of greatest national development the Germans were unaware of any limits to what they might accomplish. As a result, German history is enriched by elements of supreme grandeur. But, as Nietzsche pointed out, this grandeur shattered itself on the infinite. The German will is as limitless in its desire to be ruled as in its desire to rule over others. No other people has produced as many great leaders, or—on the other hand—shown such a propensity for submission. To us it may seem strange that arbitrary force should not be regarded as contradictory to freedom, but the German mind perceives no such contradiction. Müller-Freienfels considers this a uniquely German trait and describes it as an "unresisting acceptance of force".

The German serf always considered servility a duty demanded by the nature of things, and his lord with equal certitude considered himself the first servant of the state. The Germans more than any other people clamored for leaders who would govern them strictly. In no other nation do we find leaders becoming objects of worship and mythology while they are still alive. However, the high position of the ruler depended in turn upon the fact that he embodied the typical German traits; one may therefore say that the leader was himself led.

It is by no means an historical accident that no German government, despotic or liberal, has ever been overthrown by the German people themselves. The fact is easily explained by the undemocratic disposition of the Germans, who would prefer to be ruled by a powerful sovereign rather than by the will of their own majority. The German people demand that they be subjected to force, even in their relations to God, whom they made over in the image of a Prussian drill-sergeant. (6)

The peculiar relationship that arose between the people and the state is best characterized by the political theories of German philosophers, and especially by those of Hegel. "Up to the present day," writes Müller-Freienfels, "it has never been customary in Germany to consider the state in the light of theories of the social contract. In this respect it is questionable whether a president chosen by the people *viva voce* could ever satisfactorily represent their idea of the state." (5) In Hegel's conception the state became a metaphysical entity, entirely distinct from the people.

Furthermore, the Germans feel that they are a chosen race and that they are predestined to rule over the inferior peoples of the world. Their ambitions are comparable only to the ruthlessness of their methods of achieving them.

The Junkers' Prussia answered Germany's need for a strong ruling power. The Prussian dynasty, which took the lead in the unification of Germany, rested on an aristocracy that exploited the conquered Slavs. Under their influence regimentation, militarism, and standardization became the pattern throughout Germany.

Müller-Freienfels considers this new German order with its drill and discipline as a typical reaction of over-compensation. He finds the same tendency toward uniformity even in the Social-Democratic movement. There again we are confronted with the strange mixture of contradictory values, such as freedom and submissiveness. He sees as significant the fact that Bebel was the son of a Prussian officer.

There is indeed a great deal of valuable material for the elucidation of our subject in the work of Müller-Freienfels. This psychologist comes very close to solving the problem under investigation. In order to determine the validity of his conception of will and the relation of the German mind to freedom and coercion, it is necessary to trace the genesis of the phenomena that he attempts to explain. For just as the genetic method is important to the study of individual psychology, it can be of great value in helping us to discriminate among inherent structural and acquired characteristics of the national psyche.

The following observation of Müller-Freienfels gives us the key to our problem. "Regimentation of the Germans and the division of Germany into patriarchal states," he says, "strengthened in the people their inherent aversion to making rational decisions, but also corresponded to their inclination for voluntary submission based on emotional motives."

Feudalism, therefore, left its traces not only on the social structure of the German Reich, but on its psychic make-up as well. Apparently the historical growth of Germany did not entirely eliminate the earlier dependence of the feudal vassal on the sovereign. In the field of individual psychology, a similar relationship can often be observed: the dependence of the child on his father. This relationship is responsible for both the desire for complete submission and the tendency to idealize or even worship the admired object. The image of the father becomes the embodiment of religious emotions and is invested with magic omnipotence in the childhood of the individual as well as in primitive stages of social development.

The relationship between the child and the father is hypostatized by the child, and the image of the father becomes a permanent substitute for the real father. This image undergoes many changes and becomes the main component of the superego, which is a formation within the limits of the ego as such. The superego develops into a psychic agency embodying ethical standards, and serves as the internal prototype of laws, customs, and morals. It is composed of two basic elements—the positive which bids, and the negative which forbids. In the case of the German mind we have an accumulation of old and recent factors sanctioned by existing social conditions. The superego eventually becomes very powerful, regulating thought and feeling, and directing future development of the psychic structure of the individual or group.

To satisfy the need to submit to an external authority, individuals who fulfill certain requirements are substituted for the father image and become objects of worship. Their images supply the superego with a new content. In this manner, the relation of dependence is brought into the psychic field, which then takes on a character corresponding to the external situation.

The intimate relationship between the image of the father

or leader and the dominant superego gives a higher and almost religious character to the social structure. As the discoveries of the French school of sociology have disclosed, the social structure of a nation is closely connected with its religious life. Even social ties and the rules governing social behavior have preternatural sanctions. The primitive conception of a mysterious supernatural power, ethnologically known as *mana*, seems to be closely linked to the pressure exercised by the collectivity. The individual is usually more sensitive to this pressure in primitive than in civilized societies.

In the German mentality—which, as has already been pointed out, still contains traces of feudalism—we can discover a similar elevation of social sanctions to the rank of transcendental religious entities. Although the primitive *mana*, the Hegelian concept of the State, and the modern German idea of race, may at first seem to have little in common, careful study makes it clear that the mystic aura surrounding such notions in the German mind has its source in a primitive and prelogical mentality. Close analysis of the new version of the old myth discloses further evidence that such primitive tendencies still dwell fast in the German mind.

Early historical sources provide a clear picture of the basic tendencies in the German character. Tacitus' work on Germany yields interesting material as to what extent old ethnic elements have influenced the modern national character.

The most characteristic qualities of the Germanic tribes as revealed in his work seem to have been their militarism and their loyalty to the leaders. The cult of heroism is a case in point. "It is considered an ignominious and permanent disgrace to live after the leader has died on the battlefield. For it is a sacred duty of every man to protect the leader even at the sacrifice of his own personal fame.

The leader fights for victory and the army fights for the leader." (6)

Thus the worship of power and the extolling of conquest led the vanquished to enslave themselves voluntarily to the conqueror. Although young and strong, they allowed themselves to be bound and sold. Such submissiveness was considered a proof of fidelity. The conquering lord, made ashamed of his inglorious victory, sold them into slavery.

Another characteristic of the ancient Germans was their love of battle. "If any republic grows feeble after a long period of peace, the young nobles travel to other countries that are embroiled in wars and participate in their battles. For the Germans hate idleness. They desire to attain fame through enduring the hardships of war. It is much easier for them to inveigle each other into war with an enemy than into the cultivation of fields . . . these people, who love inaction, cannot rest. They submit willingly and even fanatically to the will of their leader because they see in him the embodiment of their most sacred ideals. With equal fanaticism they yield to the will of a foreign conqueror and gladly exchange their freedom for the fetters of bondage. . . ." (6)

During the medieval period, the Monastic Order of the Teutonic Knights established its headquarters in East Prussia, and from there made warring expeditions against the Lithuanians and the neighboring Slav peoples. This most aggressive of societies masqueraded as a group of Christian missionaries. In the hypocritical guise of defenders of the Church, the Knights committed the most atrocious crimes, claiming their ethical superiority as sanction for their methods. They applied the same methods at a later date in the persecution of Christianized Poland and Lithuania. Pride, brutality, cunning, and fanaticism brought them ill-repute and the very name of the Order became an object of loathing. The general character of this small Order, which enslaved the neighboring peoples by means of brutal discipline, had a great influence on the direction of subsequent German development.

After great upheavals and the disintegration of the Empire into several hundred small states, there ensued the trend toward unification. From the very beginning, Prussia was the moving force behind this slowly evolving process, with the result that she left an indelible imprint on the total German temperament and mentality.

The actions of Frederick the Great illustrate vividly the psychological principles that underlie all German policy. *Anti-Machiavelli,* written by Frederick before he reached the height of his career, is a masterpiece of idealism, a hymn to peace, and a condemnation of acquisitive militarists. (7) In this work we find even the revolutionary assertion that the heroic warriors were brigands, whose only claim to greatness was the notoriety they achieved. But after he came to power, most of Frederick's ideals receded from his consciousness, and he employed the few that remained in justifying his aggressions or in attempts to weaken the vigilance of his enemies. The cynicism and hypocrisy he displayed has remained unsurpassed until very recent times.

In his *Foundations of Germany,* (18) published during the First World War, Baker J. Ellis relates the political theories of Frederick II to the war policies of Wilhelm II. In reading the documents collected by Ellis, one is impressed by the similarity between the Germany of Frederick's time and modern Germany—it often seems as though only dates and names had been changed. One month before he marched into Saxony in 1756, Frederick vowed that his military preparations had no sinister motives. When he was on the point of attacking Austria he issued an appeal to the Austrian people, assuring them of his good intentions; then, addressing an official note to the European powers, he declared that his occupation of Silesia was not motivated by any evil intentions toward the Vienna Court; finally he sent Austria an ultimatum claiming his desire to save her from impending disaster, asserting that the freedom of Germany and the integrity of the German Empire were at stake. He even promised to sign an agreement with Austria and to defend her from her enemies, provided that she cede Silesia to Prussia.

Frederick organized a fifth column on an extensive scale. He sacrificed large sums of money in order to bribe foreign officials or their mistresses. He placed his secret agents in high diplomatic positions and through them tried to bring about a rift within the government he was preparing to attack. Just as he insisted on his good intentions before he attacked, he trumped up all kinds of motives to justify his acts after the campaign was completed. One instance of his ex post facto arguments is particularly interesting. After the occupation of Dresden, Frederick had the government archives searched for documents containing military agreements among Saxony, Austria, and Russia. These documents were then presented to the world as evidence of a nefarious conspiracy against Prussia. His own motives are explained in his *Mémoire Raisonné* as being "based on the most exact rules of equity and justice. They are not motives of ambition or self-aggrandizement."

Ellis' observation that "Germany's assertion that a conspiracy was formed against her by King Edward and Sir Edward Grey, finds its exact counterpart in Frederick's assertion of 1756", is a statement which could be expanded further. The present work, however, is not a comparative study of political history but a compilation of facts for psychological analysis.

One basic trait of the Germans may be described as idealism—with an exception clause. A German is an idealist, or at least pretends to be one as long as he is weak. But as soon as he becomes powerful, all the idealistic ballast is thrown overboard. Once power is obtained, it serves as a basis for further expansion and greater aggressiveness. At this point we come to another basic trait. Personal power is identified with the power of the state, and the aim of attaining maximum strength for the state involves the augmentation of the leader's control over the people. It was precisely in this sense that Frederick spoke of himself as the first servant of the state.

The German outlook on international law and morality reflects an aggressive absolutism. Frederick made a valuable contribution to our understanding of this trait in his work on the Seven Years' War. "If a ruler wishes to make war he is not restrained by the necessity to justify himself to the people. He simply outlines a course of action, makes war and leaves the matter of justifying his acts to some industrious pettifogger."

Making war is an exclusive privilege of the king, and the common people have no voice in it whatsoever. "When kings gamble for a province the people are mere pawns." A German ruler's intentions are always for the best, simply because they are his intentions. The interests of the adversary are not worthy of consideration and his very existence is a crime. The idea of *Lebensraum* made its first appearance in politics during Frederick's rule. The extent of the *Lebensraum* was bounded only by the King's aggressiveness and egoism. That is why the very existence of interests that conflicted with his own constituted an attack on his rights.

A third significant German trait is an unusual proclivity for projection. This point deserves special consideration. Projection attributes one's own secret intentions and wishes to factors in the outside world. In relation to one's adversaries, projection takes on a special character: the adversaries become the instigators for aggression directed against them. In this manner, projection supplies the real aggressor with a pretext for attacking his victim. If he has already launched the attack, he claims that it is a necessary means of self-defense, while if he is merely in the process of preparing the attack, he calls attention to the suspicious moves of the enemy as a justification for his own military preparations.

Frederick II, who always posed as the wronged party, exclaimed with hypocritical indignation when he met with reverses in the course of the Seven Years' War: "A conspiracy! A disgrace and a crime against morality! Has the world ever before seen three powerful rulers conspire against a fourth who had never done them any harm?"

At the end of the Seven Years' War, the famous Prussian idea of encirclement was introduced to the public: "May the Prussian rulers of the future not have to use measures as rash as those which must be used now in order to protect our country from the jealousy and hatred of all Europe. They wish to destroy the house of Brandenburg and the name of Prussia!"

It is, of course, absurd to think that Frederick himself really believed these fantastic statements. Nevertheless we may regard the lies he uttered as factors that in their turn influenced the collective psyche of the German people. The pattern of the lie or fantasy we study is therefore not a matter of indifference to us. Furthermore, we must always distinguish between a conscious lie and its effects on the unconscious. What the leader may regard as simply a useful fabrication can very easily take root and become a deep conviction of his followers.

It will be seen that such projective mechanisms played a large part in forming the policies of a more recent German leader who became known as "the Restorer of German territory". To a certain extent these projections seem to reflect a distinctive trait of the collective German psyche.

We may succeed in discovering why the Germans tend to be influenced by this kind of projection and why they develop collective delusions as a consequence. As modern German history has demonstrated, the fear of encirclement grew into a real delusion. When tiny Prussia was preparing to attack her neighbors in order to attain the rank of the greatest power in Europe, Frederick, despite his confidence in future greatness, was acutely aware of his inferior status among the other monarchs of Europe. Such a combination of youthful imperialism and a sense of personal and group inferiority was the foundation for aggressiveness reinforced by projective mechanisms. Suspicion of encirclement and fear of attack sprang up together with personal ambition and greed.

The mysterious transformation of Frederick the Great from an idealistic young prince tyrannized by his overbearing father into an aggressive and cynical ruler in his own right is easily explained: ascending the throne he obtained the means of satisfying the ambitions which he had previously been compelled to hold in check. At last he could achieve full identification with his hated father. Alfred Rosenberg aptly calls him "Friedrich der Einzige" ("Frederick the One and Only").

This desire for power, this "will to coerce", plays an important part in the thought processes of later German intellectuals. Two such men—Treitschke and Nietzsche—are outstanding because each contributed characteristic points of view, without which it would be impossible to understand the psychology of German nationalism.

Hegel in his philosophical works had already created the metaphysical basis for the apotheosis of the state. In his treatise he devoted only one page to international law, outlining the role of the state during a war: "War brings attention to the importance of the state as against the individual citizen. The fatherland becomes all-powerful and the individual becomes a nonentity." (9)

This Hegelian concept of the state had a lasting influence

on German thought. It was further developed by Treitschke in the following way: the sovereignty of a state involves freedom from any international control. The place that a nation occupies in the world is achieved by the sword and is limited only by the extent of the power of the state. The state is supreme. No social institution is of greater importance. Moreover it is the moral duty of the state to increase its power. Weakness is the most despicable of all political mistakes. It is a sin committed against the sacred spirit of political policy.

All the recent doctrines that express German imperialist aims are based on the theories of this historian, who worships the state and upholds its incontestable right to supreme power. Every war, every annexation, every policy of racial persecution ends by finding its justification in Treitschke's theory. And of course, the concentration of power in the hands of a leader and his élite takes place concomitantly with the strengthening of the state's authority.

There is no need for a detailed analysis of Nietzsche's ideas about power. It will be sufficient to point out two factors that have a special bearing on our study. The first is the psychological source of the craving for power, the continuous affirmation of one's own strength and the expression of contempt for the weak. It is well known that Nietzsche suffered deeply from the sense of his own weakness. (10) A really schizoid type, he was extremely sensitive about his relations with other people and he approached everyone with great diffidence. The slightest contretemps pushed him back into his introspective solitude. The following passage expresses a characteristic admission:

"Philosophers require special means of enduring life because they suffer in a special way. That is, they suffer as much because of their contempt as because of their love for humanity."

At the same time, his belief in his genius must have

created in him an acute awareness of the discrepancy between his desires and the possibility of satisfying them. This feeling of inferiority had to do only with practical problems. He therefore sought over-compensation in the idea of power and in dreams of the superman. "What does one repent most? One's modesty. The fact that one has not lent an ear to one's most personal needs; the fact that one has failed to recognize oneself; the fact that one has lost all sensitivity to one's instincts. A man never forgives himself later on for this waste of genuine egoism." (11) It is really shocking to find this refined and sensitive intellectual praising such a beast as Caesar Borgia and attacking morality as an expression of timidity. (1)

Nietzsche imposed his own resentment on others. This tendency had a great influence on his theories of morality and on his criticisms of Christianity and socialism. We must consider these criticisms as attempts to free himself from the personal resentment which his inferior position in life and his deep sense of his own weakness caused him. "I shall have nothing to do with any of you," he cries, "I despise your weakness, I deny any sympathy for you; I wish to be strong among the strong, to be bold and ruthless . . . The savage in each of us, even the beast in us must be acknowledged. Precisely on that account, philosophers will have an advantage." (11)

What a mass of compensatory mechanisms in these unremitting outcries! How much passion is expressed in the wish to obviate any possibility of identifying himself with the weak and destitute!

A careful study of Nietzsche's relation to his contemporaries reveals his deep aversion to the middle classes. Unusually sensitive to world currents, he was forced to develop a new set of reactions and to seek new means of liberation from the middle-class society of central Europe and particularly from that of Germany. He characterized his society as a conglomeration of the deluded and underprivileged who combined to make up a hypocritical democracy. Because of the nature of his psychic structure the new set of reactions did not lead him to identify himself with the weak and the oppressed. He had no desire to fight for their emancipation or to work toward the realization of progressive social ideals. Instead, he identified himself with the strong, venting his personal resentment by unmasking the resentment of the masses and by frustrating their efforts at sublimation (Christianity and socialism). At the same time, his idea of the superman compensated for his sense of personal inadequacy. He repudiated any affiliation with the oppressed masses and helped to frustrate their attempts at self-liberation. In contradistinction to the socialists, who expressed the ideal of a classless society, Nietzsche propagated class particularism and defended the division of society into masters and slaves.

One must recall the hatred which Nietzsche expressed toward the masses, and the contempt with which he spoke of socialism. "Socialist tendencies," he said, "have one outstanding symptom. The lower strata of society are treated with too much affability—the expectation of the forbidden happiness already sharpens their appetite. But it is not hunger that causes revolutions. People develop an appetite while eating." (11)

The reactive character of Nietzsche's thought is illustrated by his anti-humanitarianism. He says, "The demand for humanization contained in a formula, which is supposed to be the only definition of what is human, is merely a form of hypocrisy used by a certain type of man who seeks to reach the seat of power. It is an expression of the herd instinct." (11)

To a man motivated by intense narcissism, all democratic ideas must appear as a lawless assault by the masses on the rights of the select individual. In the belief that only men like himself have a right to enjoy a full life, he wishes to reduce the masses to the status of helots.

In Plato's *Theaetetus*, there is the following pertinent passage: "Everyone would like to be master of mankind and, if possible, a god. This attitude must be reinstated among us." (12) Nietzsche's psychotic state made it possible for him to entertain similar delusions of grandeur.

This attitude may be expressed in the following sociological terms: An aristocracy should rule—that is, those who are best fitted for governing. Psychologically, the idea may be expressed as: I wish to rule; I want to be like the gods and to forget my shortcomings, but I must also forget that those who do not deserve to be strong are in reality stronger than I.

Indications that Nietzsche's ideas originated in projective and reactive mechanisms can be seen in the paragraphs dedicated to his future disciples and to the ideal of the great man. "The great man who desires to suffer has a different attitude toward cruelty. He does not hold it to be detrimental or wicked in itself." (11) A great man must "win his greatness with colossal and awe-inspiring energy. By breeding out or rather by annihilating millions of the unfit, he makes possible the shaping of the future man but does not himself perish, despite the suffering he causes. Such suffering has never before been equalled." (11) An almost autobiographical characterization of his disciples follows: "The type of disciple with whom I would concern myself is one for whom I would wish suffering, destitution, illness, abuse, and humiliation. I would wish him that deep self-contempt, the torture of distrust of oneself and the distress of the loser. I feel no pity for him because I wish him that which can prove his worth if he stands firm." (13)

Nietzsche with his will to power and Stirner with his cult of the individual have become the representatives of the European intellectuals who suddenly discovered their psychic and social isolation. They looked for salvation in the camp of the powerful and ruthless masters. The slogans and myths of Superman, Nation and Race, which express this tendency, are, of course, secondary. The destructive force of these ideas became manifest in the earliest days but they survived until the present time. These ideas form the ideology of National Socialism which became the affliction of an entire nation. It was, as we shall see later, a manifestation of an exaggerated wish to compensate for the feelings of weakness and resentment that affect the nation.

Nietzsche's continual struggle against humanitarian tendencies proves that they actually had a deep hold on his mind. But his aggressiveness and his narcissism led him to oppose these tendencies with great passion. The sense of his own weakness aroused in him a fear of becoming one of the weak and underprivileged. Because of their reactive and purely personal character, Nietzsche's intentions to save mankind from pessimism and resentment and from the so-called "morality of slaves" made him reject the good with the bad by fighting against humanitarianism and true morality. This led to the release of aggressive and destructive drives. "The characteristic attributes of life—injustice, false-hood, exploitation—are most accentuated in great men. To the extent that the influence of such men was overwhelming, their character was misunderstood by people and mistakenly considered good." (13)

Foreseeing the rise of Caesarisms, Nietzche quite naturally desired to be one of the rulers and not one of the ruled. A similar desire was indicated by the part played in history by intellectuals who, unable to fight for social justice, tried instead to identify themselves with the powerful of the world and thus helped to pave the way for dictatorships. "In the future there will be a favorable disposition for large empires of a kind such as we have never seen before. But the most important thing is that out of the societies of men who devote themselves to the aim of cultivating a race of lords the future Masters of the Earth will arise. A new, frightful, self-determined and law-making aristocracy will come to power. From among them will develop philosophical men of power and artists of tyranny whose will shall endure through the centuries." He says in regard to the great man: "The great man believes that his power over his nation actually depends on his coincidental convergence with a nation and a millenium. The magnified sense of oneself as the cause and the voluntas is misconstrued as 'Altruism'. Can he not lead? Then he goes alone." "I am delighted", confesses the future Superman, "at the military development of Europe and at the anarchic conditions that will prevail. The period of quietude and 'Chinadom' which Galiani prophesied for this century is now ended. Manly personal ability, bodily capacity, recovers its value. Fine men have again become possible." (11)

The basic motives for this kind of social—or rather asocial —thinking are deeply rooted in the German mind. After Nietzsche, these theories reappear in the works of the lesser intellects. We find them asserted with similar passion and with scientific trappings in Spengler's *Decline of the West*. (14) Spengler's work, like that of Müller-Freienfels, was written in the first years of the Weimar Republic. The pretentious and, at times, brilliant presentation of his historical morphology is climaxed by the conclusions drawn in the second volume, which are so cleverly stated that they seem to follow necessarily from the analysis that precedes them.

First of all we may say that this distinguished intellectual is an admirer of brute force. He sings its praises in many different aspects. He writes convincingly about the ancient conquerors. "We cannot in our own times imagine their ardent love for heroic deeds, their *joy in slaughter* and their desire for a heroic death." (Italics mine.) According to Spengler, only the man of deeds lives in the world of reality, the world of political, economic and military action. "Here, a good blow with the sword is worth more than a good syllogism, and it is not without good reason that the soldier and the statesman in all ages and at all times had nothing but contempt for the ink-slinger and the bookworm."

In terms of a false pragmatism, Spengler expounds the idea that only those who attain visible and brutal success are important and that only their ideas are valid. All history is brutal and its brutality should be applauded. The arts and sciences are tied to the war chariot. In a realistic history of this sort, Archimedes plays a less important part than the soldier who killed him in the battle of Syracuse.

The struggle for power is closely connected with aggressive and destructive drives. War is extolled as the most magnificent force in history. "War is the creator and hunger is the destroyer of all great things." War can be the only true racial and natural relationship between nations. A fighting man experiences a feeling of power that is never experienced by the mere seeker after truth. A warrior needs no conscience. Here, Spengler quotes Goethe: "The man of action is always unscrupulous. Only the contemplative man has a conscience."

Wars between nations are deflected into the internal life of nations and become inter-party wars. These struggles, says Spengler, result in the decline of democracy and the rise of dictatorships, no matter what ideals lead the people into battle: "Whether one orders the partition of property, as in Syracuse, or one carries a book of his own making, like Marx, is of only superficial moment. It does not matter which slogans ride with the wind while doors and skulls are being smashed. Annihilation is the only true drive and Caesarism the only result."

Historical analysis shows that Spengler's conclusions are analogous to Nietzsche's aphorisms. According to Spengler, the laws of politics and the determinations of history make inevitable the rule of strong and ruthless individuals and the rule of strong and ruthless nations. He concludes as follows: "Imperialism is so inevitable an outcome of every civilization that it seizes a nation by the neck and forces it into the role of Master, even if the nation objects to acting such a role."

With regard to the position that the author takes, his relation to the occurrences of which he writes and the laws that he formulates, we find him to be the spiritual heir of Nietzsche (and, we might add, a precursor of Hitler). He takes an affirmative stand on the use of force by saying: "The rule of force in all the relationships between people is not the tragic fate of humanity, but a healthy and beautiful fact. One must understand it and prepare for it properly. The rule of gold (democracy) is bound to be superceded by conquest through blood and iron."

We might add that, side by side with some extraordinary flashes of brilliance, one finds in Spengler many examples of hazy and autistic thinking based on turbid conceptions and emotional moments. In this category belongs the racial idea that is supposed to be the alpha and omega of historical processes, the moving factor behind the destiny of peoples. It is typical of the German mind that it elevates all such notions to the rank of absolute metaphysical entities. "From an incongruity of purely metaphysical measure arose the hatred of one race for another such as that of the French for the Germans or that of the Germans for the Jews, and from the self-same beat arose, on the other hand, the true love between man and woman, a love so closely related to hatred."

This brief sketch of German psychology and of the development of certain basic ideas in German thought suggests several general conclusions. It seems clear that boundless nationalistic egoism, the lust for power, and worship of brute force are basic traits of German statesmen and philosophers. These tendencies are often concealed behind rationalizations. The haziness of the German mind provides an appropriate foundation on which to build concepts and theories that seem quite scientific, but actually merely serve the purpose of justifying ruthless aggressiveness and fiendish anti-humanitarianism.

It also seems clear that the German collective mind did not succeed in getting rid of feudal residues. It was unable to overcome either its pusillanimous submission to a stronger will or its aggressive drive toward subjugation of the weak. To obey and to rule remain its principal ideals.

ADOLF HITLER

Hitler's father Alois was a modest craftsman. At the age of seventeen he conceived ambitious dreams, which were realized twenty-three years later when Alois Schickelgruber (the change of the family name to Hitler occurred later for reasons not quite clear) became a minor official in His Imperial Austrian Majesty's Customs Service. Even after his retirement Hitler Senior insisted on being addressed by his full official title. At that time, he also became inordinately restless and forced his family to change residence several times. He tyrannized over his wife and children and used to summon his son, Adolf, by whistling through his fingers.

In brief, Hitler Senior was a man characterized by feelings of personal superiority and social dissatisfaction; he was despotic in his relations to his immediate family and scornful of his environment. Hitler Senior was a typical representative of the disgruntled petty bourgeois, who gazed with disgust upon their own milieu, despised the working class and liked to identify themselves with the haughty and powerful.

We find these basic attitudes along with greater unrest and frustration in the son Adolf. Moreover, these attitudes to those in power compact at once with rebelliousness, spitefulness and abject servility, were exacerbated in the son by a suppressed hostility to his father. Consequently when confronted by authority of his teachers, Adolf Hitler transferred to these the malevolent feeling he entertained for his father. Manifestations of superiority by virtue of class, achievement, or even ordinary physical prowess never failed to elicit the most envenomed responses of resentment and spite.

The Fuehrer's autobiography contains several interesting inaccuracies which were exposed and analyzed by Olden (1) and Heiden, (2) the authors of two excellent monographs on Hitler. The purpose of Hitler's distortions of his own past was to elevate his person, to throw some degree of glory on the drab chapters of his life and to obliterate details which did not conform to the desired pattern. Hitler's great ability to deceive others as well as himself, his capacity for auto-suggestion are revealed in his autobiography. Under the influence of wishful fantasies Hitler's thinking lost the vaguest semblance of objectivity, and distorted and trans-formed reality.

Hitler's passion for exclusive power and his resentment of those who retained it were manifested early in his life. The craving to cut a grand figure hindered him, even as a boy, from adjusting to reality. He was a bad student but it might have sprung from the fact that his father thwarted his ambition to become an artist. Alois Hitler insisted that his son enter the civil service. Thus, sharpening his develop-ing megalomania, a consequence of his fantasies, were the recurring bursts of resentment of those in authority and of the powerful father who frustrated the road to his imagined greatness as an artist.

Unable to shape reality to his desires Adolf withdrew into himself, hiding his injury deep within his mind, seeking com-pensation in fantasy, or falling into fits of depression and discouragement.

After leaving school he stayed with his family for a time, refusing any employment. Later he led an abject ex-istence in Vienna doing menial jobs, sleeping in night shelters, reduced at times to begging. At no point did he attempt to do any systematic work, to adjust himself to a definite place or profession. This behavior was to some ex-tent caused by his perpetual fantasies of greatness. The dreams of an artistic career were blighted by his failure to pass the examination at the Academy of Fine Arts (in *Mein Kampf*, Hitler still seems to wonder at this unexpected, and therefore, to his way of thinking, "undeserved" failure). Then dreams of an architect's career (without the necessary studies, without practical experience or any consistent effort), and finally political dreams, were the stages not clear-cut at first, but nonetheless distinct in his gradually crystallizing megalomania.

At some point in his early life, Hitler transferred his inferiority feelings to his mother country, Austria, which under the inept Hapsburgs had "betrayed her German soul". At the same time, he centered his ideas of grandeur on Germany. These nationalistic dreams and leanings were intensified under the influence of a certain teacher (history was one of the few subjects which interested Hitler at that time) and the reading of a book on the Franco-Prussian war of 1871, reputed to have been the only book in his parents' home.

In projecting his complexes into the outside world Hitler reproduced on a large scale his divided attitude toward reality. Reality was split into an inferior and a superior portion; the former was his own, intimate, accessible reality; the latter was distant and beyond reach.

Hitler's social views were also shaped during this Vienna period. Hungry, miserable, he had no interests in common with the people around him to whom he felt so superior. Nor did any community of feeling bind him to his next of kin. He rarely corresponded with his family and after the death of his mother—the only person he ever loved—he broke with them entirely for several years. Only after World War I did he resume relations.

He reacted with contempt and hatred to his immediate society. In *Mein Kampf*, (3) he speaks of his proletarian milieu with utter loathing, after the fashion of a deposed prince inveighing against unspeakable plebeians. His resentment became transformed into hatred for his companions in distress. He felt that his proper place was among the strong and the powerful, but for the time being he could only bide his time and seek to penetrate the mystifying secret of their success. Did he not possess superior qualifications and abilities? Here we have to deal again with the splitting of reality into two spheres—one splendid and inaccessible; the other, his own, wretched and contemptible. Furthermore, to him this horrible reality seemed foreign and imposed arbitrarily from outside.

Although in later and more grandiose days Hitler used the strongest terms of contempt when referring to Parliament, this institution made a tremendous impression upon him in his youth. Even the building appeared to him as an outstanding artistic achievement. From the gallery he listened to the debates for hours on end, and alternately envied and hated those well-fed, well-dressed, and handsomely remunerated representatives of the people. He certainly could speak better than these incompetent idlers!

He despised the working class, yet he was dependent upon that class even for his pittance. He was adamant against joining a labor union, conceiving it an insult to his pride. Inevitably these arrogant airs and insufferable attitudes led him into conflicts with older and more skilled fellow-workers. In retrospect these conflicts appeared to him as based on political differences. His unusual conceit made him exclaim: "I was struggling at that time with my distress. Are these people really human, worthy of belonging to a great nation?" Even twenty years later he was subject to fits of anger against the "humiliated and wronged ones", a group to which he had once belonged. "To many people this also means the wretched recollections of the lack of culture among the lower classes, of the brutality so frequent in their relations with each other, and one's own position in the social scale—be it ever so humble—

makes any and all contact with such a superannuated phase of our culture and life become an unbearable burden."

Hitler's exceptionally strong narcissism and his tendency to hasty generalization lifted these personal conflicts, which were for the most part of his own making, to a more universal, political level. To be sure, then and in later days his opponents were always to blame. At the time referred to, they were the organized proletariat—Marxian Socialism, Social Democracy. In typical paranoic fashion Hitler saw in Socialism a personal enemy and an enemy of Germany, while the working class appeared to him to be just as much a victim of party organization as he himself had been.

Nevertheless, the socialist organization impressed Hitler with the fact that large sections of labor followed it. In other words, any display of strength was alluring to him despite his overt aversion. Hitler probably conceived the idea of bending this organization to his own purposes in his years of adversity and poverty. And it seems equally probable that at the time this embittered individual unconsciously began the process of absorbing someone else's ideas, of assimilating them, and then revamping them for his own use. Had it not been for his personal resentment and overweening pride which created an unbridgeable gulf between him and his environment, Hitler might well have become a revolutionary socialist. But as Olden rightly says, "he hated the toilers even more than the well-to-do". His envy made him hate those who were strong and powerful; his desire to identify himself with them enabled him to understand the socialist ideas of the exploitation of one class by another. Moreover, he believed that the Socialists were placing stumbling blocks in the path of Germany's power and preventing Austria from becoming an outpost of Germanic expansion. In his accusations he also included those fellow toilers who—in his opinion—were to blame for his own difficulties and humiliations. With his hazy mind, prone to jump at conclusions, he thought he saw the issue clearly. And so Social Democracy became the prime enemy for a time.

But this enemy was not sufficiently removed and alien for a perpetual scapegoat. After all, the Social Democrats were working men and women, misguided to be sure, but still they were Germans, blood kinsmen. What was hiding behind them, Hitler wondered; what satanic force ruled them, upsetting his plans and purposes, blocking him from achieving his objectives? The answer was simple: the Jews.

The startling impression of outlandishness made on Hitler by the Galician Jews in their typical garb, whom he first saw in Vienna, associated itself in a peculiar manner with the anti-Semitic pamphlets he had read. He realized with sudden surprise that the Jews in his native town did not differ at all from its other inhabitants ("their appearance had become human", he says bitterly), that their disguise was perfect. It was they, he declared, who had created socialism and who stood at the helm of the Social Democratic movement, then controlling the working class. He concluded from this that they wielded great power for their own secret purposes. Thus, this was the devilish power at work to thwart him in art, literature or politics. Hitler became convinced that the Jews controlled all possible fields of endeavor, and by means of their "lucubrations" poisoned the souls of the Germans. "That was a plague, a spiritual plague worse than the Black Death in the days of yore."

The passion and violence, unusual even in him, with which he seethed first against the alleged control of the Jews over Vienna's prostitution industry and later against their debauching of innocent German girls, show that his anti-Semitism had an extremely personal and emotional origin. Let us quote the pertinent passages from *Mein Kampf*: "These black parasites on the bodies of all nations systematically prostitute our inexperienced young, blonde girls, thus destroying something which in this world can never again be replaced." He speaks of the "seduction of hundreds of thousands of girls by those bow-legged, abominable Jew bastards," and further: "the black-haired Jewish boy, with satanic joy on his face, lurks for hours waiting for the innocent girl whom he defiles with his blood." Olden comments: "But what if this was not just imagination? Perhaps it was an experience actually lived through? An experience in the description of which he shuffled and transposed the situations and the characters? Perhaps it was some other male, black of hair too, but an *Aryan* who lurked waiting for hours, while the vainly awaited girl innocently made some Jewish rival happy?" Be it as it may, the moment of sexual jealousy apparent in Hitler's paranoiac anti-Semitism seems a clear cut projection of his own repressed—or frustrated—sexual impulses. Further development of these ideas, especially their resulting in the fanatical and absurd persecution of "Rassenschande" (race pollution) that is of the pollution of the "Aryan" race, a crime equated for some obscure reasons to the incest, is indicative of some deeply unconscious sexual sources. (4) The sexual jealousy of a rejected psychopathic individual may have provided the force that linked together all the ramifications of his resentment around one single nucleus— Jewry. Hitler offers a perfect illustration of what the Swiss neurologist Monakow termed "agglutinated, emotional causality", which unifies the most varied, unrelated subjects and reduces them to a common denominator on the basis of strong emotions of love, jealousy, and hate.

Hitler's mind was also primitively antithetic. While all evil began to concentrate around the myth of the Jew, a myth saturated with emotional elements deriving from the most primitive drives, all that was bright, good, wholesome, pure, and noble began to concentrate at the opposite pole. This opposite pole was the "Aryan" race. Hitler states:

"If we Germans are the chosen of God, then they (the Jews) are the people of Satan. The Jew is much farther removed from the animal than we Aryans. He is a being alien to the natural order—a being outside of nature."

Hitler, like any man possessed by an idea and a craving for action, had the ability to transform his own delusions into weapons. Paraphrasing Voltaire's remark on God, he remarked: "If the Jew did not exist, he would have to be invented. What is needed is a visible and not an invisible enemy."

The same complexes shaped Hitler's attitude toward the city where as a youth he met with disappointment and failure. He left Vienna because he hated it, as the "incarnation of blood pollution". His native Austria was to him a beautiful country—after all it was his mother-country—but it was oppressed by the Hapsburgs and the Social Democrats, who kept it from achieving its great German destiny, just as they blocked his own path. The beautiful capital appeared to him as the prey of black devils who defiled it, just as they defiled young maidens. For the time being, the future dictator could only withdraw; he was not sufficiently strong yet to take revenge or put things in order. But deep in his soul was stored up his desire for retaliation and for setting things to rights, for the destruction of Jewry and the rescuing of Austria, above all the city of his own humiliations, poor, outraged Vienna. Many years later, Rauschning, the dictator's confidant, speaking of Hitler's plans for Austria, noted: "A personal animosity, an intense resentment were perceptible in his plans. One felt that he wished to avenge himself for his years of privation, his frustrated hopes, his life of poverty and humiliation."

But how was this passion for politics formed in Hitler's soul, how did he discover his true vocation? A complete answer to this basic question is difficult. We have seen that Hitler's experiences in society were deemed by him as a series of humiliations and insults, which in later years changed into a feeling of deepest resentment. His passion for a change in his status led him to a study of social problems. Incapable as he was of thinking objectively, he formed a distorted but dogmatic picture of the situation and its causes.

Rudolf Hanisch, once Hitler's comrade in misfortune, a companion of his night shelters and a collaborator in the early days, relates how one evening Hitler chanced on a film, *The Tunnel,* by Kellermann, in which a demagogue by force of word alone, mobilizes the labor masses. The impression of this film on Hitler was so great that for days on end he spoke only of the power of words. He often stopped his work and for entire days read pamphlets and newpapers and discussed politics with his companions at night shelters and in restaurants. "He was always suggesting that we form a new party", says Hanisch.

Hitler who tells of having been a little "ring leader" in school, again felt within him the desire to lead, to force upon others his manner of thinking and to escape from a frustrating and humiliating situation. His personal desires took on greater force and a stronger impulse toward realization when they were closely interwoven with general ideals of a seemingly unselfish nature. He was concerned, at least, for public consumption not with his own welfare, but with the welfare of other victims of existing conditions; not with his own career, but with the grandeur of Germany and the German nation. But for the time being he was unsuccessful in forming a new party and all his passion failed to attract adherents. He had first to mature and crystallize his convictions as to his real vocation; and the German masses had first to be tried by war, defeat, and revolution, before being susceptible to the virus of "new" ideas and a new mission.

Hitler's first, though probably not deliberate step on the road to the achievement of his great objectives, was his departure from detestable Austria to admirable Germany. In Munich, from 1912 to the outbreak of World War I, he kept up his interest in politics, read newspapers and discussed in beer halls his favorite theme, the inferiority of Austria to Germany. His convictions became strengthened and in his soul there swelled the desire for violent events, which might bring a change in his situation as well as in that of Germany and the land of his birth. Very likely this was all one general feeling of tension, restlessness, and expectation, so characteristic of periods of crises in the life of psychopaths. In this connection it should be added that Hitler frequently experienced periods of apathy and depression, along with moments of violent excitement.

In August 1914, the ardently desired change came at last. "Verily," Hitler wrote later, "the German nation was not forced into this war, it rode with joy into the lists for the sake of a great cause." And of himself: "As for me, those hours seemed a deliverance from the irritating feelings of youth. And even today I am not ashamed to declare that, moved by an impetuous enthusiasm, I fell on my knees and thanked the heavens above from the bottom of my heart filled with joy, that I was permitted the good fortune of living in these times."

No wonder that with such an attitude which, as he rightly stresses, was in harmony with the sentiments of millions of Germans, Hitler counts his war years as among the happiest of his life. This restless and maladjusted individual no longer needed to seek an outlet for his violent emotions; he was doing war duty, believed in victory, and looked forward to his own advancement and a proper niche for himself.

He discovered that other people did not think altogether as he did. Wounded in the fall of 1916, he spent five months behind the lines in a hospital near Berlin and in the Reserve Battalion at Munich, and found in these places an atmosphere of dissatisfaction and defeatism. He naturally attributed these manifestations of German war weariness to the intrigues of Jewish financial circles, which he believed had gained control of the entire production machinery and were paving the way for the revolution.

Thus Hitler's ideas developed logically from his earlier delusions. The germs of a mania of persecution, fed by new sources, reawakened, and defeat and revolution brought them into full flowering. Even in the normal course of his pre-war days Hitler had experienced periods of depression and outbursts of excitement: the collapse of his grandiose hopes for Germany and himself caused a tremendous shock in him, a veritable mental upheaval. His fanatical mind had not even for a moment visualized the possibility of a German defeat. In his eyes, Germany's cause was great and just, her strength was invincible. Dazzled by the power of Prussian militarism, Hitler was unable to give even a thought to the strength of the adversary, to say nothing of the adversary's point of view. He could understand the German collapse only by invoking some mysterious power which had helped the despicable adversary. Hitler's mind flashed back to the ideas brought along from his Austrian homeland: Marxism and Jewry or Marxism in the service of international Jewry, or the Jewish financiers—all variations of the same theme. These evil forces which at an earlier time had prevented the young and ambitious Hitler from achieving a position he deserved and which now vanquished the German Siegfried, were responsible for Germany's ruin. But not for long—or at any rate not forever. "I, however, determined to become a politician"—with these words Hitler concludes his description of the German defeat and revolution.

This is psychologically speaking the most difficult moment in the biography, in the evolution of the dictator, the moment of his "hearing the call"—the moment when he realized his mission. The feeling that one has a mission can manifest itself with elemental force. In Hitler, it broke forth during a period of psychic collapse, toward the end of the war. The immediate cause of his collapse was gas poisoning, but the defeat of Germany contributed the major share of the shock. Hitler allegedly heard voices which commanded him to save Germany. It is impossible today to make a clinical diagnosis of his condition at that time. However, there is no doubt that all pertinent evidence was destroyed and the professor of psychiatry who is reported to have mentioned Hitler in his lectures as a rare instance of hysterical blindness was forced, like so many others, to flee abroad although he was a pure "Aryan".

Nevertheless we may attempt to describe the psychological mechanisms of Hitler's "calling". When all the foundations of his conscious faith in life collapsed, hope and comfort came from the deep strata of his unconscious. "Germany will rise again and you will be her savior"—spoke the voice which was the reflection of all his deepest emotions. Thus in one stroke he solved both his personal anguish and the general problem. Adolf Hitler and Germany were to rise from the depths of humiliation together. So close a correlation of his own and the public cause was made possible by the fact that for many years he had identified himself with Germany.

An immense narcissism was of course required to make of his own person the focal point of his mission and to assign to it such an important part. Until then this narcissism had failed to find even a modicum of gratification; it had prevented Hitler from adjusting himself to reality and achieving normal satisfaction in life. Consequently he continually experienced wrongs and frustrations. His "revelation" and the subsequent course of events showed the real extent of his tension.

The feeling of his mission, which stemmed from irrational sources, naturally did not supply him with any practical suggestions. He had to glean those from the situation as it developed, and Hitler proved himself a master at this. His faith in himself enabled him to await the proper moment, to struggle through all difficulties, and to go on unperturbed by failures.

Whenever his ultimate objective was involved, even false steps and blindly executed moves mattered little. At first the mission of savior of Germany did not inhibit his opportunism. After leaving the hospital—then ruled by the soldiers' councils, he tried to join the only active political movement, i.e., the Social Democrats. According to the reports of soldiers, he even acted the part of a confirmed Social Democrat at one of the meetings. Of course, no references to slips of that nature can be found in his autobiography. The Fuehrer tried to convey to his readers the assurance that even in those days he looked upon all Marxists as "scoundrels" and "miserable, low criminals". Actually, Hitler tried to establish a contact with those in power, so as to be able to play his part with their assistance. Having failed again to gain recognition or to establish proper connections he felt hurt, all the more so, because this failure was a repetition of experiences in his youth. With an ego now bolstered up by his recently acquired conviction of greatness, the resentment that had been smoldering in him for many years was bound to flare up in a great blaze.

The right moment, however, was not yet at hand. He left Munich, then a hotbed of "criminal" Marxism—and took refuge in apparent inactivity and apathy; but his ideas and convictions ripened in his spiritual solitude. It was a period of internal concentration analogous to those experienced by many prophets and founders of religions. Remaining aloof from Socialism, then in power for a short period, Hitler bided his time until the "real Germany" should speak out and call him.

It would be valuable if we could learn more about the spiritualistic circles in which Hitler moved at that time. In these circles, an ex-clergyman, with the instincts of a charlatan and the behavior of a mystic, conjured up the spirit of a deceased woman "saint" who demanded that the fetters of the "dictate" of Versailles be shattered and proclaimed the slogan: "Germany awake!" Through spiritualistic circles, Hitler is said to have met high-ranking army officers. Unfortunately, our curiosity concerning this period must remain unsatisfied. The Fuehrer saw to it that evidence of such discrediting incidents in his past were destroyed. This mysterious period, however, is highly interesting from a psychological point of view.

If, as we have been told, the seances in question disclosed some "talent" of Hitler, we may assume that this referred to his "mediumism". It may be that Hitler simply proved a good medium, that is, a sensitive receiver of inspirations flowing from the world of spirits. We do not possess and probably never shall possess any information concerning his behavior during those seances. But we may easily imagine it, on the basis of observations from other sources, as well as from data in his own biography. A certain type of psychopath with a considerable tinge of hysteria is most easily susceptible to suggestion, provided it follows the line of the individual's emotions or desires, and fits into the general scheme of his own ideas. What, after all, is any spiritualistic seance, if not an experiment in mass suggestion, based on certain emotionally tinged ideas, conscious or unconscious, radiated by individuals who are either particularly sensitive or intentionally fraudulent? Among "specialists", an individual who is particularly sensitive to suggestion and able to express it forcibly is considered a good medium. Such individuals are usually prone to adopt fantastic ideas and to act out the emotional thoughts conceived by themselves or impressed upon them. They fall easily into trances, that is, half hypnotic states, during which they seem possessed by an external force, the spirit itself, as it were, whose thoughts and emotions they interpret. Such properties of the medium must also impress the members of his audience, who in their turn succumb to suggestion. The medium thus involuntarily acts the part of the suggestor, and in case of strong collective hysteria, even the part of hypnotist. We may easily imagine what a medium Hitler must have been, considering the tremendous tension of his emotions, his lack of mental balance and the fact that the commands of the spirits miraculously coincided with his own thoughts and impulses.

As thorough an expert on Hitler as Rauschning frequently mentions his mediumism and his affinity to matters supernatural. This affinity is intimately connected, as we know, with his original inborn narcissism. "Nothing was known about him," said Rauschning, "his head was full of grandiose edifices bordering on the supernatural." (5)

His mediumism may have contributed to his belief in his mission. Under the impact of one's own unconscious complexes—autosuggestion—or of external suggestion, there may form certain ideas surcharged with emotions and conveying the feeling of absolute certitude. But such ideas are only weakly connected with consciousness and seem to come from another world. It should also be borne in mind that unconscious processes of long duration sometimes suddenly become conscious. Moreover, the medium is not merely a passive receptacle but also a subject emanating additional powers. This observation recalls Nietzsche's remark on "leaders who are being led", and as we shall see, helps to explain Hitler's influence on the masses. The Fuehrer, source of an exceptionally powerful mass suggestion, remained receptive to ideas coming from outside.

Hitler could never have gone beyond being a medium if his psychic structure had not contained active, so-called "sthenic" elements, and if he had not been aided by external factors, the same factors which discovered in him the medium and which later—no longer in secret circles but in army barracks—discovered him to be a first class spell-binder. The medium became a hypnotist and his psychological qualities began to have effect in the political arena.

At that moment the German reactionaries had begun to organize. The General Staff was preparing its coup against the Social Democrats and its future war of revenge. Courses were organized among the soldiers, to inculcate them with the proper spirit. We know that Hitler was "discovered" during one of these courses. It appears that he succeeded in defeating his opponent in a debate and in carrying his audience. It must be said that the subject of the debate was very close to his heart. His opponent had dared to stand up in defense of the Jews. Hitler's ability as an agitator was rewarded: he was appointed officer-instructor. The first official recognition determined the future course of history. The German reactionaries trained their medium, made him the receptacle of their own tendencies and through him propagated their ideas. The men behind the scheme were in the first place the ranking officers of the Reichswehr and the various nationalistic groups.

We do not propose to follow all the stages of Hitler's career. The subjects of our study are 1. Hitler's ideas, 2. the form they assumed in his mind, and 3. this mind as supreme leader of Germany. This carries us into the field of social problems and mass psychology. In regard to Hitler's ideas, we have seen that they contained distinct elements of nationalism for some time. These elements were gradually expanded by various influences. There was, for instance, the idea of race. The apotheosis of Germanism became transformed very quickly into an apotheosis of the Germanic or Nordic race, or in a larger sense, the Aryan race; other races, especially the Semitic race, were declared to be inferior. Hitler's conception of the Jew as an inferior being, and the malignant spirit of evil and darkness acquired support from a number of pseudo-scientific arguments. His contacts with intellectuals had become increasingly frequent; they made him read the works of Houston Stewart Chamberlain, and under the influence of his books, the myth of race became one of the chief weapons of Hitler's new doctrine. (6)

One of his main sources of information and suggestions was Alfred Rosenberg, who supplied a "philosophical" background for the chaotic welter of ideas seething in the future leader's mind. Rosenberg's *Myth of the Twentieth Century* is one of the most deceptive products of the human mind. (7) Seemingly based on logical arguments, it is steeped in primitive emotions, bitter hate, and fantastic pride. It is full of pseudo-concepts and pseudo-ideas, hazy and confused, which are presented with insolent assurance. It is easy to imagine what the *Myth of the Twentieth Century* with its glitter of sham erudition, must have meant to the half-baked intellectual whose vague and fanatical ideas now seemed to have scientific foundation.

In the Third Reich the idea of race, laden with the dynamic attributes of pride and hate, influenced German science and legislation. Since it confused right with wrong and wisdom with absurdity, it became the source of an endless chain of sufferings and tortures.

It is by no means a matter of small moment or an accident, that Hitler himself was not at all certain of the purity of his Germanic descent. This tallies perfectly with his general psychic structure, with his primitive superego which always desired something from beyond its own sphere and consequently elevated that very thing to the first place.

The Socialist part of the National Socialist doctrine originated through external influences. Here, too, Hitler acted with unerring instinct. He realized that without some sort of social program he could not expect to win over the masses. His first contacts with socialism awakened in him only hate and disgust, but early in his career as an agitator he had the good fortune to come upon a conception of socialism which could be easily made to fit in with his other ideas. At one of the lectures he attended, Hitler met an engineer, Feder, who preached the theory of two categories of capital: predatory, interest-bearing, Jewish capital, and productive Aryan capital. Hitler immediately perceived the connection between "socialism" and "nationalism" which up to that time had escaped him. Feder himself belonged to a group of people who tried to make Marxism a reality "in spite of Marx" and he even concluded his "manifesto on the abolition of interest-slavery" with the immortal words of the *Communist Manifesto.* (8)

Hitler was completely dazzled by Feder's pseudo-scientific hodge-podge. "When I heard Feder's first lecture," he says in *Mein Kampf,* "it forthwith flashed through my mind, that here was where I found a way to one of the most important platforms for the founding of a new party."

The thought of founding a party as an instrument of power had been dormant in Hitler's mind for many years. Now the opportunity came at last. His sole desire was to wield influence, to hold power, to struggle, to hate. The ideological content came, of course, from without. In spite of all appearances to the contrary, that content was not a cut and dried formula. It was fluid, varying, adaptable, always presenting a front which was best suited to the given situation of the conflict, always attuned to those whom it was necessary to win over or to appease. To the very end, Hitler could, if necessary, play the part of a champion of labor.

Having become, on the recommendation of the Reichswehr, a member of an insignificant group which called itself the German Labor Party, Hitler found his first suitable field of action among the "small people", not among the intellectuals, who still aroused in him a rankling feeling of inferiority. Here he became a master of propaganda, tireless in inventing, shouting, and spreading slogans, and in organizing meetings and demonstrations. For the first time in his life he took the helm into his hands. It is also very important that Hitler entered this organization at the bidding of the Reichswehr and that he found his support in the "small people". From now on, in all of his activities, he could feel safe. The Army and the great nationalistic organizations were the sources of his security and strength, whereas the small bourgeoisie was to supply him with impulses, dynamic impetus, and possibilities for constant expansion. It was to them that Hitler spoke, it was they he had to convince. And it was to his great advantage, that, as an English biographer has remarked, "he was not afraid of being platitudinous".

We shall refrain from presenting in this study the amazingly rapid progress Hitler made from the miniscule "German Labor Party" to the powerful political machine of Nazism and from a mere propaganda officer and member No. 7, to Fuehrer. All that has been discussed many times. What interests us are only certain fundamental psychological problems.

What methods did Hitler apply and what methods did he preach? What laws of evolution do we discern when we examine the growth of the party and its leader and to what extent are these laws psychological?

There was nothing very original in his ideas; he encountered similar ideas among his first companions. Such kinship of spirit could have hardly filled him with joy, jeopardizing the advantage of priority and absolute originality so dear to his unusual narcissism. However, instead of throwing a crumb of grateful sympathy to those former unassuming, unknown, and harmless companions, years later he ridiculed them without mercy.

As for Hitler's methods, we shall first note that at an early date in his career, he consolidated them into a complete and coherent theory which he checked, developed, and perfected through practical application, like a scientist. His satisfaction in gathering the fruits of these methods is revealed by the brutal frankness with which he made them known to anyone who was willing to listen. In view of Hitler's overweening narcissism, his cynical frankness in disclosing the technique of his future crimes is less surprising than the failure of his future victims to take adequate precautionary measures.

What were these methods? How did it happen that before Hitler became dictator of Germany, he had for a long time, as Olden tells us, been dictator in beer halls, at meetings, in the city at large? Apparently, Hitler, who during his lean years in Vienna was first impressed by the power of organization and propaganda, had also learned to value the power of the spoken word and was resolved to make use of it with all his characteristic ruthlessness. He believed—it could not possibly have been otherwise—that his political and military opponents had used lying as a means of propaganda, and he decided to imitate them on a vast scale. He imagined he would defeat socialism by "improving" upon the ideological weapons of socialism. Lacking any intellectual culture and feeling sadly out of place "among the fine gentlemen", he knew that he could count only on those who knew even less than he did himself. Hence the slogans of his propaganda had to be as simple as possible. What they lacked in substance was replaced by emotional violence and the irresistible force of endless repetition. In the pamphlets and articles which formed the Fuehrer's only intellectual diet, he found a source of simplified ideas which after passing through his hazy, undisciplined and distorted mind, grew even more simplified than before.

Neither in his addresses nor in his entire propaganda did Hitler fear banality. The success of this method was based on two factors. First, the technique of suggestion, repetition,

and oversimplification proved effective when applied to the
minds of the small people, to an extent surpassing the
Fuehrer's boldest dreams; second, quite unexpectedly to
Hitler, it acted as a protective mechanism, by misleading the
intellectual classes and blinding them to a danger, which, on
the surface, seemed negligible.

These methods were the complements of a large-scale
mass hypnosis which Hitler applied to a constantly increasing
degree and which he eventually brought to real perfection.

"Whoever wishes to get results in politics," said Hitler,
"must take equal consideration both of the weakness (in
another place he spoke of the cowardice) and the bestiality
of the human masses." This formula, properly interpreted
and carried out with the accuracy and completeness of which
only a thorough fanatic is capable, contains the secret of
Hitler's success as a leader and organizer. Fear and hate, the
two chief weapons in his arsenal, were intended to exploit
weakness and sadism in human nature. Hitler's instructions
were unmistakable: opposition was to be overwhelmed by
terror. Hitler recalls one meeting, at which his henchmen
brutally assailed his opponents, with real satisfaction: "And
now a wild shooting affray broke loose. One's heart almost
leapt with delight at such an echo of old war experiences."

Brutality, terror, violence, these were the means with
which he sought to overwhelm the opposition. Whenever the
latter failed to give sufficient motive for their use, an excuse
had to be contrived. The slightest attempt at obstructionist
tactics on the part of the opposition was met with utmost
violence. The propaganda meetings organized by Hitler's
party anticipated the future dictatorship, and the so-called
"Order Troops", from which developed the "Storm Troops",
became the organs of brute force. "They were imbued with
the tenet that once reason was silent and force alone had
the last word, the best weapon of defense was the attack,

and that our order troops should have the reputation of being not a debating society, but a combat unit ready to do its utmost."

Thus Hitler deliberately sought to arouse fear of himself in the opposition and in the masses at large. He also proceeded to implant in the masses the fear of greatly exaggerated or fictitious enemies. At the same time he frightened legal governments with the bogey of Bolshevism.

It is interesting to note how easily the masses are made to fear imaginary foes and how they try to protect themselves from every side. Many moves of governments, too, originated in fears of the same nature, moves that psychologically might be described as resulting from a deformation of the instinct of self-preservation. Some of Hitler's bogeys, especially "international capitalism" and "international communism" proved so effective that they not only impressed the German industrialists including the Jewish financiers, but also served as an instrument of international blackmail on a grand scale. It should be noted that even in the field of common crime the borderline between blackmail and hypnosis cannot always be determined with complete exactness.

In accordance with the principles of the Fuehrer, fear was to be sown throughout the land. The violence aroused by fear could easily be blamed on the adversary. The theory of provocation was accordingly worked out, and its wholesale application in the burning of the Reichstag was only one example among an endless number of other less spectacular but more successful incidents. An overdose of cynicism and of the spectacular element seems to interfere at times with the phenomenon of collective hypnosis, and similarly a certain degree of reserve favors the success of hypnosis applied individually.

The cracking of opponents' heads was but one of the stages of a well prepared campaign of hate. Not every one had the good fortune to enjoy a part in that stage of Hitler's campaign. The participants were mostly strong, husky, frequently armed youths. To hate, however, was everybody's privilege and the Fuehrer tried to teach hate to all. Next to fear, hate was his principal weapon. Psychologically we may conjecture that Hitler's use of fear was an attempt to transfer a considerable portion of his own unconscious fear to his adversaries in order to get rid of it but the endopsychic origin of hate is so obvious that no conjectures are required. The personality of Adolf Hitler was made up to a considerable extent of sadistically-aggressive tendencies, of which hate was only one manifestation. A psychoanalyst may study here the various aspects of these tendencies and their combined outward manifestations.

Hitler discovered that hate is a powerful weapon because it unites the masses against a common enemy. For this reason the enemy must be easily identifiable, not too dangerous, vulnerable to various criminal charges and suitable as a scapegoat for all the national misfortunes and shortcomings. From this point of view, first Marxism and later the Jews proved priceless and irreplaceable. This explains Hitler's remark that if there were no Jews, they would have to be invented, and the reason he repeatedly attacked them in his speeches and urged the Storm Troopers on to their sadistic pogroms.

Such concentrated hate, both in the case of one individual, and even more so in the case of a collective body, serves as an outlet for a huge mass of suppressed or frustrated emotions: greed, envy, and resentment. In the post-war years large groups of Germans were animated by such feelings. The country teemed with secret organizations which sentenced and executed such alleged "traitors". All of these organizations owed their existence to the widespread dissatisfaction, wounded national pride, poverty, inflation, and unemployment which beset Germany at that time. The concurrence of the collective hate with the hate of one man, of the resentment of the masses and of powerful national organizations with the resentment of a fanatic psychopath, created an exceptionally fertile soil for the growth of Nazism. The old school-book adage, "hate divides and love unites", beautiful though it may be, is not always true. Hate can unite people and even transform an amorphous mass into a powerful solid body.

Hitler taught the masses to hate a common enemy and to suspect hostile conspiracies in every quarter. It was not so much the masses' ideas, often very hazy, as their fears and their hate that made them rally around a leader and a strong party organization. Each victory over the enemy fortified those mystic ties in the souls of the followers, intensified the desire for further aggression, for the annihilation of the menacing foe. Whenever an internal enemy was no longer conveniently at hand, after having been annihilated or tortured to death in the dungeons and concentration camps of the Gestapo, an external enemy was conjured up, the same external enemy who for centuries on end, ever since the time of Frederick the "One and Only", had been lurking ready to pounce on docile, hard-working, virtuous Germany: France.

The hatred which dwelled in the Fuehrer himself contained specific characteristics related to the structure of his personality. His hatred for ideological enemies or political adversaries was always a personal hatred as well. To begin with, Hitler never forgave anyone for anything. Just as he had never forgiven the Socialists the humiliations of his Vienna days or the intellectual classes his intellectual inferiority, he never forgave all those who during his long climb to power dared to place obstacles in his path. Nor did he ever forgive many of those who even actually helped him, but whose images evoked in him memories injurious to his narcissism. And all this because—and this point is of special importance—hatred in Hitler was tied up most intimately with his narcissism. As Spinoza said, every creature desires to continue existing, but Hitler belonged to those creatures who, for the sake of their existence, must destroy other creatures. He felt that his greatness, power, merits, or mission were seriously threatened whenever a person, who in some way, be it ever so small, might claim some importance or power, appeared within the sphere of his activities. By destroying the adversary with the poisonous stream of his hate—in the days when he did not yet possess such deadly weapons as concentration camps, he had other methods at his disposal—Hitler elevated himself. When he accused the Jews or the Socialists of betraying Germany, he in the same breath was passing himself off as her saviour, almost Christ himself, pretending to have narrowly missed a martyr's fate. And when statesmen of Western Europe threatened Germany with armaments, he was the one to stretch out his hand for peace, but only in so far as it was consistent with Germany's honor, of which he, again in contrast to others, was the most watchful guardian. As they refused to listen, he began arming himself, feeling that he had a perfect right to do so. "And so we armed!" offended innocence declaimed again and again in speeches we all remember.

Throughout his campaign for power, Hitler always contrasted his own incorruptibility and his pure German blood with the corruption and the impure race of his opponents. He boasted of being the restorer of his country's honor and armed might, the champion of German productive capital against the Communists, or the champion of German labor against the "Jewish" capitalist vampires. Such militant hatred, seemingly creative and bold, was bound to rally around the Fuehrer all those who discovered in him their own emotions and passions in a highly concentrated form, without inhibitions or gradations and with prospects of speedy and full realization. There stood before them their true ideal, mouthing furious shrieks and violent threats, great though self-made, the living guarantee of Germany's honor, of social justice and the sacred rights of private ownership, the conqueror of the Jews and Bolsheviks, the modest "unknown soldier" who would restore Germany's strength, the victor over the enemies of himself and of Germany, always strong and fierce, the master, the leader—and yet a modest and plain individual, behaving almost like "the son of man". Thus hatred welded his followers into an increasingly compact group, setting them apart from other people as the salt of the earth. The Party organization with its hierarchy and its external trappings greatly strengthened what had originally been a haphazard structure.

Insatiable hate constantly demanded new objects. Two highly instructive manifestations of the workings of that hate were the burning of the Reichstag and the blood bath of June 30, 1934.

The burning of the Reichstag was, as is well known, a crude provocation aimed at demonstrating the danger of Communism and justifying the contemplated policy of ruthless terror. After their accession to power, Hitler and his intimates felt cramped by the presence of President Hindenburg and the old guard of conservative-national circles and were impatient to give free rein to their sadism and aggressive megalomania. Something had to be done to convince the world that the Communists were setting Germany on fire and that immediate counter-measures were essential. Goering, one of the Fuehrer's satellites and a quarrelsome and sadistic psychopath declared: "I need not ask my conscience; my Fuehrer has spoken and he is my conscience." This statement strikingly illustrates both, the process of substituting the image of the leader for the superego, and the dictator's lack of moral scruples. The exceptional brazenness of the crime, its clever planning, the diabolic scheme of making an unfortunate Dutchman the scapegoat, are appalling. All this was done for the Fuehrer, whose command hallowed any abomination.

In Goebbel's memoirs, under the date of January 31, 1933, that is a month before the fire, we can read: "In a conversation with the Fuehrer we did make our plans for the battle with the Red Terror. For the time being we wished to refrain from direct counter- measures. The Bolshevik revolutionary coup must first burst into flames. At the proper moment we shall strike." Promising words indeed, containing the whole theory of provocation, which forces on the adversary its own sadism and aggression, and then displays the full force of that sadism merely as a reaction. And the reference to flames—was it just a rhetorical figure?

Why do those flames fascinate us so much? On that memorable evening, as soon as the radio broadcast the news and before any investigation was possible, Hitler declared to his followers: "It is a God-given sign! No one now will prevent us from destroying the Communists with an iron fist." To an English journalist Hitler said: "You are witnessing a new great epoch in German history. This fire is its beginning."

It is pertinent to recall at this point what modern psychology teaches us about the symbolism of fire and arson. Fire is probably the most perfect means of destruction and as such is admirably suited to the venting of aggressive-destructive tendencies. In setting a fire, the psychopathic individual sometimes vents his hatred for reality, which he thus destroys in a symbolic manner, when for instance he sets fire to the home of an employer whom he hates because, as in several famous cases of crimes induced by nostalgia, he longs for his own far-away family home. Furthermore, the very process of setting a fire permits the discharge of a considerable volume of suppressed emotions. (9)

The sadistic act of burning the Reichstag was directed against the symbol of the hated old regime, against the very parliament, National Socialism had always attacked in words and deeds. Now the Nazis wanted to destroy parliament completely—and to heighten their perverse sadistic pleasure they took advantage of this opportunity to act the part of its defender.

The new epoch Hitler spoke of in such glowing terms was to see the final and complete destruction of all opposition forces in the name of saving Germany and the entire Western World, from the danger of Bolshevism. The burning of the Reichstag in fact opened a new era in the history of Hitler and of National Socialism. From dictatorship within the party Hitler and National Socialism passed to dictatorship in the country and the state. The fire became the key which opened the gates to terror, that is, to totalitarian gangster sadism. But characteristically enough, the terror and the sadism continued masquerading as salvation. The tendency to associate sadism and salvation is inherent in Hitler's personality. We find definite indications to that effect in his very first outbreaks of anti-socialism or anti-Semitism, as recorded in his autobiography. Even then his own sadism and aggressiveness were transferred to the enemy. The much vaunted Jewish plots were of such a nature that, had they been executed, "this planet would have once more circled deserted through the universe, just as it did millions of years ago".

Hitler's megalomaniac obsession was so great that even though he was perfectly familiar with the secret workings of the arson plot, he tried to convince others—and perhaps he actually did convince himself—that he was saving the world. A few months later he made the following statement to the representatives of the American Press (Olden p. 285): "When on the night of the fire in the Reichstag and in the Berlin Castle, we received calls for help by telephone, telegraph, and radio from all Germany, because of the impending Bolshevik conspiracy and revolution, I resolved ruthlessly to apply all the power I had at my disposal, all my Storm

Troops. Bend or break, was my motto. The disclosures made
two hours later justified my stand. In Berlin alone, after
an immediate occupation of the public buildings, including
the university, the libraries, and many municipal office buildings throughout Berlin, as well as other places where fires
were laid, fuses, wool soaked in gasoline and explosive
materials have been found. If in that critical moment I had
not acted for the sake of peace and order to thwart the Bolsheviks in setting Germany on fire, not only the Reichstag
and the Castle, but all the public buildings in Germany—
and who knows, perhaps all of the Western World might
have been today a heap of ruins. Future court proceedings
will open the eyes of the world to the sensational happenings
on that night by means of material that because of the
investigations that are going on could not as yet have been
revealed to the public. Material evidence guarantees the
disclosure of a Bolshevik world conspiracy." (1)

While discussing the symbolism of arson, we must mention
another great pyromaniac performance which was consciously
symbolic: the famous wholesale burning of works by Jewish,
pacifist and other authors in Opera Square. This took place
in the presence of high party and government dignitaries
to the accompaniment of yells from well-drilled bands of
youths. Here again we have a symbolic destruction of the
intellectual achievements of the past, which brings to mind
the famous words of the hero in a Nazi drama: "When I hear
the word 'culture,' I release the safety-catch of my revolver."
What is the nature of this hatred? Without doubt it is
primarily the hatred of a sub-intellectual and of his group,
resulting from envy. This explains why so many half-baked
journalists, pseudo-literary men and graphomaniacs participated in the movement. The hatred of that particular class
of envious souls masquerades behind lofty slogans, such as
the defense of the purity of German culture against Jewish
or other taints. What bliss for Hitler, the frustrated artist,

who at one time was rejected by the Viennese Academy of Fine Arts, to pass judgment on art, to throw modern art out of the museums as "degenerate" and to dictate a new artistic taste to an obedient nation!

If the burning of the Reichstag was intended to clear the way to dictatorship in the state, the murders of June 30, 1934 were intended to consolidate the regime for all time to come. This outburst of destructive hate was directed against the remainder of the opposition, against too strong or too popular friends and companions of Hitler's and was above all intended to secure the good-will and support of the Reichswehr. The crime involved a considerable amount of treachery, for instance, the destruction of Storm Troopers who had raised Hitler to the summit and who had now become superfluous. The dictator realized that the Reichswehr was still the most powerful organization in Germany. But while it approved of the new dictatorship, the Reichswehr feared the Storm Troopers, whose chiefs were the closest collaborators of the Fuehrer and had upon him a hold, based on common memories and battles and, so it would seem, on his gratitude for their help. The Storm Troopers were undisciplined adventurers without professional background. Their destruction solved a difficult problem for Hitler. Seeing on which side lay the greatest strength, he could not have acted otherwise: the destruction of the weaker, the victory of the stronger was, after all, a basic rule.

The fury of his hatred which, not satisfied with the slaughter itself, revelled in viciously insulting its victims, deserves special attention.

Hitler's outburst of fury against his close friend Roehm can be explained by his wish to break burdensome emotional ties, which involved certain obligations. The very thought that it was necessary to reckon with someone, to keep the promises that had been made, to show some gratitude, was unbearable to him. Thus the friend of yesterday became an enemy. The transition from friendship to hatred which we see here is reminiscent of well-known cases of the transition from passionate love to hate and raises the question to what extent Hitler's friendship with Roehm contained erotic components. Homosexual elements played a notorious part in the entire movement; and the erotic make-up of the Dictator himself was ambiguous. We shall return to this matter later; for the moment we only wish to emphasize the sanctimonious moral indignation, with which Hitler tried to justify his murders in the eyes of the public, by accusing his victims of immorality. Here the sadism of destruction was supplemented by the sadism of defamation, which was to destroy the murdered victims once more, this time in the memory of their fellow-men.

The bloody destruction of the lesser victims can be explained either by Hitler's hatred for those who enjoyed some amount of popularity and who dared disagree with him or who were his potential rivals in the event of a change of regime, or by his fear of those who knew too much of his past, or finally by his desire for revenge. Hitler's vindictiveness is truly without parallel: he forgave nothing and no one, least of all those who had dared at any time oppose or criticize him. Any offense to his adored "ego" was a crime which released a veritable tempest of hatred.

In the course of our study we have often referred to erotic factors. Rauschning characterizes Hitler's eroticism in the following words: "What is most abominable about him is the release of a constrained and abnormal sexuality which he exhales like a bad odor." Soldiers who served in the same units as Hitler have recorded his abnormal attitude toward women, which they describe as a strange reserve. Later observations warrant the inference that this attitude did not change and that the Fuehrer remained impotent. We are unable to check Heiden's story concerning Hitler's relationship with his niece which ended tragically, the girl allegedly committing suicide.

Taking into consideration Hitler's anti-Semitic "complex" analyzed above, we can assume that his entire inferiority complex derived from his unsatisfactory sexual experiences in his years in Vienna and, at a deeper level, from his relationship to his parents. Hitler's significant and constantly expressed cult of masculinity belongs to the same category. He never rode horseback, says Rauschning, "but the high boots and the riding crop bear witness to the bitterness which had accumulated in him over a period of years". His ideals were Frederick the Great and Bismarck. He hung their portraits in all his residences and offices. Democrats, pacifists, Marxists, and Jews were the belittlers of giants, they did not appreciate true greatness, but he, Hitler, stood up in defense of those heroes who were besmearched and threatened. It is obvious that he identified himself with them, that he felt his own greatness, his power, in brief, his masculinity threatened. In his autobiography Hitler often identifies himself with some real or imaginary hero, who was full of splendid intentions and was threatened by hostile forces or by the miserable, uncomprehending mob.

Hitler's frequent outbursts of admiration and ecstasy over the army and the young men of Germany, were a distinctly homosexual trait. The following excerpt from his work is worth noting: "In the mire of a generally spreading softness and effeminacy there sprang from the ranks of the army each year 350,000 youths in full bloom of health." (3) In his conversations with Rauschning, Hitler contrasted the German youth with "us, that is the older generation, weak, worthless . . . We are already old . . . We are cowardly, we are sentimental . . . But look at our splendid youth . . ." whereupon followed a glowing tribute to youth in which he desired to see his own ideal, the ideal of strength, wildness, brutality, and primitive masculinity realized. And he warned:

"I do not want anything weak or tender in them . . ."

We are quite familiar with such admiration for brutal masculinity from our analyses of homosexuals. They are impressed by a masculinity the lack of which they feel in themselves and which they try to compensate by becoming intimate with the objects of their love who to them seem the personification of masculinity and strength. In Hitler's elucubrations, the desire for brutal masculinity extends to the entire German nation, the future generations, the selected caste of masters, and finally himself as the ideal of an unlimited lord and ruler. "The contrast between the little awkward and ill-mannered bourgeois, in the midst of other middle-class Germans, and the ferocity of the criminal dreams to which he abandoned himself as his most habitual occupation, was grotesque." (5)

To what extent did Hitler's aggressive sadism combined with his feeling of inferiority, his eagerness for constant self-assertion, and for displaying primitive masculinity shape his political activity?

The cult of strength paired with contempt for the weak or, as we now may say more plainly, with contempt for those on whom he shifted his own feeling of weakness, his own passivity and his feminine tendencies, constitute a credo productive of incalculable consequences. Hitler's entire specific system of eugenics, subsequently developed by docile scientists, expresses a desire for absolute and maximal strength, applied to a nation or rather to a caste of picked and properly raised rulers. All that is weak and incapable of life, should be destroyed. This system is a return to the traditional Germanic cult of power. Some years before Hitler, similar ideas were expressed by Professor Binding, a physician, who suggested that all individuals incurably ill, underdeveloped mentally, and the like—in brief those who are only a burden to society—should be exterminated. Six hundred years of applying eugenic principles—says Hitler—will lead to a condition of health "which today seems inconceivable". Hitler clearly defines the purpose of such a development: "A state which in a period of race pollution devotes itself to caring for its best racial elements, must some day become the lord of the earth." Once again the destruction of the weak and the strengthening of the strong is revealed as the basis for Hitler's campaign, and as the affirmation of his own masculinity, which from now on would be completely sure of itself and which no one would be able to threaten.

Thus new light falls on all the facets of Hitler's political career. From the point of view of the single slogan of leaning on the strong all becomes perfectly clear. He who turned away from "the physically and spiritually poor" laborers, fawns upon industrialists, the employers of labor, since they are the strong and privileged. "One must defend the strong who are menaced by their inferiors," he said to Rauschning. He reasons that, as long as they are in power, they obviously must have some racial basis for it, they are stronger and therefore better. Hitler's constant flirtation with big industry, in addition to purely utilitarian considerations had a deep psychologic foundation, to wit, his desire to identify himself with the strong. Doubtless this was also the foundation of his cult of the army, which pushed him to the fore, to which he rendered services (as, for instance, by murdering his companions) and of which finally—to his supreme joy—he became the Commander-in-Chief, concentrating in his hands the most powerful of existing weapons of destruction, the most typical symbols of masculinity. "What the German people owed to the Army may be briefly put into one single word: everything."

Hitler's foreign policy, too, reflected his aggressiveness and his fear of appearing weak; here, too, the primary principle was the victory of the strong, the destruction or the complete conquest of the weak. The point of view was the same as with individuals and with classes of society; of small states he said contemptuously that Germany did not intend to give them "police protection". In his opinion the former German Reich had been lacking "actively aggressive intentions" and as a result had been driven into a "defensive union of old states which were put by history on the retired list". The New Germany was to be aggressive and picked her allies and her adversaries accordingly. We shall not analyze here all the vicissitudes of Nazi foreign policy. The most important of them, the sudden about-face from the staunchest opposition to Bolshevism to the agreement of August 23, 1939, was based on that very principle of making pacts with the most formidable powers available.

Germany full of splendid possibilities, but hindered in her development and discouraged—surprisingly like the Fuehrer himself—naturally had to widen her "living space". This slogan was nothing but a projection of aggressive egotism. Since attack was, as Hitler said, the best method of defense, the rest followed logically. Hitler spread before Rauschning visions of vassal states surrounding Germany, with the result that her ultimate power would be secured forever.

Hitler took over not only the old pan-Germanic idea of securing territories for colonization in the East but also the idea originated by Clauss, that the East be free of inhabitants. These territories, Hitler dreamed, were to become "racially pure peripheral colonies", a sort of national breeding ground. "Specially constituted race commissions shall issue individual colonization certificates, which in turn will be contingent on racial purity according to standards to be set up in the future. In this way there may in time be established peripheral colonies, the inhabitants of which would without exception be exponents of the highest racial purity and consequently represent the highest degree of racial stamina." The Poles and the Czechs, being two "inferior" peoples, could find room enough in Siberia or in Volhynia. Russia—

Hitler was then in his anti-Bolshevik mood—being dominated by the "international Jews" was doomed to perish. She would be a splendid ground for German colonization, and take care of the surplus of German population, which in Hitler's megalomaniac dreams grew to gigantic proportions. "And while now in Europe there live but eighty million Germans, after only one hundred years, two hundred fifty million Germans will live on this continent." And again: "We are chosen by destiny to witness a catastrophe which will be the most forceful confirmation of the race theory of peoples. It is fate's signal to Germany to destroy Russia and to establish colonies there." Russia, according to Hitler's reasoning, would disintegrate of herself, whereas Poland and Czechoslovakia would have to be destroyed. The persecuted persecutor cannot bear to have anything around, which savors of any degree of strength and which is so much inferior to him in value, as the no-account Slavs.

Thus he coined the maxim: "Never permit two continental powers to arise in Europe! In every attempt to organize a second military power on the German border, be it only in the shape of a state capable of organizing an armed force, you must see an attack on Germany and consider it not only your right, but your duty to prevent the rise of such a state by all means including the use of arms,—and in the event such state had already arisen—to destroy it again!" The strength of another country may be tolerated only when it is possible to increase one's own aggressiveness by means of a union. That was the ideal policy: destroy the weaker, unite with the stronger. "An alliance the purpose of which does not include the intention of war, is without sense or value." And again: "Only through common acquisitions and conquests can the destinies of nations be forged together strongly."

These inspiring passages were expunged in the English edition of *Mein Kampf,* as if such a primitive mask would suffice to lull the watchfulness of the English. The full force of Hitler's aggressiveness was turned against France. He imputed to her his own tendencies of aggression and revenge, and in accordance with his racial theories considered her weak enough to be destroyed. France was "the implacable enemy of the German people" with her "sadistically perverted vindictiveness". It was "the chauvinistic hereditary enemy", "the French executioner", "the only enemy at whom we must strike", and "on whom we must unavoidably turn the tables", at present "Jew ridden", "niggerized", "an African state on European soil"—and therefore doomed to destruction. France presented a splendid object for Hitler's aggressions. A life-and-death struggle was inevitable, a fight in which it was imperative "to strike with our whole concentrated strength", and to prepare to "aim at the heart of our most despicable enemy". (3)

While preparing for the momentous step, Hitler did not lose his sense of reality. It was necessary for him to combine with other powers, such as Italy, since he was greatly impressed by his prototype, the "great man south of the Alps", or England, for he believed in the power of the British Empire based on the Germanic race. With France out of the way, it would be possible to gratify his hatred and make German greatness and expansion secure for all time. But to this end the strength of his hatred had to be shared by all the Germans. Hitler wished that "in seventy million heads of both men and women, . . . a common hatred should become one raging sea of flames, . . . out of the heat of which should arise one single will, hard as steel and one single cry: Give us arms again! . . . In the mind of the smallest boy should live the flaming prayer: Almighty God, when the time comes, bless our arms . . . bless our struggle!"

Hitler's immense primitive hatred and aggressive-destructive tendencies became fused with the old pan-Germanic fury, clamored for an outlet, and made him prepare the tools.

From our observation of youthful criminals we know that projective mechanisms always accompany aggressiveness. The bandit who plans to rob or beat up his colleagues, fears them in his waking hours and in his sleep and claims that it was they who attacked him and that he had to defend himself. Likewise Hitler and the nation rallied about him, projected their aggressive hatred into the surrounding world and suffered from a phobia which was both offensive and defensive.

Hitler wished to force the German nation to greatness, as he saw it, and to achieve that end any sacrifice was justified. "I would not hesitate a second to take upon my conscience the death of two or three millions of Germans, knowing full well the weight of such a sacrifice." Greatness naturally signified domination, and the German nation in order to fulfil Hitler's own desires should rule Europe. In this connection, an immense transposition of his own complexes and attitudes to the field of political reality as a whole is again evident. In his mind Germany either had to conquer Europe or die. Hitler's ego always oscillated between two poles: boundless greatness and utmost weakness.

The ease with which he spoke of sacrificing several million people shows clearly the sadistic roots of his plans for world domination. The extent of his sadism and his megalomania find their glaring expression in his vision of possible defeat: "But if we do not succeed in conquering, we shall drag half the world along with us in our downfall, and no one will be able to rejoice at a victory over Germany." His primitive narcissistic sadism, which made him unable to admit the existence of objective reality, desires to destroy and transform everything. Speaking of the future powerful German race, a race of truly absolute masters, Hitler foretells its being used to "destroy history": "I have need also of a nation which will permit me to dissolve the order established in the world and to oppose history with the destruction of history."

The proper instrument for such destruction is total war, and Rauschning tells how Hitler "on his mountain savors in advance his war (total war) and his triumph". (5)

The transformation of the German nation—for that matter, why not of all humanity, as planned by Hitler—expresses absolute, megalomaniac sadism on the one hand, and absolute passivity, subjection, submission on the other. Hitler foresees a mutation of the human race into "two kinds: the Man-God and the Animal-Masses". "National Socialism," says Hitler, "is more than a religion, it is the will to create a superman." In his fantasies, Hitler sees all his desires fulfilled, and before his eyes rises an awesome, half-insane vision. "Hitler claims," says Rauschning "to have seen the new man. He is intrepid and cruel. I was afraid of him." The program of the so-called "Ordensburgen" aims at the training of a caste of master-supermen, the exponents of sadism and ruthlessness. (10)

In accordance with these plans the whole social structure would be based on the hierarchic principle. "The ideal of a culture accessible to all, has long since become superannuated. The sciences should again revert to their former character as a secret cult, reserved for the privileged." In other words, science will supply the masters with the means for world domination, while the anonymous mass of helots, deprived of all rights, will be only an impotent tool. These ideas are another expression of Hitler's contempt for the common man as well as a projection of his feeling of inferiority. The picture of the future hierarchy is a distinct revenge and compensation for his own acute deficiencies. In place of him alone, on whom anonymity had been weighing so heavily and who now was at the summit of power, there would come into being an entire immense class of anonymous workers—while on the lowest rung of the ladder would stand the conquered aliens as modern slaves.

Intoxicated with the prospects of his own boundless power,

Hitler experienced early—in his dreams of course—his role of dictator of the world and of mankind. "We shall socialize the people. We shall cultivate our unshakeable will to revolutionize the world, to a degree hitherto unknown in history. It is in this obstinate will that we shall find our secret happiness, the joy that shall be ours when we contemplate around us the masses unaware of what we are doing to them."

Accordingly we see how the desire for power and the ambition to rule, together with the conviction of the absolute justness of his judgment, enabled Hitler to look upon the human masses as so much inert clay in his hands. Such an attitude seems to be extremely characteristic of a born dictator. Hitler's plans concerning the problem of population are interesting in this connection. We have discussed his eugenic plans, that "exceptional cure" which was to change the whole German race—and know how much sadism is contained in these harsh measures which are to lead to an apparently lofty objective. However, his greatest achievements in this field are unquestionably his plans for re-settlement. He intended to (and later did) tear away entire blocks of population from their ancient homes and shift them to remote places.

Hitler's plans for "populating and depopulating", as recorded by Rauschning, provided for a speedy decrease of the Slav population. All these plans, unbelievably brutal in themselves, and even more brutal in their execution, disclose complete contempt for human beings. From the psychological point of view this is not only a manifestation of sadism and narcissistic megalomania but reveals exceptional inflexibility in the execution of ideas, conceived independently of all reality, a trait to which we should like to draw particular attention.

Thus the psychological structure of Hitler's dictatorship combined brutal ruthlessness and passive submission. We might say that the dictator attempted to concentrate in

his person the maximum of brutal masculinity and to transform others into beings deprived of any will, into embodi-
ments of passive submissiveness.

An analysis of the psychological structure of the National
Socialist Party leads to a more exact formulation of this
fundamental idea. "The Party," Hitler said to Rauschning,
"includes all, regulates all. No more free-will, no more
slackmindedness, no more isolation. The individual no
longer belongs to himself. The era of personal happiness is
closed." In this hymn of praise for the Party, we are struck
first of all by the joy in the surrender of free will, combined
with the loss of the feeling of isolation. We see here the
extremely characteristic longing for unity and group life
of a man who felt isolated and failed to adjust himself to his
social environment. On what basis does Hitler desire to
regain for himself the contact he had lost?

Hitler frequently stated that he was not a dictator, since
everything he did was done with the consent of the Party,
which decided everything. But are he and the Party not one
and the same, is it not he who decides for the Party and
forces his unquestioned will upon it? There could be no
National Socialist Party without a leader or a dictator; but
by the same token a leader or a dictator is out of the question
without a Party. What then is the basis of this peculiar
combination?

Hitler's subordinates obeyed and worshipped him, and he
needed that worship; the feeling that he was the object of
love of all these men was necessary for his very existence.
It constituted in fact the very foundation of his power and
authority. Henderson remarks: "I could not forbear asking
myself how any human brain could keep its sanity amid all
the adulatory worship which his followers accorded to him."
And about Hitler's relation to youth he says: "The youth
was being taught to accord to Hitler the attributions of
something very nearly akin to God." (11)

The worship of his subordinates exalted Hitler to the heights, elevated his feelings of well-being which had been threatened by a deeply rooted inferiority complex, filled him with the realization that he was not only a true man, but a man more splendid and more powerful than all others. He had constantly to convince himself anew of his power and of the intensity of the worship accorded him. He did this by means of speeches which kindled in his audiences a thrill of ecstasy and delight, faith and hate; he did it by means of meetings and Party conferences, where a consummate stage management created an atmosphere favorable for mass suggestion.

Though practicing mass suggestion on a vast scale, the Fuehrer himself was subject to suggestion, provided it was deftly applied. He submitted to the influence of various persons within his immediate clique thus creating an atmosphere of collective loyalty for himself, which encouraged him in his apparently frequent moments of doubt and uncertainty. "The Party controls all and regulates all"; in other words it is the source of power and authority, it is collective loyalty, a carefully nurtured cult of the leader.

Leaders of a lesser calibre, chiefs on the lower rungs of the Party hierarchy displayed their psychological attitudes even more plainly. Let us take as an example the immediate group around the Fuehrer. Passive, loyal, admiring his greatness (although it was mostly of their own making) they vied for his love, his favor and approval, at the same time identifying themselves with him as their highest ideal, as the symbol of German power. But with regard to their subordinates, to those a little lower in rank, they were brutal, arbitrary, and domineering. They practiced to the fullest extent the so-called "Fuehrer principle". The inferior ones not only loved those superior to themselves, but feared them, trembled in fear of their arbitrariness, just as they trembled before the Fuehrer. But the whole nation trembled before the Fuehrer and the Party, because the Party's brutal, concentrated masculinity was turned against all that was outside it. That "all", however, was inevitably becoming increasingly weaker. United internally by bonds of love and fear, of aggressive sadism and masochistic submission, the Party turned its sinister might, embodied in the threats of the Fuehrer and his henchmen, against the body social—and in the end upon the whole world.

If we look upon Hitler's dictatorship from the point of view of his subjects, we discover a number of features that can almost be deduced from our analysis of the Party structure. Let us first of all inquire what the average German felt in relation to Hitler.

There is a significant statement of one Dietrich, a National Socialist, reading as follows: "We have had the experience that, whenever in Germany the economic and spiritual distress was greatest, wherever it seemed most difficult to bear, confidence in the Fuehrer grew most powerfully in that section, manifesting itself in the entire community." This single sentence best illustrates the nature of the psychological and historical situation. The cult of the Fuehrer is closely connected with the frustrations experienced by the masses, with their despair and their hopes. For the "small people", the petty bourgeoisie and the unemployed, he became something of an all-powerful father, a demi-god, who could do everything for everyone and who could be absolutely depended upon. It was therefore possible, and even delightful, to give up independent thinking, to submit to a higher force, which because it sprang from "the people", knew everyone's true needs and promised satisfaction to everyone. In addition it promised the realization of a common ideal, of German power, in which all would participate. They believed in him, as in their ideal, as in one who came from their midst, became powerful, and could give them strength and wealth. They worshipped

his power and feared it at the same time; to avert his wrath
and deserve his praise was their happiness.

They submitted to him passively; not without reason did
Hitler speak of the "womanish" masses; his speeches, replete
with simple, endlessly repeated slogans, warmed their surg-
ing passion, with frenzied imprecations, violent threats, and
glowing promises, deprived them of all independence of
thought or action, compelled them to psychological loyalty
and paved the way for their fusion into a single mass with
a common ideal and a common God.

Continuous mass meetings, properly staged, intensified
these effects. In the period of the struggle for power, Hitler
displayed his own strength and emphasized the weakness of
the opposition; he maintained a steady atmosphere of struggle and violently split the feelings of his followers into one
great, consuming love and one consuming hatred. Love
centered about the person of the leader, who was at the
same time the symbol of Germany, strength, world domination, victory, and, above all, masculinity. Endowed with
all these attributes, he could convince his followers that he
would absolutely keep his promises relating to the people's
vital and burning needs. And now we are confronted with
a phenomenon in the field of mass psychology: the desires
and the hopes of the great human masses sought satisfaction
and thought they had found it in the one, solitary person of
the leader, who had a remedy for everything. It was no
longer necessary to look with fear into the future; the good
father would take care of everything. And if at times he
was awesome, threatening, and dangerous, so much the better. That made it easier to submit to him, pleasanter to
trust him, and thus to feel honored, to feel oneself a true,
good German in absolute contrast to the others, the evil
ones, the foes, the traitors and the half-breeds.

In his excellent *School for Dictators* Silone defines Fascism as the "margarine of psychological life" and thus pre-

sents its role as that of a substitute. "The technique of Fascism is truly wonderful: to the capitalists it gives protection of wealth, to Labor a substitute for Socialism, to the small bourgeoisie and to the intellectuals a satisfaction of their vanity, and to the army the promise of fame." And further on we read: "Through the cooperation of the classes, Fascism gives to socialist labor a substitute for a class-free body social and to other labor a substitute for a bourgeois life. No longer is there any mention of class, there arises an apparent brotherly fellowship between capitalism and labor." (12)

In addition to being a benefactor, Hitler appeared in the imagination of the masses as a savior. We have seen how he created fictitious dangers from which he rescued the German nation: he rescued it from Communism, he rescued it from humiliation, he restored its honor and armed strength. Such imaginary rescues, be they active or passive, belong, as we know, to the classical category of childhood dreams. In their passive variety the good father (or mother) rescues the child from some nightmarish danger, and the source of delight is not only the moment of rescue itself, but also the preceding shiver of fear. (13) Thus the classical fantasy "A Child is Being Beaten" was transferred to the collective mind: the whole nation was beaten and humiliated, it wallowed in its misfortune and in the expectation of further misfortunes, with which he, the leader, the powerful and infallible Dictator, threatened it. And amidst this masochistic rapture, brought on by the constant influx of the poison of fear and hate into the collective mind, the voice of that same leader called to the trembling nation, promising rescue, a splendid future, and the destruction of all their enemies.

Thus was created a peculiar mythology which culminated in a new religion. The leader or God functioned simultaneously as a prophet and an apostle and possessed all the divine attributes: he was all-powerful, omniscient, he knew when to strike, he knew the future and the destiny of the German nation. He himself was the symbol of that nation, he and the Fatherland were one, the greatness and the expansion of Germany were identical with the greatness and expansion of his person. This mythology had its devils with the Jew as the chief Satan, it had its demi-gods and heroes: it even had its paradise in the form of a future Germany, powerful and enduring for all time to come.

The collective German psyche performed a gigantic regression and rediscovered within itself the ancient strata of serfdom and submission, of worship of authority, which is surrounded by an aura of transcendental, supernatural reality. All the elements of the national past were concentrated in this: feudalism, the Hegelian theory of the state, the cult of strength, and the will to power. And everyone, down to the most obscure individual was able to participate in this greatness, march in the ranks, parade before the leader, supported by an unalterable belief in the latter's mission and bound by bonds of identification with the mass of other Germans, all fortified with the same mana, the same notion of the lofty German race.

A new religion and a new prophet cannot tolerate any competition: "thou shalt have no other gods before me." Thus Hitler saw dangerous competition in existing beliefs and religions; in persecuting the church, he attempted to introduce new religious forms. At a Party conference in Nuremberg, 1936, he declared: "The Christian religion had, of course, played a great part in the times of the migration of nations. Today in Germany, the Christian period has been replaced by the National Socialist period. The Christian period could have only Christian art, the National Socialist has only a National Socialist one." (14)

The Fuehrer himself has plainly defined the character of his movement as religious and classed himself as a prophet, "So it may happen that the centuries displeased with the form of their religious life, long for a revival, and that out of that spiritual urge arise dozens or more men, who on the strength of their wisdom and experience, may consider themselves qualified to satisfy this religious need, and so to function as the prophets of the new doctrine, or at least as challengers of the existing ones. Here too, to be sure, in accordance with the natural orders of things, the strongest will be destined to perform the great mission. The knowledge, however, that this strongest man was the one exclusively destined is wont to come to the others very late as a rule."

This new religion had its new profession of faith, of which the core was the adoration of the leader: "We Germans, we National Socialists, we workers and farmers, we manual laborers, townspeople, students, we all on this earth believe in Adolf Hitler, our Fuehrer. We Germans, particularly we National Socialists, believe that National Socialism is the only salvation-bringing faith for our nation." This statement was made by Dr. Ley (leader of the Labor Front) at a great demonstration in July 1936. For Dr. Ley the two thousand year history of Christianity is only "a laughable episode". Touring the country with other apostles of the Fuehrer, Ley announced to the nation that Hitler was the new savior whom the "Lord God" had sent to the Germans to "free them from hypocrites and pharisees". Kerrl, Hitler's Reichsminister of Churches, drew a comparison between the "Carpenter of Nazareth" and the "Unknown Volunteer of the World War" who "both brought to the anxiously waiting nation the annunciation of salvation." Under the patronage of the theorist and apostle of National Socialism, Alfred Rosenberg, the so-called *Weihespiele* were organized, in which Hitler was worshipped publicly as the savior. "Thou appeareth before the nation as its Savior, for thou art completely possessed in faith."

New principles and new criteria were set up to replace the

entire previous social, ethical, and religious apparatus. "Conscience is a Jewish invention," notes Rauschning, and in so far as Hitler's way of thinking is concerned, these words of his contain no exaggeration. After the destruction of humanitarian and altruistic ideals there remained the principles of blood kinship and national unity, of brutal hatred, and the cult of the Fuehrer. In the collective psyche, these criteria were to replace all previous criteria, were to become the new superego which would regulate the thoughts and actions of every German.

"I am freeing humanity from the chimera called conscience or morality," Hitler declared and added: "I abolish the dogma of the redemption of man through the suffering and death of a divine savior and I propose a new dogma of the substitution of merits: the redemption of individuals by the life and actions of a new law-giver—the Fuehrer—*who comes to relieve the masses of the burdens of liberty.*"*

The remolding of the ideal superego at all its levels was conducted with the utmost consistency. It began with family life, as the first center of training. The cult of the Fuehrer and of the National Socialist principles took precedence over the natural love of youth for their parents. The organization of the Hitler Youth Movement on the one hand, and a consistently applied espionage system on the other, resulted in the fact that the image of the parent was replaced by that of the Fuehrer at the highest level of the superego. A characteristic example of this is the story related by the French ambassador, who after June 30, 1934, met a boy acquaintance of his, the son of one of the murdered victims and looked at him questioningly. The boy looked back at him, drew himself up and replied: "He is still our Fuehrer." Of the next phase in training, the school, there is no need to speak, since here the Party held principals and teachers in its

---

* My italics.

iron grip and was able to mold the youths' thinking according to its will. The same is true of the secondary schools where the student organizations as well as the teaching staff were reorganized. Here, too, the leadership system was applied and the leaders of the student youth were subordinated to the Fuehrer, in whom they saw their highest ideal. The details we have given already on the subject of specialized education, and the education of the élite in the so-called "Ordensburgen" complete this picture.

Upon such psychological foundations, it was not difficult to build the various elements of the normative super-structure, e.g. the legal system. The result was extremely characteristic: a legal system based on force, fanaticism, and a personal cult. The principle, "Right is what benefits the German people" contradicts the very principles of law, especially if we take into consideration who decides what benefits the German nation and by what criteria. Minister of Justice Frank declared on one occasion: "When it was said in the past, that one thing was right and another was wrong, we must ask today what would the Fuehrer say about it?" Lawyers, high officials, and professors recognized *Mein Kampf*, that apotheosis of force, as the source of law. (1)

Hitler's status not only made him leader, chancellor and president, chief of the state and of the government, but also the source of German law. The psychological equations which underlie an identification so characteristic of dictatorship are set forth clearly in the official publication of Meisner-Kaisenberg. (14) "The head of the government in the German Fuehrer-State is the fountainhead of the spirit of law dwelling in the body politic, the spirit which engenders the desire for what is right and equitable. He has the same legal origin as the body politic that is the community. He is the executive organ of the people's law and consequently the head of the nationally united German Reich."

As the result of this conception of legality, every crime

committed by the Fuehrer, or at his behest, or in his name, in advance received legal sanction. It is therefore quite natural, that after June 30, 1934 the Cabinet under the leadership of the Minister of Justice declared "by statute" of July 3, 1934, that the mass murders engineered by Hitler were an act of "national self-defense". There was also found—as is generally the case in Germany—a learned jurist, Prof. Carl Schmitt, who in the periodical "Deutsche Juristenzeitung" published an article on the subject of "The Proper Jurisdiction over the Fuehrer's Actions" under the significant heading "The Fuehrer Protects the Law". Was it not Frederick the Great who said that a ruler who wishes to declare war does not have to look for legal motives, because later some subtle professor of law will take that task upon himself?

The finishing touch of the system of lawlessness and the replacement of the rule of law by that of force was the institution of the Gestapo which, by virtue of a special law, received complete sovereignty and was not subject to any control, not even by the Reich's supreme court. This situation constituted the maximal sanction of force, despotism, and hatred. The chief of the Gestapo, the infamous Himmler, became at the same time chief of police of the entire Third Reich. Through him, Hitler secured for himself the unanimity of opinion and the loyalty of his subjects and carried on the merciless extermination of anything "that does not benefit the German people". The Gestapo was the foundation and at the same time the ultimate triumph of force and absolutism. The aggressive-sadistic tendencies of the leader and of his clique found in it their most complete expression.

Jurisprudence, however, was not alone in yielding to force and in belying its very nature. In other scientific fields too, the criteria of objective truth were replaced by the worst kind of "pragmatism". To the realm of the superego belongs also, as we know, the so-called control of reality or, in other words, the function of true science. But German science in the persons of many of its representatives, subjected itself to dictatorship, foreswore its principles and criteria, thus creating for itself a new "superego". Even eminent scholars did not escape this process and with surprising elasticity bent the results of their research to the orders of the Fuehrer and the needs of "national unity".

What were the social aspects of Hitler's dictatorship? Those who were not bound by love and admiration for the dictator, were held in the grip of fear. This fear, as the expression of the threatened instinct of self-preservation, stood in direct proportion to the sum total of violence and hatred wielded by the regime which the Fuehrer headed. Accordingly, our first question of a sociological nature concerns precisely those vast quantities of sadism and hatred that Hitler mobilized within the German nation. Whence did they come? Could it be that the words of the chief apostle of hatred, Hitler himself, were really true? "Hate is more permanent than affection and the guiding force of great upheavals on this earth has always consisted not so much in the scientific knowledge of the part of the masses as in the fanaticism which animated them and at times in the hysteria pushing them ahead." (3)

It is not necessary to prove that in the Fuehrer himself reposed a vast volume of sadism and hatred.

As for the Fuehrer's closest intimates, the high tension of their hatred does not require any special comment. In part, it arose from their identification with him, and this process was facilitated by the method of selecting these intimates of whom many were psychopaths or maladjusted individuals with distinctly criminal tendencies. We are certainly justified in assuming their inborn sadism. In an atmosphere of a cult for the Fuehrer, of favor-currying and rivalry among themselves, in brief, under conditions of homoerotic competition, there are favorable opportunities for the accumulation of aggressive drives which, unable to vent themselves in the immediate environment, seek an outlet against subordinates or political adversaries.

Nietzsche called the Germans the most hate-filled nation. Is it possible that the Germans have preserved deposits of brutal and primitive aggressiveness since pre-historic times, deposits that were not sufficiently sublimated and that re-emerged under conditions of collective life favorable to regression? This inadequate sublimation may be connected with a strong inborn sadism inherited from the ancient Teutons and with the insufficient psychological conquest of the feudal system.

Among the historical factors which favored such an invasion of sadism, we should mention primarily the first World War. Several years of systematic killing, or of sadism let loose, several years of heavy privations and mental intoxication by the propaganda of hatred for the enemy and nationalistic narcissism were bound to leave their mark. The importance of the army, by no means small in Wilhelm's Germany, grew immeasurably during the war years.

Lastly the failure of the hopes connected with the war—the defeat was only the first of a series of grave psychic injuries—produced in many individuals characteristic reactions of aggressive hatred. This hatred was inspired by the desire for revenge, for the punishment of those at fault, and by a feeling of having been wronged and unjustly treated.

Such multiple injuries disorganized the collective mind. Its tension vented itself, on the one hand, in a few weak and quickly suppressed revolutionary flare-ups, while, on the other hand, it sought solace in rapidly developing mystical and religious trends. Most important of all, it provided the ideal basis for reactionary-nationalistic movements. These movements sponsored by former army officers and impoverished aristocrats attempted to control and organize the broad masses of the people and channelize their feelings of grief, resentment, and hatred. The external symptoms of these plots were the verdicts passed by secret tribunals and executed with ruthless cruelty, the attempts on the lives of eminent democratic statesmen, the abortive reactionary coups d'état, and so forth.

The first World War and its ending, so disastrous for Germany, had other equally important sociological and psychological consequences. The bankruptcy of the old social classes and political parties spelled the ruin of pre-war principles and ideals, which now seemed devaluated.

Social Democracy was unable to prevent the war, and later on the inflation, the widespread poverty, and the reparations: this discredited the socialist ideal in the eyes of many Germans. Still others were disappointed in the monarchic ideal: the emperor by the grace of God had fled the country, and many felt almost as if they had been forsaken by their father and left to their own fate. Even the German God himself had failed them—again the image of the father in its most venerable form. The mystical and religious sects and circles, which began to form, were an outward expression of the desire to find compensation in a new faith and a new sustaining force.

Given such a social and psychological situation, the background against which Hitler could operate and the militant, fanatical sect of National Socialists could develop, becomes more understandable.

Hitler himself, so full of resentment and unsatisfied ambition, was particularly well suited to the work of regimenting the universal aspirations, feeling of injury, and desire for vengeance. Socially maladjusted, he surrounded himself with others of the same kind and without great difficulty won over entire sectors of Germany's maladjusted population. Tormented by a constant feeling of deficiency, he easily became the symbol of collective privation for a distressed and sorely-tried nation, whose feeling of having been wronged had been nurtured for centuries on end. Full of innate weakness and uncertainty, yet striving for power and public approval at any cost, he concentrated within himself the desire for might and force, a desire which was inherent in the German psyche. The German nation was trained for soldiering, used to conquest, imbued with a nationalistic megalomania which sanctioned aggression. And now suddenly appeared a man who breathed aggressive hate, who was full of personal and national megalomania, who felt that the World War had been a fortunate redemption and the defeat a personal wrong inflicted on him and a crime perpetrated by Germany's enemies.

The leader's ideas were in harmony with some of the most typical elements of German ideology. Hazy concepts surcharged with emotions, often swelled with pride and hate, had been carefully nurtured in Germany by political authors, philosophers, journalists, and even poets. The concepts with which Hitler constantly deals, such as blood, race, national honor, national destiny, living space, and the like, are mythological rather than political, and it is upon them that the whole modern mythology of the militant sect is based. Indeed such a sect can exist only in a muddled emotional atmosphere in which the collective passion of hatred plays a major role. Hatred and hysteria, so the Fuehrer teaches, are the main forces directing the destinies of mankind.

Briefly formulated, the answer to the question, why the collective psyche allowed itself to be controlled by Hitler, would be that the social, economic, and political conditions prevalent in Germany had tremendously weakened the collective ego. The higher levels of the superego had broken down and there was a need of new ideals as a sustaining force. Under the influence of severe injuries, the collective ego, torn by fear, unrest, and anxiety for the future, was prepared to accept any promises and became submissive to suggestion in the shape of commands, imprecations of hatred, and ancient myths. This situation was exploited by the apostle of fanaticism, whose image supplanted the old undermined ideals. He gave the masses the certainty of future victory, the certainty that was so essential to them.

The process was greatly facilitated by the leader's own peculiar mimicry: he borrowed slogans from his greatest enemies, he took from them whatever might attract the masses, to whom he also promised the fulfilment of socialist ideals.

The revolutionary impetus of socialism seemed to have grown lethargic; socialism seemed to be waiting for the future millenium to come by itself through the workings of obscure forces. The elements of action and struggle so fundamental for keeping the collective and individual mind in a state of tension seemed forgotten. German subservience to authority paralyzed all revolutionary tensions, but that very subservience helped Hitler to destroy all the foundations of constitutional government in the nation's mind and to defame the Weimar republic. Later, when the shattered republican system of government was replaced by his dictatorship, that same subservience facilitated his control over the masses.

The factors of action and struggle, of constant dynamic tension, which socialism lacked, were energetically exploited by Hitler. His own restlessness and utter lack of mental balance communicated themselves to his activity and to the movement he led. A similar spirit of unrest emanated from the maladjusted and psychopathic individuals who joined the ranks of National Socialism and who felt happiest in an atmosphere of violence and even physical struggle, marked by the constant abuse and defamation of their opponents. The pseudo-revolutionary nature of National Socialism impressed the masses and gradually took the place of the socialist-revolutionary upheaval which, although promised and eagerly looked forward to, had failed to materialize.

For a better understanding of the peculiar link between the person of the dictator and the collective psyche, it is essential that we grasp the psychic structure of Hitler as a whole.

From the point of view of psychopathology he was primarily an unbalanced psychopath belonging to the category of so-called higher type degenerates (dégénérés supérieurs). This is evidenced by the instability of his moods and the violence of his outbreaks of excitement. His fits of depression showed distinct neurotic elements, but they receded as soon as conditions made the gratification of his desires and aspirations possible.

His emotional life shows features that point to frigidity of normal human feelings. Proof of this is his relationship to his family and to his friends, whom he was ready to betray at any time. These traits of his emotional make-up point to pronounced schizoid characteristics.

To the latter category also belong his difficulty in adapting himself to his environment, his proneness to isolation, and finally a markedly autistic and catathymic way of thinking. His entire youth was marked by ever-increasing difficulties of adaptation.

Most striking are his tremendous narcissism and megalomania, dreams of greatness, and contempt and aversion for all who were supposedly inferior to him. Beginning with his hostility toward his father, commonplace though it had been, then continuing through the frictions with his fellow-workers during the lean Vienna days, up to the antics and rantings of the dictator in later times, everything points to the strength of his primary narcissism, which led the way to his early dreams of power. Any opposition to his will or caprice caused terrible outbreaks of temper.

The moment his mission became revealed to him, Hitler's

narcissism grew to gigantic proportions. From then on he believed implicitly in the correctness of all his ideas and in his unlimited greatness. The plans he developed and outlined for monumental buildings, for instance, his residence, the Eagle's Nest in the Bavarian mountains, and the like are manifestations of his delusions of grandeur. On the subject of his architectural plans, he declared: "We create sacred monuments, symbols in marble of a new civilization."

The schizoid psychopathy of Hitler permitted him to disregard internal contradictions and to deviate constantly from ideas and tendencies which only the day before he looked upon as his credo. But Hitler saw no contradiction in such cases. One day he proclaimed the necessity of uniting all people of German blood; on the following day he annexed purely Slav territories. It is not altogether impossible that he was equally sincere in both instances. In this connection he was helped by his exceptional fanaticism.

What is the psychological essence of fanaticism? The fanatic believes implicitly in the correctness of the ideas which flash through his mind, and of the emotions which animate him. The entire fury and passion of blind hatred or extravagant enthusiasm are encompassed within a few hazy thoughts and ideas. Such ideas develop slowly and push uninterruptedly toward realization. Their distinctly autistic element consists in the fact that they take actual reality into consideration only to a small degree and attempt to bend it to suit the emotions with which they are charged. Thus "living space—blood—land", lead to the idea of resettlement, which is carried out with implacable consistency.

If we trace back such ideas, we shall see that they are closely bound to personal emotional complexes, and that around this kernel cluster many layers of rationalization gleaned from the wellknown pseudo-scientific ideology of German nationalism. Thus, from the psychoanalytic point of view, Hitler's desire to seize Austria, his original mother country oppressed by foreign elements, may well derive from his infantile relationship to his mother.

In addition to the ruthless consistency of these fanatic ideas, we find another schizoid characteristic, namely their close and frequent connection with projection. The prevalence of mechanisms of projection characterizes paranoid psychopaths, who attribute their own desires, thoughts, and drives to those around them, for instance to their enemies. In this way originate delusions of persecution, which are only an expression of their own aggressive, destructive tendencies. In practically every move of Hitler we can see projected fears and delusions of persecution of this very kind. This applies to the Bolsheviks, Jews, Frenchmen, Poles, Beneš, Chamberlain and so forth. The long list of those who persecuted him includes individuals, parties, races, and nations. Hitler, the aggressor and persecutor, who considered himself continually threatened and persecuted, represents the type of persecuted persecutor so well known to psychiatry.

In using the expedient of such projection, in accusing imaginary enemies and in attacking solely for the purpose of stealing a march on the nefarious schemes of the enemy, Hitler's mentality harmonized perfectly with certain characteristic trends of German political ideology. The Germans have at all times been faced by some hereditary enemy, at all times someone has sought to destroy them, at all times they have been denied the right to live. We have seen that this was one of the forms of their own aggressive expansion. While Germany prepared her attack on Poland, Hitler was systematically fed with information about the persecution of the German minority in Poland; in reality it had been the Poles in Germany who for years on end were subjected to severe persecution, whereas the Germans in Poland enjoyed full rights. Hitler readily believed the lies prepared for him, lies which were just as much in accord with the German mentality as with his own.

Obviously every adversary, whether attacked or threatened, might defend himself in one way or another. But Hitler's manner of thinking, in this respect also in accord with the narcissism of German national megalomania, proceeded along the line of reasoning that every attempt at defense on the part of the enemy was an insolent attack. Germans or National Socialists always had the right to attack, but woe to the Slavs or the Socialists if they tried to defend themselves. The aggressor at once became the victim, raised a loud clamor and called to heaven for vengeance, as did Frederick the Great when fate turned against him during the Seven Years' War.

Here we approach an important point in our observations: the source of fanatical ideas and fanaticism. We have called attention to the fact that Hitler does not feel hampered by any contradictions in his statements. "Hitler," as one diplomat said, "is always sincere, for he believes in what he says." This naturally does not preclude the use of a conscious and purposeful lie, of which Hitler undoubtedly —after the fashion of every true demagogue and political impostor—avails himself readily and without any scruples whatsoever. But in addition he becomes so intoxicated by his own words, his fanaticism, and his emotions, that reality appears to him different at different times. To the force of emotions and of emotionally tinged thoughts, Hitler's mentality yields completely and fully. Thus his thoughts acquire the stamp of absolute certainty and infallibility, just as in the case of the so-called "spontaneous convictions" of psychotics, which appear suddenly and unexpectedly and possess the same character of absolute certainty. These spontaneous convictions are, as we know, the germs of future delusions.

This influence of the emotions on the thinking processes

has been well described by a German psychologist, Heinrich Maier, as "emotional objectivization" and is without a doubt closely linked to suggestibility. (15) Emotions have an inherent suggestive power and react primarily upon the thinking processes of the individual, who thus becomes subjected to a sort of auto-suggestion of his own. Susceptibility to auto-suggestion and suggestibility in general may naturally be of varying degrees. The strongest suggestibility is displayed by hysterical individuals, so much so that one of the foremost theories of hysteria, formulated by Babinski, defines it precisely as a disposition to be affected by the suggestive force of imagination (pithiatism). If we add a pinch of whimsicality, i.e., of uncritical belief in one's own fantasy (pseudology, called also mythomania), and a readiness to yield to strong emotions with a spectacular external expression (what the French call the "émotif" type), we attain a complete picture of Hitler as a hysterical psychopath.

When trying from this angle to analyze Hitler's way of thinking, we discover that he received his suggestions both from within and without. An example of suggestion from within, a typical auto-suggestion, was his anti-Semitism in its initial stage, or the idea of his mission and of his leadership. External suggestions were supplied by writers on political subjects, by members of his clique or simply the great magistra vitae, in this instance magistra psychopatorum at the same time: history.

Hitler did not conceive the idea of race in his own mind, nor the ideas of living space, nor the sundry geopolitical notions, nor the supposedly socialistic elements of National Socialism. All of them were suggestions foisted upon him from without, but backed by Hitler with all the force of his passion, aggressiveness, and sadism. History provides ample material which needs only to be interpreted to suit one's own ends. He who yearns for the golden glory of Germany is bound to remember the Roman Empire of the Germanic nation, with the German Emperor at its head, and to remember that Prague was but one of the Emperor's residences. And if he looks upon himself as heir to those emperors, he will justify the conquest of Prague, although in fact this conquest was not motivated by historical, but by military considerations. Furthermore in the sphere of fanatic ideas, with which we are at present concerned, differentiation between individual elements, particularly the emotional and factual, may be entirely impossible because what rises up from the dark depths of blind emotions speedily becomes rationalized and conversely, rational ideas become forthwith surrounded by an aura of myth and emotion.

Perhaps the most powerful and at any rate the most dangerous source of suggestion for Hitler were his successes. A survey of his foreign policy shows how greatly he became enraptured by such successes, how each new success became a jumping-off platform for further feats of increasing aggressiveness, and how his notorious "dynamics" further and further exceeded the limits he himself drew. (11)

An analysis of his speeches, a comparison of them with each other and with the facts, supplies many examples of fantastic and distinctly catathymic deviations from reality. "Hitler," says Rauschning, "intoxicates himself with his own declamations, forgetting both time and place, abandoning himself to the sensual pleasure of perorating as if it were physical debauch."

The third element of hysterical psychopathy, intensified emotionality and exaggerated expression, constitutes one of the fundamental features of Hitler's personality. Henderson recalls his violent outbursts, the fears which his entourage experienced at such times, the brutality of passion with which he conducted debates or tried to impose his opinion on others. Rauschning speaks of Hitler as "a maniac deprived of all control over his emotions and whose fits went as far as a complete break-up of his personality. His yelling and roaring recall the tantrums of a spoiled and refractory child." Rauschning also relates Hitler's sleepless nights, spent in a state of strong excitement and anxiety, when the Dictator could not bear being alone, and had to have beside him one of his close companions. He even mentions nightmares: The Fuehrer woke from sleep, screaming horribly and calling for help as if he had had some terrible vision.

Hitler's emotionality and hysterical outbreaks could best be observed when he was engaged in one of his most important activities, public speaking. The general character of these speeches is well-known. The fast rising violent passion, the outbreaks of elemental hatred turning into downright rage, vilification of opponents, and the extolling of the services he himself and his movement had rendered, the final solution of all problems and the hoodwinking of his audiences with promises were common ingredients of all his speeches. But if one listened more closely to the words, if one observed the speaker himself, it was striking that the voice gradually became hoarse, changed to a scream, the wild yell of a madman; it was a voice well suited to the vulgar ranting and self-praise or praise of Germany which was his theme. The speaker foamed at the mouth, his forehead dripped sweat, his gestures were violent; they were meant to be forceful and impressive. The pictures of Hitler after his speeches are striking: his face is soft, flabby, expressionless, his hair is pasted to his forehead, his whole figure expresses weakness and exhaustion. The fit of madness was over, the inspired prophet, having spent all his force, returned to his normal self.

Hitler's behavior during his speeches, the graduation of his excitation, and his method of developing his ideas give the impression that he deliberately works himself up to a state of near-madness or ecstasy, as if he were driving or

urging himself on, forcing violence upon himself as a manifestation of strength and brutality, a proof of truly masculine
self-assertion. The riding crop mentioned before and the
boots worn by a man who never rode horseback, seem to
have had a similar purpose.

Hitler's lack of an emotional balance and his internal
restlessness left their imprint on his actions. Thus, for example, it seems that among other reasons, he was pushed
into the last war by the fear that he would not live long
enough to be able to achieve his great objectives. These fears
were the source of his "dynamic impatience". (11)

Emotional-hysterical reactions are by their very nature
short-lived. More lasting, although otherwise similar, are
the pseudological fantasies. But Hitler's ideas, even if by
their genesis they are reminiscent of mythomania, were
distinguished by exceptional consistency and stubbornness
and were developed sometimes over a period of decades.
Furthermore, another trait which runs counter to hysterical
psychopathy is that Hitler, when putting his fanatical notions into effect, showed great cleverness and far-sightedness.
"Geniuses are strange creatures," says Henderson "and Herr
Hitler among other paradoxes, was a mixture of longheaded
calculation and violent and arrogant impulses provoked by
resentment." To round out our psychiatric analysis, we
must say in this connection that the stubbornness of his ideas
and their immense vitality, as well as Hitler's ability to carry
out in practice these pseudo-rational products of purely
emotional cold calculation, are all schizoid elements. These
characteristics, combined with the above-mentioned characteristics of hysteria, are capable of producing the type of a
hysterical-paranoid psychopath, who despite all his violence
is able to calculate coldly and whose autism while distorting
his thinking does not hinder him in applying perfect realism
to the execution of his plans. His ideas are easily transformed
into delusions, but such delusions do not have the character

of autistic escape from reality, because they are active and dynamic, surcharged with repressed drives and ungratified complexes, and they unceasingly clamor for realization.

Hitler's sensitivity, and above all his extreme touchiness, are likewise schizoid characteristics. In his conversations with Henderson during periods of great tension in international politics, Hitler reverted time and again to the question of personal insult. The attacks of the English press on his person, he said, were a constant hindrance to "conciliation". Henderson himself complained of the excessive outspokenness of the English press in the following words: "It would not have mattered so much had Hitler been a normal individual, but he was unreasonably sensitive to newspapers . . ."

We have pointed to the sources and character of Hitler's suggestibility in so far as it leads to auto-suggestion. These elements were also operative in his influence on the masses. All who have studied and observed Hitler agree that in this field he was a master, and here is apparently the secret of his genius. His qualities as a medium were of a passive nature, but they have also an active aspect. The violence of his vocabulary, the unusual load of passion and sublimated impulsivity which he emanated when speaking, and the external expression of his passion pitched to a frenzied amplitude—all these constituted first-rate tools of suggestion. Crowds of listeners were simply forced to behave according to the laws of psychic mimicry and identification, while they were infected with the Fuehrer's passion and with his ideas, presented in a primitive and convincing manner. Such psychic infection and identification with the Fuehrer and with his ideas became easier and more imperative as the masses became more closely welded together and more uniform psychically by ties of mutual identification. All of them were participating, just like members of some primitive tribe or clan, in a common *mana,* that is a common blood, a common race, a national community, a common faith in Germany's greatness and a common hatred of her enemies.

The masses, bereft of will and personality to an ever-increasing degree—the function of the ordinary normal superego as the logical and moral control of reality being excluded—gave themselves over to a common ecstasy and submitted to the mad passion of a deeply convinced, but at the same time exceedingly keen, hypnotist. They adopted his emotions and his ideas, while his image combined with his ideals assumed the place of the former superego and eventually replaced it altogether.

Fully aware of his purposes and of his methods, Hitler carefully led his audiences into a proper psychic state and made them as susceptible as possible to collective hypnosis. He liked to speak in the evenings, for then his listeners were mostly tired; he used simple and forceful phrases, adapted to the low intellectual level of his audiences and repeated these phrases over and over again. He applied the method of repetition, of blaring forth appropriate slogans not only in his speeches. The same principle was followed in radio and newspaper propaganda, which used variations of the same idea, stirred up the same passions and preached the same cult for the Fuehrer. The impression of irresistible force was made on the audience not only by the torrents of eloquence, but also by the entire mise-en-scene arranged for the appearance of the Dictator. "The S.A. march into the hall with the resounding step of Prussian battalions. The bands strike up a flourish. He appears surrounded by his bodyguard, composed of the tallest of the tough and dangerous looking youths. The yells of joy from his well-drilled followers welcome him, everything is so arranged as to impress the newcomers and those half won over, to awaken in the masses that thrill which is perforce always awakened in weak souls by superiority of power."

After coming to power and gaining control of the whole

government machinery, Hitler was able to arrange gatherings and particularly Party conferences with the most elaborate stage effects so as to produce the proper atmosphere, a mystical thrill, true ecstasy, and complete fascination. Unprejudiced observers, invited as spectators to conferences in Nuremberg, were amazed by the display of lights and decorations and the marvellous control over the huge human masses. Many of the observers were hard put to resist the atmosphere thus created.

In his speeches prior to the period of "coming to power", the chief recurring motif was an aggressive sadism of the worst sort. Words and screams seemed to crush the adversary, hatred was shared by the assembled crowd. This hatred and passion of personal and national megalomania animated all his thoughts and forced themselves on the masses with unrestrained violence. Fanatical ideas, breathing a maximum strength of conviction, split away from the speaker like ectoplasm from a medium during a spiritualistic seance, penetrated deep into the soul of the audience and became an integral part of it. The haziness of these ideas and their emotional character caused them to strike at once at the more primitive psychic layers and to find a perfect aura in the primitive, prelogical mentality of the listeners. The following example is a good illustration of this:

"The Soviet Star is the star of David, the symbol of the synagogue. The symbol of the Russians ruling the world, the symbol of a rule extending from Vladivostok to the West, of the rule of the Jewry. The golden star signifies to the Jews the shining gold, the hammer signifies the influence of Free-masonry. The sickle means cruel terror . . ." (1)

The ego of the audience and of the subordinates yielded to the person of the Fuehrer. Not only did he threaten, but he made good his threats, not only was he surrounded by a body-guard and Storm Troopers ready to commit any act of violence, but he himself propagated the use of force and violence, of which he made a mystic weapon in the struggle for greatness. His words breathed such faith and such conviction as to preclude any and all doubt. Accordingly, while the lower levels of the collective ego simply submitted to strength, its higher levels were glutted with implicit conviction and salutary faith, which is a soothing balm for fear and anxiety.

Submission to overpowering and uncompromising force affords rapturous ecstasy to an individual in a hypnotic state, to a woman at the moment of surrender, and to human masses when they are subjugated and enslaved.

This then is the psychologic portrait of Hitler. In his childhood a strong oedipus complex led to reactions of resistance and spite. He wanted to remove the father and to be great himself. A mania of grandeur developed in line with the primitive development of his ego and its pronounced narcissistic attitude. Accordingly, his activity remained at a primitive level. Hitler looked upon any kind of systematic work with the greatest dislike since any systematic activity would be an insult to his burning megalomania and an acknowledgment of defeat.

His psychosexual evolution and adolescent crises can only be reconstructed on the basis of later data and of our general psychiatric experience. It seems highly probably that in addition to some organic inferiority, conflicts with his father, and a strong castration complex played a part in this connection. Fear of being wronged, exceptional sensitivity to offence and typical over-compensations in the form of stressing of his masculinity and displaying his greatness are characteristic manifestations of castration anxiety.

Sense of threatened masculinity, originating in his castration complex, found still another outlet. Whoever was in any way superior to him and whoever did not acknowledge his greatness was looked upon as a dangerous enemy. Primitivity of his ego was responsible for the predominance of projective mechanisms on a large scale and his world was populated with enemies who had to be destroyed with utter brutality and ruthlessness, otherwise he would be destroyed by them. His own aggressive drives were thus attributed to various individuals, parties, and nations and this fact determined Hitler's political and personal behavior.

Since he laid such great stress on the necessity of learning the methods of his adversaries whom he was constantly trying to imitate (Socialism, Jews, English propaganda), it is logical to assume that the prototype for this kind of attitude was the desire to take away power form his father, a desire which is irrational and unrealizable and consequently well suited to constitute a source of eternal restlessness and anxiety, as well as of every new aggression.

The repressions of his psychosexual development did not permit the proper integration and sublimation of his aggressive-sadistic drives, which, to begin with, were not utilized for the construction of normal erotic aggression. The intended identification with his father was not even psychically successful, and instead of the expected masculinity, the constantly competing passive, female attitude appeared. The masculine attitude remained, as we have seen, on a brutally aggressive level. To this was added the constant need of accentuating his masculinity so as to conceal his feminine tendencies. We know that a similar constellation exists in active or latent homosexuals.

We have already discussed Hitler's tendencies of pseudo-masculine brutality so characteristic of the latent homosexual. Passive, feminine tendencies were perhaps operative in forming Hitler's mediumism, which played such an important role at the outset of his career. The tendencies of primitive masculinity kept on struggling against breakdowns, depressions, and even suicidal impulses. Furthermore, Hitler, so feminine in his psychic structure, submitted to members of his clique and Party, who unceasingly fed his spiritual vacuum. Belief in his own masculinity seemed to win out only when the feeling of his mission awoke within him, but he became nevertheless a tool in the hands of the Reichswehr. And even when, after murdering his comrades, he definitely disclaimed his homoerotic connections, ("we need real men and not monkeys", he exclaimed in justifying the murders and in condemning the homosexuality of his victims), and when by these very murders he seemed to be shouting to the world, "see what a strong and ruthless man I am," he acted as an obedient tool of the Reichswehr, whose support he sought and without which his power was not secure. The further course of events showed that such a method of absorbing outside strength may be successful: Hitler himself became the head of that very army which he had worshipped so much and by which he had been so greatly impressed.

The trauma that produced his anti-Semitism seems to mark a breaking point in Hitler's life. (4) The abortive attempt to display normal masculinity led to an even greater aggressive-sadistic regression and the alleged cause of the failure, the unfortunate Jew, was decked out in the garb of all his former enemies and persecutors, who dared to refuse the young Adolf access to greatness, love, and happiness. In combination with social anti-Semitism that hatred achieved all its objectives, such as the ever new and much desired proofs of real masculinity and the annihilation of the diabolic enemy.

At public meetings, while bewitching and fascinating his listeners and threatening his enemies, Hitler blared to the four winds his declaration of masculinity and message of doom to others who gained strength earlier than he did and therefore, to his way of thinking, were his persecutors. Demonstrating his masculinity in this manner, he forced himself as father, ruler and ideal upon the masses, within which he mobilized passive masochistic tendencies and utmost sadism. The masses were happy to have the opportunity to love so splendid a Fuehrer and were confident that, thanks to him, they would also gain strength and happiness. They saw in Hitler a symbol of strength, which would restore to them with interest everything they had lost. Thus they agreed to a maximum of passivity in order to share at some future time in the splendid masculinity of their Fuehrer.

Postscript:

This study was written in 1941-2 when Hitler was at the peak of power. Now the case history is closed and we can add a brief epilogue to our analysis of his crimes and insanity.

Moving from one aggression to another and gratifying his paranoia by the murder of millions of helpless "enemies" in gas chambers, he continued proclaiming his innocence and posing as the savior of his beloved Germany and European civilization.

Engrossed in his delusions, Hitler lost all sense of reality. He actually convinced himself that after a few weeks of war against Russia, her army was annihilated. He also convinced himself that the English speaking democracies were degenerate and would not withstand the assault of the reborn Germany. Every paranoiac system involves such a fatal drifting away from reality. Driven by his demon, Hitler never could rest. New enemies had to be attacked, no power other than his own could be tolerated. In his march toward his own doom he transposed into reality all his deep-rooted delusions.

Hitler had anticipated this colossal projection of his disturbed mind when he burned the Reichstag. At that time he explained his terroristic measures as intended to save Germany and the Western World from Bolshevik conspiracy and revolution. Had he not acted, he announced proudly, "not only the Reichstag, but all public buildings in Germany and, who knows, perhaps all of the Western World might have been today a heap of ruins."

Thus the greatest paranoiac criminal in recorded history brought about the very disaster that he had allegedly set out to avert.

STALIN AND THE DICTATORSHIP
OF THE PROLETARIAT

Psychological problems involved in the Bolshevist dictatorship would require a special study. However, the writer feels that this work would be incomplete without, at least, a brief chapter on the Russian dictatorship.

We may recall that the psychological background of the first Russian Revolution evolved from defeats in the long war; from hunger, weariness and growing anarchy in the country as well as in the army. The corruption among the ruling classes had contributed toward annihilating the basis of former ideals, the imperial dynasty had lost its prestige. In these respects the situation was similar to that of the French Revolution.

Thus the first Socialist Revolution, hailed as an act of liberation, claimed to achieve the great ideals of the French Revolution together with abolition of the capitalistic system along the lines of a democratic socialism to be realized in the future. This promising situation altered after the arrival of Lenin and his staff from Swiss exile. The Germans permitted the Bolshevist chiefs to enter Russia so the disruptive influences could be exerted on the Russian war effort. They were not mistaken in their expectations. Lenin made short shrift of honoring Russia's alliance with the bourgeois powers. The Bolshevists induced the soldiers to throw their arms down and enter into discussions on a separate peace with the Germans.

They were successful in these manœuvres despite the opposition of the Provisional Social Democratic Government of Kerensky. From then on the principle of violence, applied

by a well organized minority, became the major tenet of
Bolshevist policy. The Constituent Assembly, consisting not
of "capitalists" but of workers, peasants, and democratic
intellectuals, was dispelled by Lenin and his loyal sailors.
The Bolshevists took advantage of the forbearance of the
democratic leaders who felt that they could not put under
arrest representatives of a Socialist Party. They had to pay
dearly for this yielding to "bourgeois" prejudice of humanitarianism.

After Lenin had sapped the power of the Constituent Assembly, he initiated the practical application of the so-called
dictatorship of the proletariat. This idea was originally
promulgated by Marx who looked upon it as a necessary
stage of transition between the capitalistic society and the
Socialist democracy of the future. The element of violence
contained by implication in these concepts helped to dis-
tort the whole socialist ideal. According to Lenin's concept,
"democracy is not identical with the subordination of the
minority to the majority". Democracy is a *state* recognizing
the subordination of the minority to the majority, i.e., an
organization for the systematic use of violence by one class
against the other, by one part of the population against
another. " . . . We set ourselves the ultimate aim of destroying the state, i.e. every organized and systematic violence, every use of violence against men in general." (1)
In addition to the force these concepts exercised on Lenin,
he was strongly influenced by Sorel, who in turn, had been
"saturated by some of Nietzsche's ideas". (2)

Sorel had written: "Proletarian violence not only makes
the revolution certain; but it also seems to be the only means
by which the European nations—at present stupefied by
humanitarianism—can recover their former energy. . . ."
And: "The violence of the proletariat exercised as a pure
and simple manifestation of class feeling, and class struggle,
appears in this light to be a very beautiful, a very heroic

thing. . . . The concept of the class struggle tends to purify the concept of violence . . . The idea of the general strike, continuously revitalized by the emotions which proletarian violence provokes, fosters an absolutely epic state of mind." (3)

Official Bolshevist theory is based on the premise that the means are justified by the end. It was Lenin who remarked aggressively: "Great questions in the life of nations are settled only by force." Trotsky wrote in his *Defense of Terrorism:* "No other ways of breaking the class-will of the enemy except by the systematic and energetic use of violence." (2)

The Socialist Martov and the Marxist theoretician Plechanov had pointed out that terror and violence employed in the interests of a proletarian dictatorship, particularly where capitalism had not entered a stage of violent reaction, would become ends in themselves. The Socialist Kautsky, opposing the concept of a proletarian dictatorship on virtually the same grounds, was branded by Lenin as a traitor—a procedure which rapidly became a familiar weapon of Bolshevism and was liberally applied to every dissident, heretic, or critic. The high ethical principles, so characteristic of Socialism, were eliminated by Lenin from politics even prior to the Revolution. With the seizure of power and establishment of terror, such bourgeois prejudices as individual liberty and freedom were completely overthrown.

In vain did Gorky, the defender of the poor and the oppressed, appeal to the Communists: "Evidently killing is easier than persuasion and this very simple method is very easy for people who have been brought up amongst massacres and educated by massacres." "All you Russians", he cried, "are still savages, corrupted by your former masters, who have infused you with their terrible defects and their insensate despotism."

Terror became an easy substitute for freedom of speech,

press, opinion, and so forth. Were those ideals of a defunct
capitalistic system anything more but convenient tools of
capitalistic exploitation? This devious and characteristic Bolshevist reasoning could invoke for its justification the great
authority of the Communist Manifesto, which says: "When
the Christian ideas succumbed in the Eighteenth Century
to Rationalism, feudal society fought its death battle with
the revolutionary bourgeoisie. The doctrine of religious
freedom and liberty of conscience simply gave expression to
the rule of free competition within the domains of knowledge." (5) It was an easy matter for Lenin and his followers
to debase and ridicule all the democratic principles which
are the common ideals of Western civilization. With some
semblance of justice, he proclaimed, for instance, that there
could not exist any freedom of assembly in a society where
the main buildings in which a meeting could be held were
owned by capitalists. Therefore the seizure of those buildings
was the necessary prerequisite for freedom of assembly.
Marx devoted the greater part of his life, writings, and
scientific investigations to disparaging freedom, equality, the
will of the majority, by claiming that every kind of freedom
is a fraud unless it serves the interest of the emancipation
of labor from the oppression of capital. He stated that
humanity could not attain Socialism other than through
dictatorship of the proletariat. "Dictatorship of the proletariat is inevitable; it is necessary and undoubtedly essential
for the transition from Capitalism. Dictatorship does not
only mean violence, although it is impossible without violence, it also means an organization of labor, which is higher
than the preceding organization." (6)

"Dictatorship of the proletariat will mean substitution of
the dictatorship of the proletariat for the actual dictatorship
of the bourgeoisie . . . It will mean substituting democracy
for the poor, for the democracy for the rich. It will mean
a substitution of the right of assembly and freedom of the

press for the majority of the population—the toilers, for the right of assembly and freedom of the press for the minority —the exploiters. It will mean an enormous world-historic expansion of democracy, its transformation from a lie into a truth, the emancipation of mankind from the fetters of capital." (7)

Dictatorship of a small minority, identifying itself with "the oppressed", invoking the great Socialist ideal of liberation of the exploited and oppressed workers, became an objective that would ultimately, it was believed, lead to a classless society. Thus suppression of freedom has become an essential attribute of a system aiming at the establishment of liberty. We may see the operation of the rationalization of power drives and egotistic desires in terms of millennial benefits for the masses, in the theories of communists preceding the actual assumption of power in Russia.

To achieve such power, it was required that theory be translated into action by a leader fully aware of its implications and with the ability to lure or coerce the masses into accepting his program.

Certainly Lenin knew not only how to handle the masses, but had the magnetic qualities of a true leader. He had prepared in a lifetime of hardship for the moment of seizure of power and meant to use it without restraint. His convictions were absolute and unswerving, based on what he believed to be utter truth. He was the man to bring Marx' predictions to fulfillment. He never doubted that his mission and the mission of revolutionary Russia was to initiate the fall of capitalism throughout the world, and thus to save mankind: "Proletarian revolution alone is capable of saving perishing culture and perishing mankind." (8)

It was Engels who had asserted that Revolution must arise from war: "We are entitled to be proud and to consider ourselves fortunate that it has been our lot to be the first, in one part of the globe, to fell that wild beast—

capitalism, which has drenched the earth in blood, and reduced humanity to starvation and demoralization and whose end is near and inevitable, no matter how monstrous and savage its frenzy in the face of death." (9)

In fact it was Lenin, cognizant of Engel's theories, who had, from the atmosphere of revolution and armed intervention, brought Russia to a pitch of revolutionary fervor.

Lenin became the leader of the Russian masses and was hailed throughout the world as the leader and savior of the proletariat, the herald of a new era of social justice and liberty. He seemed to incorporate in his person the suffering of centuries of oppression. A faithful follower gave her impressions of her visit to Lenin in terms of utter devotion: "An impression of unspoken and unspeakable suffering was on his face. I was moved, shaken. In my mind I saw the picture of the crucified Christ. . . . Lenin appeared to me burdened, oppressed with all the pain and all the suffering of the Russian people." (10)

Thus while representing endless suffering and presumably giving voice to the torments of the oppressed classes, Lenin was enabled to stimulate and fan the hatred of these classes for their alleged persecutors. Combining personal grievances and the sanction of the theory of class society, Lenin could channelize this hatred and violence to a direct and observable opponent, namely, the bourgeoisie.

"It is understandable," wrote Freud in 1930, "that the attempt to build up a new communistic culture in Russia finds its psychological backing in the persecution of the bourgeoisie. Only one cannot help wondering what the Soviets will undertake once they finish exterminating their bourgeoisie." (11)

We are now in a position to answer this question. The unleashed aggression found new objects which at the same time served as a scapegoat for all the disillusionment of the masses. Their constant deprivations and increasing frustrations could be blamed on the machinations of saboteurs, old liberals, Mensheviki Socialists, and foreign agents.

Thus, in exterminating all those "enemies of the Proletariat", the ruling group could satisfy not only their own aggressive impulses; it also could divert the aggression of the masses and enforce its power by demonstrating its "Bolshevist vigilance" and loyalty to the ideals of the Revolution. The machinations of the scapegoats became an excellent device for strengthening the ties between the rulers and the people; the struggle against common enemies and salvation from common danger provided an important factor for the formation of new ego ideals, incarnated in the person of the leader and his closest disciples.

What has become of the ideal set by Engels, and advocated with such enthusiasm by Lenin? After the seizure of power by the oppressed Proletarians the state was supposed "to wither away". Engels predicted "banishment of the whole state machine to the museum of antiquities. In assuming state power the Proletariat by that very act destroys the state as such. The first act of the state in which it really acts as a representative of the whole of society, namely the assumption of control over the means of production on behalf of society, is also its last independent act as a state. Under Socialism much of the primitive Democracy will inevitably be revived."

"The bureaucracy and the standing army constitute a parasite on the body of the capitalistic society. In these words 'to shatter the bureaucracy and military machinery of the state' is to be found tersely expressed the principal teachings of Marxism on the subject of the problems concerning the state, facing the Proletariat in a Revolution. All former Revolutions helped to perfect the machinery of government whereas now we must shatter it, break it to pieces."

And now a last, an all-important quotation: "The interference of the authority of the state with social relations will then become superfluous in one thing after another and finally will cease of itself." (1)

Nobody, not even the most enthusiastic admirer of the Soviet Union will deny that the Revolution evolved in the opposite direction. Stalin himself recognizes that there is "contradiction in our treatment of the question of the state. We are in favor of the state dying out and at the same time we stand for the strengthening of the dictatorship of the Proletariat. The highest possible development of the power of the state, with the object of preparing the conditions for the dying out of the state: that is the Marxist formula." (12) Stalin explains this apparent contradiction as a reflection of Marxist dialectics.

It is possible then to describe the evolution of the Soviet Union as an accumulation of all those evils of oppression which were characteristic not merely of capitalistic society, but of autocracy. The rationalization given for this development toward totalitarianism was the persistence of enemies within and abroad. The real psychological motives may be described briefly as a desire to perpetuate illimited power and to suppress the anarchistic and rebellious impulses unleashed by the Revolution with its shattering of the old ego ideal. The ruling group took over the ideology of proletarian violence in order to rationalize those desires and it identified itself with the interest of the masses, so that every act of oppression came to be regarded as an act in the service and actual self-preservation of the Russian nation. In fighting the capitalistic oppressors the rulers extended their hostility to all opponents.

By a searching analysis of the Bolshevist justification of violence and of proletarian dictatorship in terms of the future, that is, the establishment of freedom and equality at some unspecified future date, we may arrive at the political realities that obtain in Russia. Instead of the former masters, we have, in the Soviet system, a new set of rulers who have acquired power. But in the last analysis are they the very same proletarians who up to the moment of the seizure of power had been wronged and oppressed? The entire course of the Russian Revolution shows just the opposite to be true. The actual masters are a bureaucracy, a small group of prominent Party members. They seem to have put into practical operation Nietzsche's concept of the masters who must rule ruthlessly in order to dominate the masses. Indeed the duped masses have been so skilfully imposed upon that they believe in many instances that they have exercised a choice in the selection of their rulers. That such freedom of choice was the merest illusion can be gleaned from Lenin's remark: "It is true that liberty is precious; it is so precious that it must be rationed." The subsequent course of the Russian Revolution proved convincingly that even the immediate goal of liberating the workers and peasants, had been converted into an enslavement incomparably worse than in any modern capitalistic society. Gradually the laboring public lost all those individual freedoms that their fellow workers in Western democracies had succeeded in achieving after long years of hard struggle. The story of the peasants and their exploitation by the state is no less tragic, fraught as it is with the terrors and sacrifices in the course of frantic resistance to complete extermination. As is well known, in the course of this struggle against the "kulaks", whole rural districts were completely depopulated either through famine caused by wholesale requisitions, or by forced deportations. This, by the way, was the first application on a large scale of the principle of mass deportations continued ruthlessly by the Soviets and emulated by the Nazis.

Thus the proclaimed dictatorship of the proletariat turned into the dictatorship *over* the proletariat. In fact, the whole structure of ruthless despotism and submission to authority and eventually the submission of all to the almighty leader is really strikingly similar to Fascism.

After his death, Lenin the Leader and the idol of the masses, and at the same time Lenin the Tyrant, responsible for immense suffering, was deified, embalmed, and deposed in the great Mausoleum in the Red Square like a holy mummy, thus being imposed upon the people as an evident substitute for the former holy ikons which the masses had worshipped before the advent of the Revolution. From the remotest corners of Russia, worshippers arrived to do homage to the sacred figure. Ironically the rulers feared that such homage might be mixed with aggression, for they took exceptional pains to examine each visitor scrupulously, to inspect the tiniest package with minute care. It seemed as if they expected an outrage against the holy shrine, as if sons mourning their dead father had projected their bad conscience, their own guilt, into the masses. It is necessary to dwell on this psychological aspect if one is to understand the succession of Stalin to power.

The struggle for succession, which began during Lenin's illness, was carried on by Stalin with great skill and utter ruthlessness. He removed all potential rivals and was always extremely careful to preserve his unique position as dictator of the Soviet Republic. This struggle between the Sons of the Revolution for the succession of the beloved father went through all the drastic stages which, as we have learned, characterize primitive tribal societies in which the sons are destroyed by the most cunning and powerful among them for fear of retaliation. Thus it was inevitable that the Revolution itself foundered on the rocks of Thermidorian or Bonapartist reaction. The events after the death of the father of a primal horde, as hypothetically described by Freud and developed and expounded on the basis of abundant ethnological evidence by Roheim, give some cue for the understanding of the vicissitudes of the Revolution. (13)

After the dreaded, simultaneously hated and loved Father had been killed and devoured by the rebellious sons, they began to identify themselves with that ideal hero. Some among them attempted to take over the lead, but were prevented from doing so by hatred and jealousy of their rival brothers. At last one succeeded and imposed his authority on all the others by eliminating his most important rivals, the potential successors.

The father-murder resulted in deep feelings of guilt and fear of retaliation. The leading among the sons, that is the successors to the father feared revenge not only from the remaining brothers, but also from the slain parent. Many of their reactions derive from these sources. Since the guilt was shared by the brothers, this common factor helped to strengthen the bond between them. Through the devouring of the slain father, they absorbed—so they felt—his secret powers, and thus established an identification with him and with each other. Totemistic feasts in primitive societies bear witness to these feelings and practices which probably have laid the foundation of human society. (14)

This process of identification of the murderer with the victim is a phenomenon frequently observed in the mourning rites of the primitives and has been studied extensively by Roheim. It finds its clinical counterpart in the psychopathology of melancholia. This identification results finally in the murderers' establishing an internal image of their victim as a powerful ideal, worshipping and deifying him, thus trying to deny their guilt and to placate his vindictive wrath. In this way, their suppressed hostility becomes transformed into overgrown loyalty.

However, there is always the danger of a break through of this hostility, which would this time be directed against the successor, the new father substitute. Therefore, the successful murderer and his group have to create powerful safeguards so as to hold in check the threatening hostility of the rival brothers each of whom may aspire to the succession. This is accomplished by taboos which are so important in all primitive societies and which in a period following a revolution take the form of rigid rules, of reaction formations, characterized by absolute severity and terrible penalties.

The slain parent, who in the history of the primal horde became deified, was made the center of a cult. In a revolution, the original leader and his successors acquire similar mythological characteristics and become identified with the new ideology. Thus in magnifying and protecting his personal power, the leader seemingly protects and exalts the ideals for which was shed the blood of the revolutionaries.

Hostility of the rebellious sons, held in check by the powerful successor and suppressed by the idealized image of the slain parent breaks through in form of paranoid projection. The "sons" project the hatred on each other and especially on any groups which may differentiate themselves from the original horde. In a revolution, this is easily rationalized by ideological divergencies behind which the ruling group suspects lust for power—sometimes correctly.

After the victorious group has become cemented by the common shedding of the blood of their enemies, the suppressed hostility of its members manifests itself in paranoid reactions which center around possible opposition and also around foreign groups with different social and national structure. Thus in the process of the final merging of internationally minded Bolshevism with pure Russian nationalism, we find a peculiar fusion of revolutionary ideology with the old nationalistic ideals breaking through, as it were, from repression. In all these processes the cementing of the ruling group and of the revolutionary nation has its inevitable parallel in hatred and suspicion directed toward foreign countries. This suspicion is easily rationalized as differences of ideology and as old historical conflicts.

Interestingly enough the struggle of the son against the father had been a strong factor in forming the personality of Lenin's successor. Consequently it may have proved of benefit to Stalin's bid for power when the same struggle was to take place in the political arena. What are the cornerstones of Stalin's personality as far as we can deduce them from the available data?

The only surviving son of a crude and tyrannical peasant shoemaker, Stalin, the boy, learned early how to hate and how to suppress hostility (until the opportune moment). Despite the position assigned to the father in the traditional patriarchal structure of a Georgian family, the main responsibility of the family seemed to have fallen upon the shoulders of the mother. She toiled hard but earned very little as a servant in the homes of the rich. Naturally, she had no way of protecting her son against the brutality of the father and helplessly watched as her husband mistreated him. Undeserved, frightful beatings made the boy as grim and heartless as his father. Indeed, his suppressed hatred against the father transferred itself to persons in power and to all authority. The death of the father occurred when Stalin was eleven years old, too late to change his character pattern. Probably the boy breathed with relief upon the father's death, and felt and acted as the savior of the mother who had shown him so great a devotion. Stalin's mother was indeed ambitious to elevate her son. She determined to enter him into the priesthood as a career which for a boy in such poor circumstances seemed the only possible way of social elevation. Thus Greek-orthodox theology with its rigid dogmatism became the stepping stone on the way to satisfying both his own and his mother's ambition.

Social humiliations naturally increased his general feeling

of inferiority and his desire for revenge and compensation. In addition to social humiliations there were mortifications engendered in the domination of Russian officials over the Georgian population. It may be noted that there were also some elements of inferiority in Stalin's physical make-up: weakness of the left arm, pox-marked face, and other un-prepossessing features. According to the theory of Alfred Adler such organic inferiority plays an important part in distortion of personality through the mechanics of psycho-logical overcompensation.

Indeed, young Stalin became hard and unsympathetic: "I never saw him weep," remarks his childhood friend, Iremash-vili—"he had only a sarcastic sneer for the joys and sorrows of his fellows. As boy and youth he was a good friend to those who submitted to his domineering will." (15)

In the theological seminary where Stalin received his training for a future vocation, he went further in developing a personality in which dissimulating his hatred and biding his time in anticipation of revenge in the future, became dominant features. The rigorous discipline of the seminary instilled in him a deeper hatred for authority. In this semi-nary, punishments were inflicted for such crimes as reading a "liberal" book. The inspectors and the monks were hostile and suspicious, maintaining a strict watch over the students, observing their movements, closely searching their rooms and their persons at the slightest pretext.

Forced to submit to his masters, Stalin found an outlet in asserting his despotism in the secret circle of his comrades. "He deemed it something unnatural," writes Iremashvili, "that any other fellow-student might be a leader and or-ganizer of the group. Joseph knew how to persecute and how to avenge himself. He knew how to strike at weak spots. . . . In his struggle for mastery Koba (Stalin's nick-name) with his supercilious and poisonous cynicism fomented many personal squabbles among his friends." Thus, the future revolutionary was serving an apprenticeship in the exercise of coldness, ruthlessness, and guile. In his student days, moreover, his revenge fantasies became more pronounced.

When Joseph Stalin became familiar with the Revolutionary movement, he broke with theology and substituted Marxism for Greek-orthodoxy. It was only natural for him to embrace it with the same dogmatic fanaticism which he had absorbed from his own theological precepts. At a later period it became quite natural for him to vent his hatred on the theological institution, which had chastized him, by launching upon a ferocious campaign of atheism.

Once Stalin had embraced the hazardous career of a professional revolutionary, he found at last the opportunity to express his accumulated store of hatred and resentment. His life had prepared him well for conspiracy. He had learned to suspect everyone and with this attitude his slyness and shrewdness grew correspondingly. His hatred and envy of power and authority received further impetus from the persecution by Tzarist secret police. Moreover, the young revolutionary absorbed the technic of his persecutors who resorted to the methods of inquisition in securing "confessions". He learned, as it were, all there was to know about threats, physical violence, moral torture, falsifying the depositions of witnesses, the subornation of false witnesses and other techniques of terror and oppression. These lessons he never failed to remember and, when in power, applied them with a thoroughness that would have shamed the Tzarist persecutors.

His slyness and the insidious talent for inciting others to dangerous action while remaining safe and secure, are reported by an eye-witness who spent a year or so in various prisons with him. (15) His capacity for cunning, his adroit dodging of punishment, was such that it was impossible to upset his balance. As a result of his early experiences, he developed a strong armor of self-defenses around his ego which made him insensitive to suffering and unable to sympathize with the pain of others. During confinement in the Baku prison, Stalin's cell neighbor reported to him a dream about Revolution. "Have you a craving for blood?" Stalin asked him unexpectedly. He took out a knife that he had hidden in the leg of his boot, raised high one of his trouser legs and, inflicting a deep gash on himself, he said: "There is blood for you!" (15)

It would seem that the entire development of Stalin's personality is contained in the implications of this incident. His sadistic character had been formed beyond redemption and the course of world history was to be deeply affected by a personality formed primarily through the repressive authorities of his youth.

Stalin's ruthlessness which had its roots in the enforced submissiveness to his father became complete at the death of his first wife which desolated him.

His biographer Iremashvili wrote: "Beginning with the day he buried his wife, he lost the last vestige of human feelings. His heart filled with the inexpressibly malicious hatred his merciless father had already begun to engender in him when he was still a child. He crushed with sarcasm his less and less frequently recurring moral impulses. Ruthless with himself, he became ruthless with all people." (15)

Kameniev, one of the old guard who opposed Stalin and was liquidated in due course, remarked to Trotsky in 1925: "You imagine that Stalin is preoccupied with replying to your arguments. Nothing of the kind! He is figuring out how to liquidate you without being punished." Not unlike Robespierre, Stalin felt that any opposition to him was disloyal and criminal. He rationalized his cruelty in dealing with mere differences of opinion by asserting the need for Party harmony and Bolshevist unity and discipline.

If Stalin's irrational attitudes toward criticism are viewed not merely as a means of preserving power, we may arrive at broader aspects of his outlook. On closer scrutiny, it appears that both his and Robespierre's rationalizations expressed a megalomaniac strain to the effect that the highest purity of the ideas of the party were expressed in their person. Stalin not only identified himself completely with the leaders and theoreticians of communism but believed that he represented the purity of the absolute truth they had formulated. In the name of idealism, calling upon the past to sanction his cruel, repressive measures, he unleashed terror on an unprecedented scale. Of course there were not wanting professional apologists who would interpret the significance of Stalin's attitudes and justify them historically. Thus a Professor Tarle, an official historian accredited by the regime, praised the French Terror and Robespierre who, in practicing it, was expressing the will of the people. (16)

Certain trends may be detected in the long course of Stalin's terroristic practices. It hardly needs mentioning that he exterminated all his actual and potential rivals and opponents in the service of his unique dictatorial position. Not satisfied with this simple and efficient system, however, he liquidated the entire old Bolshevist guard, as if he feared that they knew too much of his past, and might function as witnesses in detriment to the legend formed about him. "Stalin requires that in every circumstance he shall be the leading light; he destroys the last witnesses capable of producing one day a true testimony about him. He avenges himself now on these for not having known how to keep silent. And he shows the measure of his courage, as of his 'humanism', when, secure from all risk, he insults the defeated, stamps on his prisoners, and rages over their dead bodies." (17)

Another outstanding and, from our point of view, most important tendency of a dictator, is the identification with the enemy. It is typical of Stalin, who can hardly be esteemed as a thinker of any originality, that he was not averse to adopting as his own the ideas of opponents whom he had liquidated. Thus he fought Trotsky, allegedly on the ground of Trotsky's policy toward the kulaks and collectivization, only later to proclaim the very ideas of his enemy. All the plans of General Tukhachevsky, liquidated during the mass purge of 1936, were subsequently adopted and carried out by Stalin. Among those plans was a pact of close co-operation with Hitler which formed the basis of Tukhachevsky's indictment in treachery. However, the same pact promulgated by Stalin was hailed as an act of supreme wisdom.

A peculiar combination of shrewd cunning with merciless vindictiveness enabled Stalin to organize terror on a vast scale and to create a powerful apparatus in support of such terror. The Cheka, a secret police force, was formed in the first period of the revolution and then developed into the notorious GPU and finally into the no less notorious NKVD. These immense organizations were states within a state, endowed with the greatest privileges, unhampered by existing laws, and responsible only to Stalin himself. Some of its sinister mechanisms have been revealed to the astounded world during the famous purges of 1936. Other revelations were forthcoming when Kravchenko and others divulged its world-wide ramifications. These revelations, however, would not have been so overwhelming if the world had not been shocked by several internationally famous cases of murders and kidnapping by which the NKVD got rid of Stalin's enemies.

All opposition, even that of minor political significance was exterminated without qualms. What, one asks oneself, could have been sufficient motivation for the bloody purges in the Navy? They seemed attributable only to the ideas of younger navymen who considered light units (submarines, torpedo boats, hydroplanes) preferable to large, costly and vulnerable cruisers and dreadnoughts. They were charged with serving the enemies of the people by depriving the USSR of a fleet of major proportions. Fortunately, "the glorious officials of the People's Commissariat of the Interior cut off the heads of these reptiles." (17)

Stalin's methods of systematic terror, his merciless annihilation of antagonists, remind one strongly of the long line of Russian despots, headed by Ivan Grozny (The Terrible). It was he who initiated the system of "Opriczniki", of his faithful servants, notorious for their cruelty and freedom from legal restraint, who exercised the function of a modern secret police. Their chief, Skuratov, was infamous for his brutality and absolute, blind obedience to the Tzar. The organization bore striking resemblance to the NKVD, particularly in its exemption from all law. It is only natural that today Ivan Grozny is praised by the professional Soviet writers, who compose history and art, as a great constructive monarch who was compelled to use stringent measures because of the ignorance and lethargy of the Russian masses, in particular because of the opposition of the nobility.

In spite of the analogy between the methods of Tzarist despotism and Stalinism, it must be recognized that the present ruler has magnified terror and cruelty thousandfold since the days of his eminent predecessors. Stalin, the head of a modern organization and endowed with immense power, tortured and persecuted his victims on a scale undreamed of by the former tyrant. Moreover, the NKVD, Stalin's secret police is immeasurably more efficient than the Tzarist Okhrana. Deportations of criminal and political prisoners to Siberia had been instituted by the Tzars, but their unfortunate victims numbered in the tens of thousands. It was left to the country of the proletariat to deport millions to the remotest corners of Siberia and Kazachstan. Forced labor was not invented by the country of the proletariat, however, it reached its largest scope in Soviet Russia. The total numbers in the labor and concentration camps is estimated to be between fifteen to twenty million. Great enterprises which are the pride of Soviet industrialization and of the various five-year plans, as for example Dnieprostroj, the White Sea Canal, and many others, have been executed predominantly by these modern slaves of Stalin under the whip of the NKVD.

It would seem that Stalin, Georgian, himself a member of one of the national minorities oppressed by the Tzars, had absorbed all of the latters' sadism and was revenging himself by giving it vent throughout Russia. In this process, however, he did not forget his native Georgia. The role he played in the Sovietization of this land, was marked by most relentless cruelty. The Georgians, a proud and independent people, with strong Social Democratic leanings, offered serious resistance to the Bolsheviks which was crushed in the true Stalinist manner. Lenin himself felt quite indignant when informed of Stalin's brutal tactics, but his efforts to stop him were unavailing.

One may recall at this point the parallels with Hitler's attitude to the incorporation of Austria, his homeland, into the Reich. The mercilessness and bitterness displayed by these dictators toward their native lands becomes explicable when it is understood how deeply they had suffered as children at the hands of cruel and stern fathers. Apparently the conquests of the mother country had to the unconscious the symbolic significance of both redeeming their mothers and taking revenge on the hated fathers. The conquest rationalized by flaming ideology and supported by military power served to free the mother and to compensate the conquerors for their early humiliations.

Stalin transferred all the pain and resentment of his miserable childhood from his native land to the vast area of the Tzarist empire. He, representative of a minority persecuted by the Tzarist Regime, behaved as if he identified himself with the old aggressor and once in power, he carried out the old imperialistic policy to the limits. An analysis of his foreign policy shows convincingly that he realized not only all the imperialistic aspirations of the Tzars but went far beyond them and would have gone even further had he not been halted by other powerful nations. It was impressive to witness the process of re-incorporation of independent countries which had been a part of the Tzarist Empire and had been freed during the Revolution, only to be reabsorbed by a despotism incomparably stronger than that of the Tzars. Soviet imperialism in action was much different from Lenin's eloquent appeals against annexations; it was justified by transparent fictions. Loud and pious statements rang out that the Soviets had arrived to liberate a nation from its oppressors, a nation moreover whose allegedly evil government had participated in the capitalist encirclement. It is significant that the concept of encirclement arising from cynical utilitarian reasons ultimately became a singular delusion, paranoidal in scope for the dictators.

We have now reached a point at which the identification between Stalin, the dictator, and an expanding, powerful country becomes quite obvious. Not satisfied with successful destruction of past and future antagonists, Stalin took great pains in erasing from the memory of the nation whatever could in any way prove detrimental to his mythological grandeur. In some analogy to the so-called retrospective unconscious falsifications of a paranoiac, Stalin, by a perfect and certainly *conscious* system, did everything in order to create an image of his incomparable greatness. In successive editions of the Soviet Encyclopaedia, of textbooks of history, and above all of the Soviet Bible—the so-called *Kratki Kurs*, a short history of the Communist Party, Stalin's role was exaggerated and fulsomely praised while his antagonists were vilified or simply remained unmentioned.

Almost every trite word uttered by the beloved leader was hailed by the official Pravda, as the beginning of a new era in history. Stalin's thirst for flattery was particularly active in the domain of ideas. To be considered an original and powerful thinker remained his constant desire. It was not enough that Stalin was praised on every occasion as the greatest teacher and genius of the world proletariat; nor was it sufficient that the Russian press overflowed with adulation of his person and every meeting, every speech had to culminate in an ecstatic tribute to his genius. Even on utterly unexpected occasions, such as an anniversary of Spinoza, or in an article about Kepler, he was praised as an expert on Spinoza's philosophy or as a talented astronomer. One professor of philosophy wrote that the true meaning of Kantian philosophy was revealed by a letter of Comrade Stalin's. The periodical, *Cultural Front,* stated that "in reality certain pronouncements of Aristotle have only been fully interpreted and expressed by Stalin". (18) Another professor was happy to admit that the meaning of Cervantes had at last been realized through the illuminating pronouncement of Comrade Stalin, who had declared that "Don Quixote was a great satire".

All these flowery eulogies were a proper form of over-compensation for the lack of education and intellectual training which are important factors in Stalin's unconscious inferiority complex. Under favorable circumstances it was natural for Stalin to claim praise as a great and original thinker, philosopher, and as a brilliant theoretician. Ideas of grandeur are usually determined in their content by the specific elements which originated the sense of inferiority.

Thus the "Sun of Nations" and the "Beloved Leader" of workers and peasants became standard terms in the new Soviet mythology, Homeric in nature, in which a pantheon of heroes was endowed with semi-divine, eternally fixed attributes. However, we find precedents in Russian mythology itself. Some of the hymns and eulogies dedicated to Stalin remind one of the old Russian folk tales "Byliny" in which a hero of gigantic proportions and supernatural powers performs wonderful deeds in succoring the oppressed and wronged. Since the hero is of supernatural dimensions, all the common mortals dwindle in their significance. Similarly we are told that Stalin, "the great machinist of locomotive history" is such a powerful giant that all the other statesmen on the international scene seem "so tiny, so pitiable, such pygmies . . ." (19) Not only obscure poets of the Asiatic, the so-called "autonomous" republics, exalt Stalin beyond human limits. Even the poet Alexey Tolstoi, a writer of distinction and real talent has written a hymn addressed to Stalin:

"Thou, bright sun of the nations,
  The unsinking sun of our times
  And more than the sun, for the sun has no wisdom."

Such incredible flattery reached its peak on the day of Stalin's sixtieth birthday. In *Pravda* of December 21, 1939, only one column each was devoted to the Finnish-Russian war and World War II, while seventy-one columns were devoted to the leader. In the words of an American newspaper correspondent, "a world's record was established for newless newspapers." (18)

This megalomania of the dictator was accompanied by other forms of idolatry: pictures and statues of Stalin, sometimes of immense size, can be encountered throughout all Russia, in all railroad stations and public buildings. The murdered Tzar Batiushka (Father), became reincarnated on a tremendously magnified scale, much greater than in the past, since the reincarnation was supported not only by the megalomania of the leader but also by the cynical or naive response of his followers.

This collective Soviet idolatry is sufficiently well known to require little further elaboration. However, some examples may be selected from the vast number at hand. For example, after an interview with Stalin regarding "Trotskyist contraband" in historical and artistic works, some Russian musicians declared: "In the light of Comrade Stalin's letter, new and great tasks arise on the musical front. Down with rotten liberalism, with its bourgeois resonances, inimical to class theories." They undertook to revise the scoring of the composers of the past beginning with Beethoven and Moussorgsky. "Stalin's letter has to make of each Soviet orchestra a collective struggle for authentic Marxist-Leninism."

At the Congress of chess-players in 1932, Krylenko declared: "We must finish once and for all with the neutrality of chess. We must condemn once and for all the formula: 'chess for the sake of chess', like art for art's sake. We must organize shock-brigades of chess-players and begin the immediate realization of the five-year chess plan." (17)

The full apotheosis of the leader required, as a preliminary, the complete vilification of his antagonists of any period. This was carried out by a harmonious chorus directed by the great man himself and consisting of faithful, obedient, frightened, or merely cynical followers. A perusal of the records of the trials, as far as they have been made accessible to the public, shows what an amount of obloquy it was necessary to heap upon those who dared oppose Stalin. "Traitors", "lackeys of Fascism", "reptiles", were some of the epithets accorded to the unfortunate who dared provoke Stalin's wrath. In compulsive fashion he must besmirch the victim's memory. This was particularly true in cases where the victim was of any political significance and had some important deeds to his credit. It is of considerable psychological interest to analyze some of these accusations whose complete incredibility makes one speculate as to their deeper motives. For instance, in studying the *real* source of the indictment of Bukharin, one of the most prominent members of the

old Bolshevist guard, whom Stalin charged for having prepared, in 1918, an attempt on Lenin's life, certain facts
emerge. Bukharin was well known for his boundless love
and admiration of Lenin. We may surmise that the accusation was a projection of the designs or even plans, lurking
in Stalin's mind.

In this process of moral destruction of his antagonists,
Stalin was aided by his followers. Organizations and special
meetings demanded the execution of the alleged traitors
long before the court convened. One could read in the
Journal of Soviet Psychiatry and Neurology violent con-
demnations of the "criminals", the "bloody fascist agents",
"the vile reptiles". These tirades were signed by men outstanding in the Russian scientific world.

Since every means of education and every channel of expression is dominated by the regime, the process of moulding
public opinion in accordance with the Party's own interests
presents no difficulties. Generations have been brought up
in blind obedience to the Party and the beloved leader.
Their ideas are shaped with sternest rigidity and differences
of opinion are not tolerated. Criticism of the "general line"
is tantamount to heresy and meets with reprisals no less
merciless than the Inquisition. Apparently, the fear experienced by the leader and the ruling clique is such that they
have to maintain a constant system of physical and mental
defense reactions. This explains the striking sensitivity of
Soviet rulers to every criticism from abroad. It explains also
the typical Soviet custom, so incomprehensible to the democratic mind, of branding writers and artists for "lack of
ideology" and of expelling them from professional unions
for "bourgeois deviation". Such an expulsion, especially if
followed by banishment from the Party, may mean loss of
employment, imprisonment, or deportation. The dictatorship wields all the positive and negative instruments of
coercion: positive—through the methods of incessant propa-

ganda such as press and radio, negative—through constant
vigilance of censorship and threat of merciless punishment.
Fear and propaganda are powerful enough to achieve a
monolithic public opinion, an ideal that was sought by
Robespierre but could never be realized by him. A unanimous resolution at a Soviet meeting is as easily achieved as a
standardized prison garb in a concentration camp.

Until recently, isolation from the dangerous West had
been imposed so thoroughly that people were afraid to receive and to answer letters from relatives residing abroad.
For an average Russian to know a foreigner, to be seen with
him in Moscow, was a dangerous risk to take with his
political record. Constant repetition of phrases like "capitalistic encirclement" created in the population a psychological preparedness for approving whatever defensive—in
reality aggressive measures—the regime wished to undertake.
Those measures have been recently topped by the decree
unique in modern history forbidding Soviet citizens to marry
a foreigner. This propaganda created a justification for all
the deprivations imposed by the regime on the existence of
an average citizen.

All these defensive measures, some of them petty, some
terrible, indicate constant fear of either overt rebellion or
dissidence. It is only natural that the greater the oppression
and terror the Stalinist dictatorship applies to its citizens,
the more it must fear some retaliation. It tends to react with
defensive measures on a grandiose scale.

The *"Pierietasowka"*, (Shuffling), that is deportation of
an entire population of a "liberated" or otherwise ideolog-
ically uncertain province to the farthest corners of the
Soviet Union, and importation of some remote tribe into
that province which has just been deprived of its native
population, is one of the monstrously inflated methods of
self-protection. It is evident that the population of Kal-
mouks, resettled in the newly annexed part of Poland, or

of the Ukrainians, deported to remote parts of Siberia, are uprooted and so weakened in their possible political, national, and even physical resistance, that they cannot be expected to start any irredenta. Besides, such procedures are an excellent safeguard against plebiscites in the future. Ideological purity of the country of Proletariat is also better preserved if Spaniards, who had fought against Franco in the Civil War and had to flee from their country, are settled in the Uzbekistan; they had been given all sorts of promises by Moscow, only to find themselves deported and forced to lead a meager existence, toiling in the cotton fields, side by side with the Koreans just as ill fated, transplanted here sometime between 1934-1939 after the border skirmishes, constituting a sort of an unofficial war between the Soviets and Japan.

Such methods seem completely incredible and repulsive to the civilized mind. Obviously they are indicative of a profound contempt for human individuality. One infers from this attitude that a human being has no value in himself. The mission of the individual, according to these tenets consists in utter abject abandonment to the will of the state and to the dictatorship. A mentality of this order excludes any possibility of creating an ethical structure. However, even Stalin and his henchmen are made uneasy at the prospect of appearing unprincipled. Accordingly, semantic distortions of democratic and liberal ideas are constantly performed. Words like freedom and democracy are used as labels for Communist dictatorship in the USSR and in satellite countries. They even use the term election to designate an obedient acceptance of one-list candidates, imposed by the regime on the submissive masses.

When one realizes that this system of oppression evolved from Socialist theories, which contained some of the noblest ideas ever conceived by the human mind, one cannot but wonder at this tragic paradox of history. We may reach a better understanding of the Russian phenomena if we review the main points of our analysis. Although originating in Socialism, the Bolshevist ideology culminated in hatred, lust for revenge, and violence. Those impulses replaced rapidly the original ideals and their main instrument; the Dictatorship of the Proletariat became a goal in itself. Ideas growing in an atmosphere loaded with aggressiveness and hatred, could not evolve a society based on ethical values. On the contrary, the ideas developed were fanatical, corrupt, and often tinged with paranoidal delusions.

In the final crystallization of the Russian autocracy, individuals of special mentality were required. Stalin, who possessed all the essential characteristics of a fanatic dictator, gained the upper hand. He not only knew how to exterminate his rivals and possible successors, but also how to blend his personal hatreds and resentments with powerful collective emotions. It was also natural to him to rationalize his individual cruelty by putting it into the service of collective ideals. Since he identified himself with the cause, he could impose his personal tyranny as a token of an ideological triumph. Through terror, coercion, and incessant propaganda and indoctrination, he and his followers have succeeded in imposing a new set of values and concepts on the masses superseding the old collective ego ideal. They have blended their ideology with methods and goals originating with and represented by a long series of their Tzarist predecessors. A new mythology has been created in which Stalin has become enthroned as supreme being endowed with attributes of an archaic barbaric father-image. Thus, under the guise of liberation, dictatorship laid solid foundations for a system of political and psychological enslavement, and the revolution which was supposed to deliver a definite blow to the state as an institution resulted in the creation of a super-state relentlessly exploiting the individual.

As a result of a process of thorough identification, the new rulers have taken over the methods and ideals of the Russian tyrants of the old past and under the disguise of sublime ideals made them acceptable not only to the vast masses of their own people but even to followers and sympathizers all over the world. Anxiety and frustration of the post-war world superimposed on the inherent weaknesses of our social structure have created in the masses a deep need for ideals backed by material power. This collective longing invests the Soviet system with an aura of salvation which makes sympathizers overlook the suffering and depression on which it is based.

It is possible then to describe the evolution of the Soviet Union as an immense accumulation of all these evils of oppression which were characteristic not merely of capitalist society, but of autocracy. The rationalization given for this development toward totalitarianism was the persistence of enemies within and abroad. The real psychological motive may be described as a desire to perpetuate illimited power and to suppress the anarchistic and rebellious impulses unleashed by the Revolution with its shattering of the old ego ideal. The ruling group took over the ideology of proletarian violence in order to rationalize those desires and it identified itself with the interests of the masses, so that every act of oppression came to be regarded as an act in the service and actual self-preservation of the Russian nation. In fighting the capitalist oppressors the rulers extended their hostility to all opponents and dissidents. They identified themselves unconsciously with all the powers of despotic oppression which have existed in Russian history.

This set of unconscious identifications were supplemented by a system of identifications performed on a more conscious level. On this level, they set themselves up as representatives of the masses of the formerly oppressed and now supposedly liberated Russian people. They even extended this identification to the oppressed proletariat or, if expedient, to oppressed nationalities of the whole world. In short, they have been successful in promoting Communist ideals to the point where they have formed the core of a new collective ego ideal which superseded the old one. Thus the masses learned to surrender their desire for personal freedom and happiness, exchanging these goals for the new ideal of collective achievement in the present and universal communist felicity in some remote future.

Certain situations in psychologic terms are recurrent despite certain fresh features. Stalinism in its disruption of the collective superego, built through centuries of civilizing processes, necessarily involves a regression to the archaic unconscious. Hence, it should not at all be a matter of surprise that situations arising in Russia should present so marked a resemblance to processes described as typical of more primitive societies. We recall that the successful murderer and his group have to create powerful safeguards so as to hold in check the threatening hostility of the rival brothers, each of whom may aspire to the succession. This is accomplished by taboos which are so important in all primitive societies and which, in a period following the revolution, take the form of rigid rules, reaction formations, characterized by absolute severity and terrible penalties.

In conclusion, we arrive at some understanding of the extremely complex processes which have transformed the powerful upsurge toward liberation into a system of relentless oppression. Here as in every other dictatorship we have studied, this result was possible by a cooperation of historical and sociological factors with the personality of a fanatic leader who had succeeded in imposing himself as an ideal on the suffering masses.

ORIGIN AND PREVENTION OF DICTATORSHIP

Our studies have shown that certain psychological factors favor the rise of dictatorship.

Blind obedience and submission to a self-appointed authority are made possible only when the people feel weakened in their ego and give up whatever criticism and independence they had developed. Such weakening of the collective ego may occur under the impact of anxiety, fear, and insecurity. Poverty, starvation, fears of imminent danger are important factors in producing such a condition. Disappointment following a lost war or an exhausting revolution may have the same effect.

Under such circumstances, the collective ego, harassed by its feeling of helplessness, performs a regression to a more infantile stage and looks anxiously for help, support, and salvation.

Disintegration of a social structure accomplished, or simply climaxed by a revolution, creates not only general anxiety and thus weakens the collective ego but, in destroying the social fabric, it also undermines the foundations of norms and ideals which form the basis of the collective ego ideal.

The masses are then prepared to look out for a new ideal which, due to their general mental regression, does not remain confined to abstract concepts and theories. The latter, represented as they are by some leading individuals, assume the characteristics of a new cult, while the individual in question may become endowed with superhuman attributes.

The collective ego, weakened in its feeling of security and regressed to a primitive stage of development, inclines

242

toward leaning on an individual who appears to relieve it from all responsibility and concern over the future, and ascribes to him attributes of almost divine omnipotence. This individual is trusted and worshipped by the group just as a parent is trusted and endowed with magic powers by the naive child. In its regression, the collective ego taps the deep sources from which once in the remote past had sprung magic, mythology, and religion, and thus surrounds the person of the leader with an aura of new mythology.

The leader, or rather the image, representing him in the collective mind, replaces the old ego ideal which had been shaken by the social crisis preceding and preparing the establishment of dictatorship. The image of the leader becomes incorporated into the collective mind, as it were, as a kind of a new superego. Thus, the leader becomes a supreme authority, ruling not only over millions of his faithful subjects, but also regulating their ideas, emotions, and activities. This he can accomplish with the help of his clique, by fear which they engender through the use of terror and due to the support offered by the response and compliance of the collectivity.

Analysis of the response with which the group meets the impact of dictatorship reveals many important features. In submitting to the absolute and ruthless ruler, the group satisfies its profound and partly repressed masochistic impulses. By the same token, however, many of the "subjects" of a totalitarian dictatorship may find a gratification for their sadistic lust for power and domination; since, due to the structure of a totalitarian society, there is almost as much room for domination of subordinates as there is for the submission to a superior. Moreover, a totalitarian dictatorship offers to its subjects still other outlets for their sadistic impulses: there is always in sight a campaign against an internal enemy and most likely a crusade against an external foe, threatening the country of dictatorship with aggression and "encirclement". Thus in attacking him, the dictatorship rationalizes its own sadism and anxiety by an ideological disguise and by attributing mischievous designs to the enemy.

Moreover, submission to the dictator is supported by the process of identification of his subjects and disciples with his august person. To them he seems like an incarnation of their own ideals and desires, an embodiment of their own resentment and of their own greatness. Implicitly they believe the promises of their leader, since they endow him with omniscience and well nigh omnipotence.

Infallibility being one of his main features, his image exerts a powerful fascination, eliminating whatever doubt and criticism may subsist. (It hardly needs mentioning that terror and systematic indoctrination, wielded by modern dictatorship to a perfection, are most helpful in weeding out any such unruly opposition). Thus, as a final effect, the impact of the dictator on the masses is largely reminiscent of the power wielded by a hypnotist.

Like a hypnotist, he infuses the masses with his own desires, ideals, hatreds, and resentments. Like a hypnotist, he imposes on them his way of thinking, making them blind, impermeable, and deaf to reality. They have to see, to think, and to believe according to the belief of the leader and his clique: thus is being performed a gigantic experiment in mass hypnosis with both negative and positive illusions and suggestions.

In view of this situation, the dictator, supported by his henchmen and wielding the machinery of terror and indoctrination, can infuse the masses with ideas so overladen with emotions and so unrealistic that they assume the characteristics of collective delusions, both of grandeur and of persecution. Here again, the dictatorship bases its power on primitive layers of the human mind. Their revival is favored by the general regression characteristic of mass psychology.

However, the relationship between the masses and the dictator is based on a complete reciprocity in the sense of give and take going on in both directions. Not only is it obvious that the position of the dictator is unthinkable without the material and moral support of his disciples but, moreover, they imbue him with their faith, feed him with their ideas and emotions. It is they who make him feel great and important beyond any mortal, and thus convey to him elements of their immeasurable megalomania. Surrounded by worship and adulation, he would have indeed to be endowed with an unusual amount of self-criticism to resist the temptation of sharing their belief in his calling, mission, and semi-divine power. Thus, the dictator and the masses live in an atmosphere of common delusions of grandeur and persecution; high charges of emotional ideas flow from one to another, creating a constant process of mutual identification. Moreover, they are bound by ties of common guilt and anxiety. They have perpetrated—or simply condoned—crimes and shed blood which calls, so they unanimously believe, for punishment. Finally, they have every reason to fear retaliation from enemies whom they have antagonized, or whom they plan to attack.

It is this identification that was the psychological basis for Robespierre acting as a representative of the "people", for Hitler expressing the unalienable rights of the German "Volk" and proclaiming the sanctity of the Party, for Stalin being worshipped as the defender of the "proletariat" and of the purity of the Party and its ideology.

What are the men apt to act both as recipient and powerful source of such collective fascination? Dictators, we have studied, although representing a great variety of background and personality, have certain trends in common. Some of these are manifest and almost self-evident: excessive narcissism, aggressiveness, hatred, and lust for power. However, deeper analysis reveals that this facade conceals feelings of weakness and inferiority often based on early frustrations and on inadequate virility. The people "suffer plundering, wantonness, cruelty, not from an army, not from a barbarian horde, on account of whom they must shed their blood and sacrifice their lives, but from a single man; not from a Hercules nor from a Samson, but from a single little man. Too frequently this same little man is the most cowardly and effeminate in the nation, a stranger to the powder of battle and hesitant on the sands of the tournament; not only without energy to direct men by force, but with hardly enough virility to bed with a common woman!" (1)

Yet, with all these neurotic features, the dictator is an individual who has intuitive understanding of the masses and the capacity to lead them by the power of his suggestion. This he can achieve due to the special structure of his personality. Similar in this to an artist, he never gives up his early emotional conflicts and frustrations, never resolves them except in action, so that they provide continuous fuel for his activity. The power of his convictions, based on emotions with deep unconscious roots, is such that they successfully resist the pressure of logic and reality; in this way, they assume the characteristics of hypervalent ideas known in psychopathology as a preliminary of delusions. Such ideas form the core of fanaticism no matter how well disguised they are by ideological rationalization.

Fanaticism, with its powerful load of repressed and conscious emotions, enables the dictator to strike a response in the masses since it appeals to similar emotions in them. Moreover, he succeeds in imposing on them, through suggestion, his own megalomaniac identification: he makes them believe that he really is their best representative, their ideal, their savior, the guarantee of their greatness and happiness.

While the passive trends of his personality enable the dictator to absorb all the turbid emotions and ideas of the masses and to act like a medium in a spiritistic seance, his active, aggressive and sadistic tendencies allow him to concentrate on the subjugation of the masses and on the physical or spiritual extermination of his antagonists.

The personality structure of a dictator contains numerous trends well known to psychopathology. At times, he seems to be on the verge of a definite psychosis, a paranoia both of grandeur and of persecution. However, what distinguishes him from most of the typical psychotics is the direction of his ideas toward reality. Unfortunately, for the masses and sometimes for humanity at large, fanatical ideas of a dictator do not remain confined to his morbid imagination. They are full of dynamics and of dynamite and if delusions they are, they are nevertheless delusions tending to action and to realization. Here lies their danger and the final doom of every dictatorship, since no matter how realistic, shrewd, and schemingly practical may be the dictator and the rule of his party, in the last analysis they must butt and break against one powerful element of reality which they disregard in their frenzy: love for freedom so deeply ingrained in human beings.

* * *

What are the conclusions we can draw from our studies concerning prevention of the social disease called dictatorship?

It would be simple enough to dodge the whole question by making the answer dependent on society and human beings as such reaching a degree of perfection possible probably only in an utopia. However, there are many other social and individual diseases which we cannot yet eliminate and nevertheless we are trying very hard to prevent them or at least render them more innocuous.

Some of the factors weakening the collective ego can be eliminated only by altering the economic conditions so as to assure freedom from want to all members of a society and—by implication—to humanity at large. This postulate seems indispensable as a measure of pure social prevention, aside from all moral and humanitarian considerations. It becomes then a question of political and economic planning how to achieve a universal distribution of indispensable goods. Historical experience and our analysis clearly indicate that this cannot be accomplished by violence which inevitably leads to political dictatorship and moral disintegration of the leaders themselves and of their disciples. On the other hand, the fact remains that without such planned and, therefore, more equitable distribution poverty and starvation prevailing throughout the world create continuous tension and anxiety, resulting in permanent weakening of the collective ego with all its dangerous consequences. A similar effect is produced by economic depressions followed by unemployment which create the feeling of general insecurity.

There are in our social fabric some other elements seemingly unavoidable and yet most damaging to the ego of the masses. They are linked with our industrial civilization which brings in its wake regimentation and mechanization, that is, a uniformity almost incompatible with the development of the individual. Even modern techniques of recreation such as the movies and the radio contribute to molding the collective emotions and ideas in a certain standard way, preparing the masses, as it were, for easy acceptance of any slogans imposed by a power-hungry demagogue.

Since every mass production- and consumption-culture inevitably leads to a certain degree of uniformity, individual and independent thinking should be developed and encouraged by an increasingly high quality of scientific and artistic production offered to the masses. Obviously this could be achieved only if people responsible for recreational industry were aware of their high social responsibility at least as much as of their material interests.

Inspiring results of scientific research should be made available to larger groups of the population so as to incite them to more independent thinking and to offer opportunities for sublimation as a counterbalance against overgrowth of the "appetitive soul" in the sense of Plato, characteristic of our acquisitive civilization.

This point brings up the whole essential problem of mass education in the direction of helping the ego of the masses to achieve more maturity, to feel less need for dependence and submission. It might seem that at a time when psychological science is being geared on a large scale to education, and group therapy is gaining wide recognition, methods could be devised how to influence the people not in the sense of dictatorial indoctrination but of moral elevation and maturation.

What should be the objectives of such education meant as prevention of tyranny, in other words education for democracy?

At the outset of this discussion we have to remember one basic truth: to be really effective, such education must start in early childhood, since, according to our present knowledge, that period is decisive for character formation. Even Plato was fully aware of this fact, since he wanted to have exiled from his utopian ideal city "all inhabitants . . . who are more than ten years old, and . . . take possession of their children who will be unaffected by the habits of their parents". (2)

This early education for democracy should, according to our present psychological knowledge, steer a middle course between submission-domination characteristic of authoritarian social structure and undisciplined looseness leading to anarchy, eventually inviting tyranny. To express it in psychoanalytical terms: it is equally wrong to impose upon the child the imprint of a severe, intolerant superego

as it is to bring it up—if such a fiction were at all possible—
without an ego ideal.

The ill effects of the authoritarian misconception are too
apparent and well known to need any further elaboration.
The errors of the opposite deviation are likely to produce
individuals with too little concern for other human beings,
with inadequate social feelings to counterbalance narcissism
and primitive aggressiveness of the "appetitive soul". Insufficiently critical of themselves and insufficiently aware of
social bonds as an important part of reality, they are likely
to become involved in neurotic or otherwise anti-social conflicts. Thus they may become a real danger to democracy,
either as candidates for prospective dictators on a large or
on a small scale or as material for a group of amoral psychopaths from which a dictatorship might draw its pretorian
guard.

Individual narcissism and primitive aggressiveness can be
countered and sublimated only when education is based on
true ideals. They are as necessary in education as they are
in maintaining mental equilibrium in adults. A vacuum in
this respect invites the misleading ideologies of demagogues
who exploit the craving of the masses for some ideology.

Since individual narcissism and primitive aggressiveness
find their most significant outlet in group narcissism and
group hostility, education for democracy must counter this
dangerous development by actively stressing bonds of sympathy between all human beings regardless of race, creed, or
political adherence. Group therapy with children has devised methods of actively combatting anti-social aggression
and hostility, and still more stress must be laid on eliminating every trace of bias and group conceit. It is most fortunate
that religious leaders, at least in this country, display increasing tolerance and respect for creeds different from their
own. Obviously it is most alien and dangerous to the spirit

of democracy that any religious or political group should believe itself in possession of absolute truth and therefore superior to other groups. This important change in the approach of religious leaders should enable religion, enlightened through modern knowledge of human nature, to play again its important role in social sublimation.

Such tolerance is by no means equivalent to cynicism and belief in relativity of essential human and moral values which form the basis of democracy. Such values, headed by profound respect for human dignity, promoted as they were by the great founders of American Democracy, should form the supreme goal inspiring society and its educators. This ideology, when really believed in and lived in education and in every day life would form a powerful bulwark in defense of freedom. It would not be freedom of Caliban who kneels in abject worship before the drunk knave who made him share his bottle and made him believe his promise to liberate him from the civilizing rule of noble Prospero. Freedom then would be not only freedom from shackles imposed on individuals by an imperfect traditional social structure, but it would rather be freedom for full development of individual dignity in the frame of a society rendered more perfect and more flexible due to the growing evolution and moral sublimation of its members.

Such evolution then, and not violent upheavals, would help to evolve better forms of social structure which would not be imposed from the outside by self-appointed reformers and saviors but would be natural stages of a truly human development.

Availing themselves of the impressive progress not only of physical science and technique but also of knowledge of human nature, statesmen, similar more to social scientists or to Plato's king-philosophers than to rulers in the old sense of this word, would help to find better forms of social existence.

If all this seems utopian, we should bear in mind that what is really demanded is nothing less than a more rational shaping of history, that is a more rational planning of human evolution. Even if this demand is based on deep desires of every serious student of society, still this writer believes that it is more than just wishful thinking. After all, the real foundations of this demand lay in the entire course of evolution of the human species from its subhuman origins toward true humanity. Sub specie aeternitatis, that is in the light of evolution, all horrors of cruelty and deprivation are but outbursts of revenge of repressed animality and should not blur our vision toward the ideal goal of human evolution: freedom and nobility.

A Brief Reminder of Chronology

JULIUS CAESAR

AND THE DEATH OF THE REPUBLIC

Establishment of the Roman Republic	500 B.C.
Lucius Cornelius Sulla's reign	138-78 B.C.
Birth of Julius Caesar	102 B.C.
Julius Caesar starts his political career on Sulla's death	78 B.C.
First Triumvirate organized by Caesar	60 B.C.
Caesar gets the Consulship of Gaul (Gallic Wars)	58-54 B.C.
Caesar's march on Rome and seizure of power	50 B.C.
Battle of Pharsalia, Caesar's great victory	49 B.C.
Battle at Munda, Caesar's victory over Pompey's legions	45 B.C.
Caesar's assassination	44 B.C.
Battle of Philippi, final defeat of the Republican party	42 B.C.

OLIVER CROMWELL

AND THE PURITAN REVOLUTION

Birth of Oliver Cromwell	1599
Reign of Charles I	1625-1649
Cromwell gets a seat in the Parliament	1628
Charles convokes the Short Parliament	1640 (3 weeks)
Charles convokes the Long Parliament	1640
Long Parliament	1640-1649
Civil War starts	1642
Charles escapes London	1647
Charles's execution	1649
Cromwell's war with Ireland	1649
Cromwell's war with Scotland	1650
Rump Parliament dissolved by Cromwell	1653
Cromwell becomes Lord-Protector	1653
First great speech of Cromwell in his Parliament	1654
Rule of Oliver Cromwell	1653-1658
Long Parliament reconvened	1659
Charles II Stuart enters London and the corpse of Cromwell is dragged through the streets	1660

ROBESPIERRE

AND THE TERROR

ADOLF HITLER

Birth of Adolf Hitler	**1889**
Years of Poverty in Vienna	**1910-1913**
Wounded in the army, during World War I	**1916**
Defeat of Germany	**1918**
Treaty of Versailles	**1919**
Constitution of the Weimar Republic	**1919**
Program adopted for the National Socialist German Workers Party	**1920**
Beer Hall Putsch	**1923**
Hitler sentenced to imprisonment	February, **1924**
Writing of *Mein Kampf*	**1924**
Hitler appointed German Chancellor. Party comes to power	January, **1933**
Reichstag Fire	February, **1933**
Blood Purge	June, **1934**
Death of Hindenburg, President of Germany. Hitler becomes President	August, **1934**
Occupation of Austria	**1938**
Occupation of Czechoslovakia	**1939**
Outbreak of World War II	**1939**
War with Russia	**1941**
Suicide of Hitler and Eva Braun	**1945**

STALIN

AND THE DICTATORSHIP OF THE PROLETARIAT

Publication of Communist Manifesto	1848
Organization of Russian Socialist Democratic Labor Party	1898
Birth of Vladimir Illyich Ulianov: Lenin	1870
Birth of Joseph Visarionovitch Djugashvili: Stalin	1871
Stalin graduated from Gori Theological School	1890
Stalin expelled from Tiflis Theological Seminary	1899
Formation of Bolshevik Party	1903
Outbreak of World War I	1914
Revolution starts in Petrograd	March, 1917
Formation of Socialist Government of Kerensky	March, 1917
Arrival of Lenin from abroad	April, 1917
Dispersing of the Constituent Assembly by Lenin. Formation of the first Soviet of People's Commissars. (Dictatorship of the Proletariat)	November, 1917
Signing of Peace Treaty in Brest Litovsk	1918
Execution of the Tzar	July, 1918
Death of Lenin	1924
Stalin's fight for power and liquidation of his rivals: Trotsky	1929
Bukharin, Rykov and Tomsky	1932
Deportations of the Kulaks	1932
Purges of party members	1936-38
Outbreak of war with Germany	1941

BIBLIOGRAPHY

JULIUS CAESAR

AND THE DEATH OF THE REPUBLIC

(1) Ferrero, Guglielmo, *The Greatness and Decline of Rome*. New York, G. P. Putnam's Sons, 1910.

(2) Plutarch, *Lives (Vitae Parallelae)*, vol. 4, "Life of Sulla" London, W. Heinemann, 1914-26.

(3) Mommsen, Theodor, *History of Rome*. New York, Chas. Scribner and Co., 1869.

(4) Syme, Ronald, *The Roman Revolution*. Oxford, Clarendon Press, 1939.

(5) Plutarch, *Lives (Vitae Parallelae)*, vol. 7, "Life of Julius Caesar". London, W. Heinemann, 1914-26.

(6) Suetonius, Caius T., *XII Caesares*, "De Divo Julio". Paris, 1828.

(7) Boissier, Gaston, *Cicero and His Friends*. New York, G. P. Putnam's Sons, 1922.

(8) Sallust, C., *De Bello Catillinari*. London, W. Heinemann, 1921.

(9) Plutarch, *Lives (Vitae Parallelae)*, vol. 6, "Life of Brutus". London, W. Heinemann, 1914-26.

(10) Bychowski, Gustav, Zur Psychopathologie der Brandstiftung; *Schweizer Archiv. f. Psych. und Neur.*, 1919.

(11) Jaspers, Karl, Heimweh und Verbrechen, *Archiv f. krimin. Anthropol.*, 1910.

OLIVER CROMWELL

AND THE PURITAN REVOLUTION

(1) Carlyle, Thomas, *Collected Works*, "Oliver Cromwell's Letters and Speeches". London, Chapman and Hall, 1870-82.

(2) Firth, Sir Charles Harding, *Oliver Cromwell*. New York, F. De Fau & Co., 1900.

(3) Morley, John M. P., Viscount, *Oliver Cromwell*. New York, The Century Co., 1900.

(4) Cardiner, Samuel Rawson, *Oliver Cromwell*. London, Longmans, Green and Co., 1901.

(5) Buchan, John, *Oliver Cromwell*. London, Hodder and Stoughton, Ltd., 1934.

(6) Hayward, Frank Herbert, *The Unknown Cromwell*. London, G. Allen and Unwin, Ltd., 1934.

(7) Taylor, George Robert Sterling, *Oliver Cromwell*. Boston, Little, Brown and Co., 1928.

(8) Kittel, Helmuth, *Oliver Cromwell, seine Religion und seine Sendung*. Leipzig, W. de Gruyter and Co., 1928.

(9) Oncken, Hermann, *Oliver Cromwell; vier Essays über die Führung einer Nation*. Berlin, G. Grote, 1935.

(10) F. Kapelusz: Religioznyj durman w period anglijskij rewolucji XVII wieka. *Pod zanamieniem marksizma*, 8 1940.

ROBESPIERRE AND THE TERROR

(1)   Le Bon, Gustave, *La Revolution Française et la psychologie des revolutions*. Paris, E. Flammarion, 1929.

(2)   Bychowski, Gustav, Zur Psychopathologie der Brandstiftung, *Schweizer Archiv. f. Psych. und Neur.*, 1919.

(3)   Sorel, Georges, *Reflections on Violence*. New York. P. Smith, 1941.

(4)   Robespierre, Marie Margueritte Charlotte, *Mémoires de Charlotte Robespierre sur ses deux frères*. Paris, Depot Central, 1835.

(5)   Robespierre, Maximilien, *Oeuvres Complètes*. Paris, V. Barbier et C. Vellay, 1910.

(6)   Barère de Vieuzac, *Mémoires*, Carnot et David, 1842-44.

(7)   Robespierre Maximilien, *II Discours sur le Jugement de L. Capet du 28 Dec. 1792*. Dijon, Capel, 1793.

(8)   Robespierre Maximilien, *Speeches*. New York, International Publishers, 1927.

(9)   St. Just, Louis Antoine Leon, *Oeuvres*. Edition de la Cité Universelle, 1946.

THE SPIRITUAL BACKGROUND OF HITLERISM

(1) Nietzsche, Friedrich Wilhelm, *The Complete Works*, vol. 12, "Beyond Good and Evil". New York, MacMillan Co., 1910.

(2) .... *The Complete Works*, vol. 13, "The Genealogy of Morals". New York, MacMillan Co., 1910.

(3) Fouillée, Alfred Jules Emile, *Esquisse Psychologique des Peuples Européens*. Paris, F. Alcan, 1903.

(4) Hegel, Georg Wilhelm Friedrich, *Vorlesungen über die Philosophie der Weltgeschichte*. Leipzig, F. Meiner, 1919-23.

(5) Müller-Freienfels, Richard, *Psychologie des deutschen Volkes*. München, C. H. Beck, 1930.

(6) Tacitus, P. C., *The Germania*. London, Taylor Walton Moderly, 1851.

(7) Frederic le Grand, *Examen du "Prince" de Macchiavelli*. La Haye, J. Van Duren, 1741

(8) Baker, J. Ellis, *Foundations of Germany*. Oxford Pamphlets, 1914.

(9) Barker, Sir Ernest, *Nietzsche und Treitschke. The Worship of Power in Modern Germany*. Oxford Pamphlets, 1914.

(10) Herzberg, Alexander, *Zur Psychologie der Philosophien und der Philosophen*. Leipzig, F. Meiner, 1926.

(11) Nietzsche, Friedrich Wilhelm, *The Complete Works*, v. 14-15, New York, MacMillan Co., 1910.

(12) Plato, *Theaetetus*. Cambridge, University Press, 1881.

(13) Nietzsche, *Vermächtnis*.

(14) Spengler, Oswald, *The Decline of the West*, New York, A. A. Knopf, 1932.

ADOLF HITLER

(1) Olden, Rudolf, *Adolf Hitler*. New York, Covici Friede, 1936.

(2) Heiden, Konrad, *Der Fuehrer*. New York, The Lexington Press, 1944.

(3) Hitler, Adolf, *Mein Kampf*. New York, Stackpole Sons, 1939.

(4) Kurth, Gertrud M., The Jew and Adolf Hitler. *Psychoanalytic Quarterly*, vol. xvi, #1, January, 1947.

(5) Rauschning, Hermann von, *Hitler Speaks*. London, T. Butterworth, Ltd., 1940.

(6) Chamberlain, Houston Stewart, *Die Grundlagen des 19. Jahrhunderts*. München, F. Bruckman, 1932.

(7) Rosenberg, Alfred, *Der Mythus des 20. Jahrhunderts*. München, Hoheneichen Verlag, 1932.

(8) Marx, Karl and Engels, Friedrich, *Communist Manifesto*. New York, Labor News Co., 1934.

(9) Bychowski, Gustav, Zur Psychopathologie der Brandstiftung. *Schweizer Archiv. f. Psych. und Neur.*, 1919.

(10) *Encyclopedie Française*, XV, Pédagogie Nationale Socialiste.

(11) Henderson, Sir Neville, *Failure of a Mission*. New York, G. P. Putnam's Sons, 1940.

(12) Silone, Ignazio, *School of Dictators*. New York, Harper and Bros., 1938.

(13) Erikson, Erik H., Hitler's Imagery and German Youth, *Psychiatry*, vol. v, 1942.

(14) Alexander, Edgar, *Der Mythus Hitler*. Zürich, Europa Verlag, 1937.

(15) Maier, Heinrich, *Psychologie des emotionalen Denkens*. Tübingen, J. C. B. Mohr, 1908.

STALIN AND THE DICTATORSHIP
OF THE PROLETARIAT

(1) Lenin, Vladimir Ijlich, *State and Revolution*. New York, International Publishers, 1932.

(2) Spearman, D., *Modern Dictators*. New York, Columbia University Press, 1939.

(3) Sorel, Georges, *Reflections on Violence*. New York, P. Smith, 1941.

(4) Trotsky, Leon, *Terrorismus und Kommunismus*. Hamburg, Westeuropäisches Sekretariat der Kommunistischen Internationale, 1920.

(5) Marx, Karl and Engel, Friedrich, *Communist Manifesto*. New York, Labor News Co., 1934.

(6) Lenin, Vladimir Ijlich, *The Deception of the People by the Slogans of Equality and Freedom*. London, Martin Lawrence, Ltd., 1934.

(7) .... Democracy and Dictatorship, *Pravda* 2, Jan. 3, 1919. *Coll. Works*, 23.

(8) ....*Letter to American Workingmen from the Social Soviet Republic of Russia*. New York, The Socialist Public Society, 1918.

(9) .... Prophetic Words, *Pravda*, July 2, 1918. *Coll. Works*, 23.

(10) Zetkin, K., *Reminiscences of Lenin*. London, Modern Books, 1929.

(11) Freud, Sigmund, *Civilization and Its Discontents*. London, L. & V. Woolf, 1930.

(12) Stalin, Josif Vissarionovich, *Problems of Leninism*, vol. II. Moscow, 1933.

(13) Freud, Sigmund, *Totem and Taboo*. New York, New Republic, 1931.

(14) Roheim, Geza, Nach dem Tode des Urvaters, *Imago*, IX, 1923.

(15) Trotsky, Leon, *Stalin*. New York, Harper and Bros., 1941.

(16) Tarle, E., *Textbook of Modern History*. Moscow, Government Publications.

(17) Souvarine, Boris, *Stalin, A Critical Survey of Bolshevism*. New York, Longmans, Green and Co., 1939.

(18) Lyons, Eugene, *Stalin, Czar of All Russians*. Philadelphia, J. B. Lippincott, 1940.

(19) *Stalin, A Collective Volume published on the occasion of his sixtieth birthday*.

ORIGINS AND PREVENTION OF DICTATORSHIP

(1) de la Boetie, Etienne, *Anti-dictator. Les discours sur la servitude volontaire*. New York, Columbia University Press, 1942.

(2) Plato, *The Republic*, Book VII. London, Cambridge University Press, 1930.

APPENDIX

POSTSCRIPT TO "ADOLF HITLER"

Since the writing of this study, events have moved at a rapid pace. Today, looking back at this tragic chapter of modern history, we can base our thinking and conclusions on a wealth of accumulated data.

While nothing basically new can be added to our reflections and conclusions, we are able to perceive certain points in a sharper light and focus.

I turn first to the formation of the Fuehrer's personality. When we piece together the available information concerning his miserable adolescence, it becomes evident that some serious turning point in his development had led to an increasing failure in adaptation.

Young Hitler was turning away from reality to such an extent that one might even suspect the onset of a schizophrenic process. I suspect that this would be the psychiatric diagnosis my venerable teacher Eugen Bleuler, the creator of the concept of schizophrenia, might have made of the future Fuehrer, had he had the opportunity to examine him. Young Hitler avoided schooling, was idling his time away with some pseudo-artistry and appeared to be aiming for goals for which he was completely unsuited and unequipped: entrance in the Art Academy or School of Architecture. He chose not to engage in any work or gainful employment and withdrew altogether from human relationships with men as well as women. This behavior was accompanied by regressive over-dependence on his mother whom he let support him, while pursuing his vague fantasies of some future grandeur.

Finally, and here the impression of serious psychopathology

becomes particularly poignant, all this progressive maladaptation culminated in Hitler's leading the existence of a tramp, a vagabond, sleeping in miserable flophouses in the capital of the old Austro-Hungarian monarchy and severing all ties of friendship and family. The future leader of the German nation and the Supreme Commander of German Armed Forces shunned his military duty and dodged conscription.

While many a future prophet or leader had his Hegira, the future Fuehrer never sought the solitude of inspiration and meditation. It was rather his growing inability to cope with reality that led to his aimless drifting.

Nevertheless, and here I come back to the problem of psychiatric diagnosis, future development of Hitler's personality precludes the diagnosis of a schizophrenic process. The other alternative then would be to speak of a crisis in adolescence which led to a distorted personality development. In this development we can detect at an early time the germs of future hypervalent ideas, culminating in overpowering and fixed delusions.

One point of view would be to speak of a paranoia developing out of a general background of paranoid-hysterical psychopathy. Another point of view might be developed according to a recent concept, introduced by Frosch, of psychotic character.

To put it briefly: the psychotic processes in these individuals become an integral part of their character structure. "These processes resemble those seen in the psychotic process, as reflected in the role that reality plays in all areas, in the closeness of the ego to the id, and in the nature of object relationships. Therefore, they show a propensity for disturbances in these areas. However, the basic feature which establishes the fact that these people are not psychotic is this: the capacity to test reality, while often quite defective, is relatively intact."[1] The disturbances in reality, and this point is of particular importance for our consideration, are mainly reflected in the relationship to reality and in the sense of reality. However, the capacity to test reality, though impaired, is relatively well preserved. To clarify our view we now have a considerable amount of additional material.

One such characteristically striking episode is the deep impression made on Hitler by Wagner's opera, "Rienzi." Obviously, Hitler identified himself with the popular tribune Cola di Rienzi who in the first decades of the 14th century led a rebellion against the Pope and Roman nobility. Here was grandeur as well as self-destruction: after a brief period of power, the popular tribune was overthrown by the aristocracy and killed by the populace, who were disillusioned by his cruel rule; his corpse was burned and the ashes strewn to the winds. Reminded after many years by his companion in those days, of that evening at the opera, Hitler admitted: "It began in that hour."(2)

Although there is not much data on the development of ideas of grandeur, it is likely that the incubation of these ideas occurred during the years of aimless drifting, misery, loneliness and successive defeats. Descriptively speaking, this ideational content developed as compensation for the ongoing experience of deep inferiority. In psychoanalytic terms, one might speak of a narcissistic fixation and regression with a fantastically grandiose image of the self taking the place of a more realistic image of one's own inferiority.

However, we have more data regarding the origins of ideas of persecution which were destined to play such a gruesome role in Hitler's *Weltanschauung* and politics.

Thus, we find early sources of his anti-Semitic delusion, with all its implications of a sinister and powerful enemy, an idea which became an early focal point of his system. In those years of his destitute youth his reading consisted mainly, if not exclusively, of cheap pamphlets. Among them was a revue published by a strange individual, a son of a teacher, a former monk and now a self-appointed "aristocrat" who, characteristically, changed his name from Adolph-Joseph Lanz to Georg or Jorg Lanz von Liebenfels. He founded an order "The New Temple" which boasted a flag on whose golden background shone a red swastika.

"What this lower middle-class Austrian teacher's son with aristocratic yearnings was preaching, was—when considered with sobriety—an extremely silly, mystical doctrine of a universal mission and an everlasting struggle between the 'blond, blue-eyed master race' of the Aryans and the dark, inferior race of 'the monkeys of Sodom,' represented by the Jews. We find in Lanz von Liebenfels ideas of racial purity of the foundation of an Order of those who 'know the truth' and many other things all of which were put into practice by Hitler and his paladines" [author's translation](2).

It must have been a triumph indeed for the defeated self-esteem of the tenant of a flophouse, Adolf Hitler, to realize that, with all his humiliations, it was he who belonged to the superior race, it was he who could look down on those who "made it," who had power, money and education.

In later years another influence contributed to the formation of the focal delusion of the Jew as the source of cosmic evil. It was a writer from the circle of the famous poet Stefan George who gave a cosmic, almost metaphysical foundation to anti-Semitism. He discovered Jehovah (Yahweh) as the origin of all evil. Yahweh equals Satan equals Moloch was from the very beginning the origin of all evil.(3)

Finally, there came the political implications of anti-Semitic ideology with its furious struggle against the Austrian Sozial-Democrats. Feder's brochures and other similar tracts allowed Hitler to crystallize his paranoid ideas around the Jews as the chief enemy, the pullers of the strings behind the hated Democracy and Socialism, who were thus responsible for all the misery and humiliations of the naïvely trusting German nation. It is obvious that here Hitler found a most gratifying, simple and absolutely convincing explanation of his own humiliations and defeats. This set of ideas allowed him to deny his own inferiority and to rationalize his hatred. At this junction the latter found its focal point and, as Hitler himself admits, everything began to fall into place, light sprang up where there had been darkness and confusion.

It would require a more extensive study to trace all the stages in the development of Hitler's system and his main delusional ideas. Suffice it to observe that with these delusional germs in his mind, he became attuned to events and impressions which he selected from the rich input of information coming from the world of reality, like a magnetic pole attracting ferrous limes. He absorbed ideas which confirmed and elaborated upon his own irrational convictions and he interpreted events in keeping with his own distortions of reality. In this way, these distortions gained in power and overwhelmed the sense of reality, to be sure, merely in this special way and in these selected areas.

Thus, the misery of the workers did not evoke sympathy in him: to deny his identification with the have-nots he seized upon his own megalomaniacal narcissism and made the Social Democrats and, in the last analysis, the Jews responsible for his own misery. The truly paranoid division between Good and Evil which at that time was already in operation in his mind, allowed him to see in the Jews the ultimate cause of all evil and misery.

Hitler seized upon the ideas of struggle for existence and the survival of the fittest and expanded them into an apology of brutal force and cruelty put in the service of the great German Cause. In this way he could project his own basic strivings on the screen of great causes and general ideas of magnitude, surpassing any individual, purely selfish aspect. He could rationalize and extol his own boundless cruelty and lust for power by seizing upon the idea of the Superman and the chosen Leader, thus appointing Nietzsche as one of his ideological masters. As his circle widened and he found many intellectuals to lend support and more elaborate foundations to his own ideas, the latter became more firmly entrenched in his mind. Progressively they assumed the monstrous destructive form of the struggle for racial purity and the struggle for life-space for the superior German-Aryan "Race," all of which was inevitably bound with the idea of annihilation of the Jew as the Devil Incarnate and of the destruction or enslavement of non-German elements which should be placed in the service of the German masters.

It is truly fascinating to observe how in the course of years this completely uneducated, ignorant man of evil genius, extracted from perfunctory readings and from growing contact with his better-educated acolytes, every piece of information or every scrap of an idea to strengthen the scaffolding of his own system.

I should like to mention one example from the new material which was not available at the time of publication of the English original of this study.

In his *Secret Book* Hitler extols the right of a strong nation to "adapt its territory to the size of its population." He continues to discuss the misery of a nation which, contrary to the law of survival of the strongest, prevailing in nature, resorts to the control of its birth rate. How wise were the Spartans who "gave free rein to the number of births but cut down on the number of those remaining alive. At one time the Spartans were capable of such a wise measure but not our present mendaciously sentimental, bourgeois-patriotic nonsense. The rule of six thousand Spartans over three hundred and fifty thousand Helots was only thinkable in consequence of the high racial value of the Spartans. But this was the result of a systematic race preservation; thus Sparta must be regarded as the first folkish state. The exposure of sick, weak deformed children, in short their destruction, was more decent and in truth a thousand times more humane than the wretched insanity of our day which preserves the most pathological subjects, and indeed at any price, and yet takes the life of a hundred thousand healthy children in consequence of birth control, or through abortions, in order subsequently to breed a race of degenerates burdened with illness."(4)

It should be obvious that this harangue, so clear in all its implications, heralds some of the revolutionary measures introduced by National Socialism which were to horrify the civilized world. Here were foreshadowed and rationalized the extermination of inmates of psychiatric hospitals, of institutions for crippled and mentally retarded and of the racially "inferior" Gypsies and Jews. In this way was highlighted a chapter in the systematic destruction of basic principles evolved during the course of centuries by civilized ethics and society and advocated by all great religions.

From such premises Hitler could evolve complex measures with

careful planning and scheming. Once conceived and firmly entrenched in his mind, these "principles" inevitably led to his
politics of racial extermination, to military conquest and subsequent total subjugation of lands needed for life space for the
superior German race.

In order to establish a more solid basis for a psychiatric
understanding and evaluation, we must add Hitler's distorted
interpretation of events in his personal and political life. From the
available material it is amply evident that he distorted the
meaning of events in his personal life, in ascribing his unfortunate
youth to injustice and persecution.

As an example of delusional distortion of political events I shall
cite another illustration from the *Secret Book*. "On November 11,
1918, the armistice was signed in the forest of Compiegne. For this,
fate had chosen a man who was one of those bearing major guilt
for the collapse of our people. Matthias Erzberger, deputy of the
Center, and, according to various assertions, the bastard son of a
servant-girl and a Jewish employer, was the German negotiator
who affixed his name to a document which, compared and
measured against the four and a half years of heroism of our
people, seems incomprehensible if we do not assume the deliberate
intention to bring about Germany's destruction."(4)

Thus, German defeat, just like personal failures, was interpreted
by Hitler as a result of diabolical machinations of all the evil
enemies. How else could a war be lost that was fought by the great
and noble German nation and the great "Socialist" instrument of
the German Army?

When one follows the development of Hitler's ideas and their
application in reality, one is struck by the increasing delusional
distorted interpretation of facts along with an admirable execution
of plans. This remark will be of value for our final conclusion.

I shall offer one more illustration of increasing distortion of
events, important as a basis for understanding future disastrous
planning, quoting again from the *Secret Book*.

In discussing the political structure of Soviet Russia, Hitler makes a typical sweeping statement that "Slavdom is lacking in state-forming forces. . . . Russia is indebted to this Teutonic upper stratum for her political state as well as for what little exists of her cultural value. A great Russia would neither have arisen nor would she have been able to preserve herself without this really German upper and intellectual stratum."(4)

This upper stratum, Hitler goes on, has been largely destroyed in the world war, "and the last remains were finally extirpated by the revolution and Bolshevism." Behind this disastrous event there lie again the diabolical machinations of the Jews. The Russian Bolshevik leaders are the exponents of Jewry.

"Jewry, pressing toward the upper strata and therefore toward supreme leadership, has exterminated the former alien upper class with the help of the Slavic race instinct. . . . Thus, present-day Russia, or better said, present-day Slavdom of Russian nationality, has received as master the Jew, who first eliminated the former upper stratum and now must prove his own state-forming power." In continuing this historical analysis, Hitler comes to the conclusion that the struggle will end with the destruction of Jewry within Russia and, finally, with "Russia as insignificant in governmental power as she will be deeply rooted in anti-German attitude." Ultimately the vast Russian territory will become "a source of eternal unrest and eternal insecurity and a perfect objective for the aspirations of other states and nations."(4)

On the basis of such cogent reasoning, it seems almost natural to wonder with Hitler how Germany could miss this opportunity for expanding her life space through colonization and subjugation of the subhuman Slavs.

In such a maze of distortions and false interpretations lie some of the sources of Hitler's fateful decision to attack Russia, thereby sealing his own doom. Here then we must conclude that, despite careful registration of facts, the distortion in their understanding was such that it inevitably led to poor reality testing and, ultimately, to a catastrophic end.

The material now available sheds sharper light on the develop-

ment of the Fuehrer's personality along with his fabulous success
and his sinister end. It was only natural that his political success
would confirm his ideas of grandeur, his absolute belief in his
mission as the chosen leader and saviour of the German nation
and, ultimately, the leader and ruler of Europe.

Although the premises of his main ideas were irrational, a
considerable amount of rational scheming and planning went into
the execution of his plans. Yet, in the final analysis, it was the
utter irrationality of his delusional ideas that proved his undoing.
With the characteristic rigidity of a paranoiac, he was unable to
alter any of his ideas and, despite the evidence to the contrary,
believed almost till the last moment that all his ideas and
intentions would ultimately be proved right.

Particularly revealing are, in this respect, the records describing
his activity as the Commander-in-Chief of the German Armed
Forces. In this activity, as in any other, his narcissism was fed and
his ideas of grandeur confirmed by his acolytes.

According to the Gauleiter Wagner, he was the greatest artist of
all times. His hypnotic fascination convinced the industrialist
Wilhelm Keppler that "Der Fuehrer hat eine Antenne direkt zum
lieben Gott."(5) According to Ley: "Der Fuehrer hat immer
Recht. Er ist ein Mensch, der sich als einziger auf der Erde in der
ganzen Geschichte der Menschheit niemals irrt."(5) And, according to Goebbels, he was "der grosste Feldherr aller Zeiten." (3)

Finally, the characteristic given of the Fuehrer by one of his
most ardent admirers coincides in its essential trends with his own
self-image as the Great Individual as outlined in *Mein Kampf.* This
parallel offers a most eloquent contribution to the understanding
of the interrelationship between the Fuehrer and the German
people. To quote Speer: "For Hitler was one of those inexplicable
historical phenomena which emerge at rare intervals among
mankind. His person determined the fate of the nation. He alone
placed it, and kept it, upon the path which has led it to this
dreadful ending. The nation was spellbound by him as a people
has rarely been in the whole of history." And so had Hitler

effectively become hypnotized by his own grandiose self-image, so clearly outlined in *Mein Kampf*.*

This latter part of the Hitler myth received a thorough analysis by Guderian, one of his surviving generals. His insistence on imposing his plans and "intuitions" on his military experts, his inability to listen to their arguments and to discuss with them the complexities of world-war strategy, became particularly striking in times of crisis and impending defeat. Guderian's descriptions of Hitler's hysterical rage, during which time he was unable to exercise the slightest degree of self-control, convey the picture of a raving madman.

Naturally, given his distorted perceptions, no defeat of the otherwise invincible German army was ever seen as being due to the superiority of the enemy forces or to his own mistakes and miscalculations, but inevitably to treason and, in the last analysis, to the international Jewry.

In this way Hitler could preserve intact his grandiose self-image. To leave it untarnished, he made deliberate efforts to avoid confrontation with reality: when the doom of defeat became visible beyond any doubt, he limited even the input of information which could reach him from the crumbling battlefronts. In his bunker, first in East Prussia then in the underground chancellery in Berlin, "he lived in a private world of his own, from which the ugly and awkward facts of Germany's situation were excluded. He refused to visit the bombed towns, just as he refused to read reports which contradicted the picture he wanted to form. . . . On no account was the war or anything connected with it permitted as a subject for discussion during the tea hour."(6)

The self-image Hitler managed to preserve almost till the end was that of one of Hegel's "World Historical Individuals." To be sure, he was a man chosen by Providence to act as the agent of the World Historical Process. His escape from the attempts at assassination, the number of which he placed at seven, was to him another convincing proof of Providence watching over his mission and his elected person. This was proven more particularly by his

*p. 231.

last escape on July 20, 1944. While exhibiting the scene of the unsuccessful attempt on his life to Mussolini, "he began to reenact the scene and his voice became more excited. 'After my miraculous escape from death today I am more than ever convinced that it is my fate to bring our enterprise to a successful conclusion.' Nodding, Mussolini could only agree: 'This was a sign from Heaven.'"(6)

It is within the framework of the psychological structure of dictatorship that in this process of denial of reality Hitler was substantially helped at first by the Germans at large and, in the years or months of impending and obvious doom, by his entourage. While he was modeling his self-image after Frederick the Great, he was assisted in this by the faithful Goebbels who read to him from Carlyle, and who in President Roosevelt's death saw a most meaningful analogy with the death of Catherine the Great. The death of the Tzarina marked the turning point in the waning fortunes of Frederick during the seven year's war. For the magically and mystically minded Nazi leaders it was obvious that the same change of fate would from now on favor the cause of the Fuehrer. "The German people were reminded how, in the eighteenth century, even the great Frederick had seemed doomed, when his allies fell away, and his enemies closed in, when the Russians took Berlin and he was outnumbered on all sides and alone. Yet he had survived and triumphed in the end, thanks to his oriental endurance, his brilliant strategy, and the certain favour of Providence, which had sown dissension among his enemies. Since the Germans of 1944 were ruled by a leader of no less resource, the greatest strategical genius of all time, no less favoured by Providence (as events had recently shown), might not they, too, hope, if only they showed the same endurance, for a similar delivery?"(5)

In the last period of the hopeless struggle, as it was becoming more and more impossible to deny dreadful reality and the impending doom, certain trends of the Fuehrer's personality emerged with greatest clarity. They had been covered up by rationalizations, by nebulous ideas and bombastic promises, masterful planning and diabolical terror, all of which culminated in unheard of successes. Now, with the last hope for victory gone, Hitler displayed his basic hatred and lust for destruction. In his utterances, in his orders and, finally, in his last will he laid bare the mainsprings of his complex and poorly integrated personality.

It had been characteristic of him that when reality contradicted his desires and his predictions, he would fly into a rage with wishes to kill and to destroy. Such a characteristic scene was described by General Halder, chief of the Army General Staff. "For practical purposes, Hitler announced in October, 1941, the war was over; 'the Russians no longer exist!' he would shout at doubting generals. . . . When the Chief of the Army General Staff produced figures of Russian tank production, Hitler flew into a rage and ordered the technical department which had compiled such 'defeatist' figures to be silenced. . . . He went off the deep end—he was no longer a rational being. . . he foamed at the mouth and threatened me (Halder) with his fists. Any rational discussion was out of the question."(5) Just as Britain was only apparently unbeaten, so Russia was only apparently standing up.

However, with the enemy at the gate of his capital, Hitler's rage and wish for destruction knew no bounds. We have already mentioned that he saw in treason and weakness surrounding him the only true cause of defeat. In this way he could preserve, maybe until the last moment, the grandiose image of himself while projecting his true miserably inferior and weak self on the German people at large. This German nation which during the incubation of his delusions and their organization into a coherent system, and which during the time of success was extolled by him as the epitome of all perfection, was now rendered utterly worthless and despicably inferior.

Already during the scene of mad fury following the last attempt at his assassination, while shouting orders into the telephone, Hitler uttered the portentous statement of the megalomaniac: "I'm beginning to doubt whether the German people are worthy of my great ideals."(5) Now, facing the inevitable doom, he gave vent to his hatred of the Nation which had extolled him to the peak of idolization. "If the German people were to be conquered in the struggle," he told a meeting of Gauleiters in August 1944, "then it had been too weak to face the test of history and was fit only for destruction."(5)

And indeed destruction it was, the ultimate undisguised release of basic primitive destructive hostility underlying the structure of the Fuehrer's personality and of Nazi ideology. In this hour of Goetterdämmerung, Nazi propaganda began to extol general destruction of Germany as well, and Goebbels was jubilant about "the bomb-terror that spares the dwellings of neither rich nor poor; before the labour offices of total war the last class barriers have had to go down."

Hitherto Hitler's cruelty and lust for blood were directed against all the various imaginary or real enemies. "Nature is cruel, therefore we, too, may be cruel," he said in 1934, when discussing the Jews and the Slavs; "If I can send the flower of the German nation into the hell of war, without the smallest pity for the spilling of precious German blood, then surely I have a right to remove millions of an inferior race that breeds like vermin! . . ."(5) "Throughout the war Hitler continually gave evidence of this lust for blood, this physical delight in the intellectual contemplation of slaughter for its own sake."(5)

Now, since the German nation proved to be weak, it had to be destroyed. No thought and consideration for coming generations of Germans could prevail upon the Fuehrer and make him stop the senseless slaughter. Not content with destruction which had been wrought so far by the war, particularly by the Allied bombings, Hitler ordered the scorched earth policy which, if carried out, would have left the whole of Germany in ruins never to be rebuilt. Sending for Speer who "wrote to him declaring that militarily and economically the war was lost, and if the nation was not to be lost also, it was essential that some material basis be preserved upon which the life of the people, however primitively, might be continued, Hitler announced: 'If the war is to be lost, the nation also will perish. This fate is inevitable. There is no need to consider the basis even of a most primitive existence any longer. On the contrary, it is better to destroy even that, and to destroy it ourselves. The nation has proved itself weak, and the future belongs solely to the stronger Eastern nation. Besides, those who remain after the battle are of little value; for the good have fallen.' That day new orders of destruction were issued by Hitler and Bormann: the fight was to be continued 'without consideration of the German people.' "(5)

The history of Hitler's last days spent in his underground chancellery in the bunker, shows this strange combination of destructive rage and utter lack of reality sense. "On 21st April, Hitler, who in all these days personally directed the movements of every battalion, ordered a final, all-out attack by the troops in Berlin . . . 'any commanding officer who keeps men back,' Hitler shouted, 'will forfeit his life within five hours . . .' So Hitler ordered; but his orders bore no relation now to any reality. He was moving imaginary battalions, making academic plans, disposing nonexistent formations."(5)

Finally, in his political testament Hitler disposed of "traitors" disclaiming any responsibility for the disaster of the defeat, and tried to perpetuate the Nazi administration, the Nazi war and the Nazi myth.

The parting shot of this unique document deals with the essence of Hitler's personal and political paranoia: his successors must "above all else, uphold the racial laws in all their severity, and mercilessly resist the universal poisoner of all nations, international Jewry." Thus, until his last moment, Hitler remained faithful to his basic ideas and delusions. His suicide was the turning of unabated fury against himself, insofar as it was no longer possible to turn it against his various and sundry enemies, traitors and persecutors.

It is important to note that not even in the face of ultimate doom did he change any of his basic ideas or, to put it differently, was he ever illuminated by what we call insight. Perhaps this fact should carry significant weight in our final evaluation of Hitler's personality.

However, before formulating these final conclusions, we must mention briefly the wealth of medical, in particular neuropsychiatric data concerning his last years. It seems that there was taking place a rapid progressive deterioration manifested by such organic neurological symptoms as generalized trembling, left-sided motor weakness, paralytic gait, seizures of epileptoid character. In 1942 he agreed to a visit with the famous surgeon Sauerbruch who was struck by this picture of deterioration and who observed the bizarre quality of such announcements as: "I must go to India . . . ten enemies must die for one slain German." His entourage had been struck by moments of growing euphoria and expansive ideas of grandeur which bore no relation to reality. After such descriptions the psychiatrist is not surprised to hear at least from one personal witness of a syphilitic infection which Hitler had acquired in his youth. If to all this we add definite addiction to drugs administered by the sinister Dr. Norell, we must agree that the final clinical picture becomes very complex and difficult, if not impossible, to analyze.

We will not attempt here a final psychiatric diagnosis. To be sure, we cannot exclude some slowly progressive organic deterioration of the brain originating in a never properly or thoroughly treated syphilitic infection, and resulting from prolonged use of narcotics.

However, these changes are of secondary nature. What emerges as personality background are elements of a paranoid personality with strong hysterical features. On this psychopathic basis there developed a distortion of the ego characterized by a deficient sense of reality and a distorted grandiose image of the self. Regardless of this interpretation, our last remarks call for a qualification. To be sure, Hitler's sense of reality was distorted but not altogether deficient. After all it enabled him to conceive of and carry out complex political and strategic schemes on a grand scale. In the final analysis, however, his sense of reality failed him because of a distorted ego which was overwhelmed by delusions.

The intensity of his primitive hostility, the intricate elaboration of his system, the rigidity with which he stuck to his original premises and delusions, and his suggestive, indeed hypnotic, power, qualifies him as a daemonic paranoiac on a grand maybe unique scale.

BIBLIOGRAPHY TO APPENDIX
POSTSCRIPT TO "ADOLF HITLER"

(1) Frosch, John, A Specific Problem in Nosology: The Psychotic Character Disorder, *J. Amer. Psychoanal. Assn.*, 1960, 8:544-548.

(2) Goerlitz, Walter, *Adolf Hitler* (Persönlichkeit und Geschichte, 21/22). Gottingen, Berlin, Frankfurt, Messerschmidt Verlag, 1960, pp. 18, 22.

(3) Buchheim, Hans et al., *Fuehrer ins Nichts*. Rastatt/Baden, Grote, 1960, p. 39.

(4) Hitler, Adolf, *Hitler's Secret Book*. New York, Grove Press, 1961, pp. 17-18, 76, 135-136, 138-139.

(5) Trevor-Roper, H. R., *Hitlers letzte Tage*. Frankfort, Ullstein, 1965, pp. 12, 31, 45, 46, 63, 64, 73, 102.

(6) Bullock, Alan, *Hitler: A Study in Tyranny*. New York, Bantam Books, 1961, pp. 363, 377.

POSTSCRIPT TO "STALIN AND THE DICTATORSHIP OF THE PROLETARIAT"

The historical events which occurred between 1948 and today call for some reflections and amplifications.

Let me begin with a general comment which should have been made in the original English edition of this book, but which is nonetheless valid.

One of the most striking features of the Stalinist era were the purges and the extraordinary trials accompanying them. We are rather well informed about the techniques of moral and physical torture which were a part of the so-called brainwashing method, a technique which was subsequently utilized effectively by the Chinese Communists. Yet, all our knowledge notwithstanding, time and again one could not help but marvel at the uniformly self-destructive character of the "confessions."

A renewed study of Dostoyevsky, this most extraordinary literary genius, who in his novels prophetically anticipated many events in the development of Russian Socialism and Communism, proves most illuminating. It puts into sharp focus certain basic trends in Russian mentality which manifest themselves again and again throughout Russian history.

To state it as briefly as possible. In his study on Dostoyevsky Freud writes: "He reminds one of the barbarians of the great migrations, who murder and do penance therefore, where penitence becomes a technique to enable murder to be done. Ivan the

---

*Compare this with the historical anti-Stalinist speech by Premier Khrushchev: "And how is it possible that a person confesses to crimes which he has not committed? Only in one way: because of the applying of physical pressure, torture, bringing him to a state of unconsciousness, deprivation of his judgment, taking away his human dignity."(1)

Terrible behaved in exactly this way—in fact this compromise with morality is a characteristic Russian trait."(2)

In *The Brothers Karamazoff* the towering figure of the Great Inquisitor, drawn after the notorious reactionary Minister of the Interior and arch-enemy of all liberalism, Pobedonostzeff, could serve as a prototype of Stalin himself and some of his henchmen. Similarly, in "Biesy" (in English translation, the Possessed, while in reality the word means the Evil Spirits) Dostoyevsky presents us with the picture of mental degeneration of Russian revolutionaries, truly prophetic of the vicissitudes of Communism. The main common trends in all this are as follows: the inherent belief, indeed the conviction that human beings, vicious and depraved though they are, have to be coerced into the acceptance of ideas for which they are not ready but which, ultimately, will serve them well. To achieve this goal, no means should be shunned, no cruelty spared. In their abysmal ignorance and sinfulness they do not know, poor innocents, what is good for them. Therefore, freedom of choice, in fact, any trace of liberty is not for them; in fact, it would mean their undoing. They themselves are, or can become so convinced of this, that they prepare to renounce their sins, to confess and to repent, in submitting to the superior knowledge and power of those who are truly enlightened (the Church, the Party or the Government). Here then, by virtue of a perverse and cruel dialectic, freedom of thought and freedom of choice, become the supreme evil, worthy of supreme punishment. In this context and from a broad perspective, it becomes really and truly irrelevant whether the sinner is a young liberal student who, like Dostoyevsky himself, kneels in abject submission before the Tzar and the orthodox church and reneges on the ideals of his brief *Sturm und Drang* period; or whether he is a social-revolutionary or some other heretic who beats his breast and submits to the authority of Stalin, that is, of the Party reigning supreme and in the possession of absolute Truth. When one reflects on Dostoyevsky himself and the vicissitudes of his life and ideas, one cannot help being struck by the analogy between his spiritual fate and the fate of Russian socialism as embodied by J. V. Stalin. I quote Freud: "Nor was the ultimate result of Dostoyevsky's moral struggles anything very glorious. After the most violent battles to reconcile the impulsive claims of the individual with the demands of the community, he ended up, retrograde fashion, with submission both to the temporal and the spiritual authorities, with veneration for the Tsar and the God of the Christians, and a narrow Russian nationalism, a position which lesser minds have reached with less effort. This is the weak point of the great personality. Dostoyevsky threw away the chance of becoming a teacher and liberator of humanity; instead, he appointed himself its jailer. The future of civilization will have little to thank him for."(2)

As to Stalin's personality, I am not aware of any new material which might significantly add to the understanding of its formation. However, to put things into a sharper focus, I cannot resist, at the risk of being repetitious, to quote again from Freud: "If the father was hard, violent, and cruel, the super-ego takes these characteristics from him, and in its relation to the ego, the passivity which was supposed to have been repressed ,reestablishes itself."(2)

Some interesting new data have reached us relevant for the functioning of Stalin's mentality. I turn first to personal observations of which there are obviously not too many.

Achmed Amba was a young Turkish idealist who came to Russia in 1933, joined the ranks of the Red Army and was singled out for distinction by the Dictator. Stalin took him into his personal guard in the Kremlin where the young convert could observe his hero for two years. Yet, despite his favored position, he too, fell victim in the period of the great Purges, was thrown into prison, and barely escaped execution.

Amba speaks of the duality characteristic of Stalin who could on the one hand cajole him, play lovingly with his child and show his warm and friendly understanding, while on the other, allowed him to be engulfed by the wave of incredible terror and cruelty which he himself unleashed. Amba draws an interesting comparison between this duality of his beloved hero and the Russian mentality at large. "This incredible humaneness of men who shared the guilt for the most horrible of all wars—this is Russia as though reflected in a drop of water"(3)[author's translation].

Some of the most personal and lively impressions are those gathered by a man who at the time of his contact with Stalin was one of his most convinced admirers. Milovan Djilas, one of the closest friends and comrades of Marshal Tito (which did not prevent him in later years from falling from grace and languishing for many years behind prison walls), had between 1944 and 1948 three encounters with Stalin: he was a member of the official Yugoslav Mission to the Soviet Government. As an old and trusted Party member, he arrived full of admiration and idolization of Stalin, only to end in deep disillusionment. He was struck by Stalin's suspiciousness, and when he quotes Stalin's comments on his western allies, one can almost hear the rumblings of the Cold War.

Since Stalin identified himself and his personal power with the power of the Party and the State, his personal suspicions could be aroused as easily by opposition to his opinion as by anybody who, to his suspicious mind, might in some remote future become a threat to himself or to Soviet power and hegemony. "Everybody beyond the control of his police was a potential enemy."

It was for these reasons that Stalin was wary of revolutions in other countries and "helped (them) only up to a certain point—up to where he could control them—but he was always ready to leave them in the lurch whenever they slipped out of his grasp."(4)

Stalin's attitude toward violence, as disclosed in Djilas' observations, cannot surprise a student of the Russian dictator. He never forgave Djilas for allegedly insulting the Red Army by accusing it of rape and violence in the liberated Yugoslav territory. "Can't Djilas understand it if a soldier who has crossed thousands of kilometers through blood and fire and death has fun with a woman or takes some trifle?"(4)

Djilas made notice of Stalin's cynicism in avowing anti-Semitism and advocating most brazenly pure and simple imperialism. "We have no special interest in Albania. We agree to Yugoslavia swallowing Albania . . . . Yes, yes. Swallowing! But we agree with you: you ought to swallow Albania: the sooner the better."

Finally, Djilas makes subtle and most pertinent observations on Stalin's self-adulation and, correspondingly, his idolization by the Russians and Yugoslavs alike. The latter is, of course, best illustrated by his own example.

And yet, after his personal encounters and his political disillusionment, Djilas reached a significantly different image of the beloved leader. He considers him as capable of every crime of violence. "Every crime was possible to Stalin, for there was not one he had not committed. Whatever standards we use to take his measure, in any event—let us hope for all time to come—to him will fall the glory of being the greatest criminal in history. For in him was joined the criminal senselessness of a Caligula with the refinement of a Borgia and the brutality of a Tsar Ivan the Terrible. . . . All in all, Stalin was a monster who, while adhering to abstract, absolute, and fundamentally utopian ideas, in practice recognized, and could recognize, only success—violence, physical and spiritual extermination."(4)

On the basis of his deep inside knowledge, Djilas explains the role of Stalin in ruling the Party. "The ruling political bureaucracy of the Party found use for just such a man—one who was reckless in his determination and extremely practical in his fanaticism. The ruling party followed him doggedly and obediently and he truly led it from victory to victory, until carried away by power, he began to sin against it as well."(4)

We find valuable material in the study of that profound student of Soviet Russia, the former American Ambassador to the Soviets, George F. Kennan.(5) He confirms our opinion of the personality of the Dictator by pointing out that Stalin was able "to see the world only through the prism of his own ambitions and his own fears." His fundamental motive was the protection of his own position . . . and this is the key to his diplomacy."(5) Kennan, like many others, establishes the fundamental analogy between his attitude toward his real or potential enemies in personal as well as in political life. "His strategy was a simple one. It could be summed up in the single phrase 'divide and rule.' "

Stalin vented his immense hostility in his personal life, where ultimately it led to the untimely death of his wife. It is characteristic of the man that the question remains unanswered whether she killed herself or whether it was Stalin who shot her. "That he drove her to her death seems inescapable." His mourning reactions offer a poignant illustration of a Russian trend of mind to which we alluded at the opening of this chapter. Kennan writes: "He showed afterward signs of remorse and sadness; gave her a curiously Christian sort of burial; followed the hearse on foot through the streets of Moscow; loved to talk about her with those who had known her well."(5)

It appears that Stalin did not hesitate to murder even such a universally beloved and venerated figure as the great Gorky, possibly because in the latter's criticism of his strategy of terror he heard the voice of his own superego which he did his best to repress and deny.

Kennan's analysis of the great Purges demonstrates once more the combination of incredible cunning and cruelty which went into the staging of this terror on a grandiose scale in the disguise of a mockery of justice. In an astute observation Kennan remarks that Stalin learned a great deal from his German counterpart: he was deeply impressed by Hitler's Blood Purge of June 30, 1934. "This exhibition of ruthless brutality against Party Comrades evidently made a profound impression upon Stalin. Alone among his leading associates he is said to have insisted that this act would strengthen, not weaken, the Nazi regime. He was, I am sure, filled with admiration. From now on, there was no stopping him."(5)

However, even prior to his German model, Stalin had been using mock trials as a sure way of deflecting his own culpability. Three times, in the course of the years 1928 to 1933, great propaganda trials, involving foreign specialists and Russian technicians served the objective of demonstrating to the suffering and constantly frustrated Russian people that their hardships were the result of sinister machinations of foreign saboteurs and Russian traitors, rather than the bungling on the part of their own Government. Here, too, Stalin played cunningly on the old, inveterate Russian suspiciousness of the hostile West—a strategy which he resorted to on numerous other occasions.

In a famous and often quoted article, "Dizzy with Success," published in 1930, Stalin criticized the excesses of agricultural collectivization which was inflicting terrible suffering on the farmers. The article was his attempt to disclaim responsibility for this drama, since it was he, after all, who signed all the laws promulgated to that effect. Thus, the fault would lie not with him but with some inept officials.

A similar alibi was attempted by Stalin after the period of terror and purges in 1936. At first, no longer satisfied with his chief of Secret Police, Yagoda, he insisted on the appointment of one of his most sinister henchmen, N. T. Yezhow. From that moment on "the purges took that fantastic course which defies the powers of description and nearly defies the imagination. Heads rolled by the thousands, the tens of thousands, probably even the hundreds of thousands. . . . In a vast conflagration of mock justice, torture and brutality, at least two thirds of the governing class of Russia literally devoured and destroyed themselves."(5) And yet, once the vast destruction of all real, potential and imaginary rivals and enemies had been successfully carried out, Stalin proceeded to destroy the Grand Inquisitor Yezhow himself. He had to go not only as one of "the witnesses" who had seen too much and knew too much, but also as a scapegoat upon whom Stalin could conveniently blame the excesses of his cruel "justice."(6)

Kennan notes that with increasing political terror, inspired and directed by Stalin, his mental abnormality became more and more apparent. This is confirmed by some personal observations recorded by a small number of observers. Even Djilas speaks of signs of senility by which he meant increased vulgarity in speech and manners, and primitive rudeness of behavior.

Much has been written about Stalin's megalomaniac self-

adulation which received reinforcement from eager acolytes or—
especially in earlier years—from true admirers. Yet, such was his
cunning and astute forethought, such was his duplicity, that even
here he tried to disclaim his part in this process of deification of
the living Caesar of the Communist world. In one of his articles he
protested against the Personality Cult long before the 22nd
Congress of the Party. Not content with this, in his short biography, written and corrected by himself, he praised himself for his
lack of vanity!

Political analysis by men like Kennan, Basseches, Uralov and
others, demonstrates the intricate connection between Stalin's
paranoid personality and his political machinations. It is, for
instance, apparent how, in complete analogy with his German
counterpart, he created or rather remodeled the Secret Police as
the extended arm of his vicious cruelty and vindictiveness.

It is also apparent that his "paranoia" took advantage of the
political scene inside Russia as well as abroad, to raise political
adversaries to the rank of personal mortal enemies (viz, for
instance, the struggle against Trotzky); and vice versa he rationalized personal hostility by making as its object those he considered
to be traitors and counterrevolutionaries, thereby justifying their
ruthless "liquidation." We know that no lie, no defamation was
beyond him in this process which affected the living and the dead
alike.*

In conclusion, our review of new material illustrates how, with
his personal psychological background, and given the social and
historical events and configurations of the times, the Russian
Dictator, from his start as a leader, became a ruthless dictator, a
criminal paranoiac of the type described by the French classic
school of psychiatry as the *persécateur persécuté,* the persecuted
persecutor. In view of these considerations, we gain a better
understanding of some of Stalin's more sinister political maneuvers
which otherwise would be difficult to comprehend—for instance,

---

*One of innumerable examples is the execution of Alter and Ehrlich, the two
famous Polish Jewish Socialist leaders, as Hitler's spies.

his handling of the Spanish Loyalists or his love affair with Adolf Hitler.

Through an examination of the collective processes which made this development possible, we have pointed out how the collective ego through love and admiration, but also through dread and terror, had incorporated the image of the leader and resulted in his deification. The events of the post-Stalin era provide a unique illustration of the process of dethronement of the dead leader. His successors, in their desperate attempt to disclaim their own culpability and complicity in his crimes, set out to abolish the so-called Cult of Personality. However, they went much further: they did everything within their power to eradicate the holy image from the collective mind of his faithful subjects and mourning sons. The holy mummy was taken out of the Mausoleum, the names of the cities were changed and, first the faithful comrades, then the general populace were shown the hideous face of the cruel, demented paranoiac emerging behind the façade of the universal Genius, the Father of the Russian masses, and oppressed proletarians throughout the world.

In his secret speech to the 22nd Congress, Khrushchev described Stalin's cruelty as unmatched in the bloody chronicle of history, pointing to the delusions of grandeur which completely distorted his sense of reality.* Thus, even before the corpse was cold, or his memory had begun to dim, the orphaned sons began to wrestle with the Father's ghost.

Indeed, one of the authors, analyzing the speech of Premier Khrushchev, and comparing his interpretation of historical events with the official Soviet version in Stalin's time, chose for his book the appropriate title, *Autopsie du Stalinism.* Unfortunately, we lack sufficient data to analyze the full impact of this autopsy on the Russian masses.

*For instance, speaking of Tito, Stalin said: "I will shake my little finger and there will be no more Tito."

POSTSCRIPT TO
"STALIN AND THE DICTATORSHIP OF THE PROLETARIAT"

(1) Wolfe, Bertrand *Khrushchev and Stalin's Ghost.* New York, Frederick A. Praeger, 1957.

(2) Dostoevsky, F. M., *Stavrogin's Confession.* New York, Lear Publishers, 1947, pp. 88, 99-100.

(3) Amba, Achmed, *Ein Mensch sieht Stalin.* Hamburg, Rowohl Verlag, 1957, p. 39.

(4) Djilas, Milovan, *Conversations with Stalin.* New York, Harcourt, Brace and World, 1962, pp. 132, 143, 187, 188, 191.

(5) Kennan, George F., *Russia and the West under Lenin and Stalin.* Boston, Little Brown & Co., 1960, pp. 252, 258, 281, 302, 307.

(6) Basseches, N., *Stalin.* New York, Staple Press, 1952